Lecture Notes of the Institute for Computer Sciences, Social Informatics and Telecommunications Engineering 713

The LNICST series publishes ICST's conferences, symposia and workshops.

LNICST reports state-of-the-art results in areas related to the scope of the Institute.

The type of material published includes

- Proceedings (published in time for the respective event)
- Other edited monographs (such as project reports or invited volumes)

LNICST topics span the following areas:

- General Computer Science
- E-Economy
- E-Medicine
- Knowledge Management
- Multimedia
- Operations, Management and Policy
- Social Informatics
- Systems

Ayodeji Oluwatope · Folashade Dahunsi ·
Glory Enaruvbe · Kalaivani Chellappan
Editors

Towards New e-Infrastructure and e-Services for Developing Countries

17th EAI International Conference, AFRICOMM 2025
Ile-Ife, Nigeria, November 24–25, 2025
Proceedings

Springer

Editors
Ayodeji Oluwatope
Obafemi Awolowo University
Ile-Ife, Nigeria

Glory Enaruvbe
African Regional Institute for Geospatial Information Science and Technology,
Obafemi Awolowo University
Ile-Ife, Nigeria

Folashade Dahunsi
Federal University of Technology
Akure, Nigeria

Kalaivani Chellappan
Universiti Kebangsaan Malaysia
Selangor, Malaysia

ISSN 1867-8211 ISSN 1867-822X (electronic)
Lecture Notes of the Institute for Computer Sciences, Social Informatics and Telecommunications Engineering
ISBN 978-3-032-38681-6 ISBN 978-3-032-38682-3 (eBook)
https://doi.org/10.1007/978-3-032-38682-3

This Springer imprint is published by the registered company Springer Nature Switzerland AG
The registered company address is: Gewerbestrasse 11, 6330 Cham, Switzerland

Preface

We are delighted to introduce the proceedings of the seventeenth edition of the European Alliance for Innovation (EAI) International Conference on Africa Internet Infrastructure and Services (AFRICOMM 2025). Hosted by Obafemi Awolowo University, Ile-Ife, the conference was held from November 24–25, 2025. This conference brought together researchers, developers and practitioners around the world who are leveraging and developing Internet and ICT infrastructure in order to improve e-government services in Africa. The theme of AFRICOMM 2025 was "e-Infrastructure and e-Services for Developing Countries".

The technical program of AFRICOMM 2025 consisted of 15 full papers, including 1 invited paper, in oral presentation sessions. The conference tracks were: Track 1 — Emerging Networks; Track 2 — Cybersecurity; Track 3 — Artificial Intelligence/ Machine Learning; and Track 4 — Applications of AI in Health and Agriculture. These papers were selected from 54 submissions. Each submission was reviewed following a single-blind process with a minimum of 3 reviews per paper. Aside from the high-quality technical paper presentations, the technical program also featured one keynote speech. The keynote speech was delivered by Michael Ajibola Olajide, the CEO of Sidmach Technologies Nigeria Limited (Sidmach).

Coordination with the General Chair - Ganiyu. A. Aderounmu, Obafemi Awolowo University, Ile-Ife, Nigeria and the General Co-Chair — Kalaivani Chellappan, University Kebangsaan Malaysia, Malaysia was essential for the success of the conference. We sincerely appreciate their constant support and guidance. It was also a great pleasure to work with such an excellent organizing committee team for their hard work in organizing and supporting the conference. In particular, the Technical Program Committee, led by our Program Chair, Folasade Dahunsi and TPC Co-Chairs, O. Osunade and Beman Kamagate, coordinated the peer-review process of technical papers and made a high-quality technical program with the help of a host of reviewers whose names appear in the list of reviewers.

We strongly believe that AFRICACOMM 2025 provided a good forum for all researchers, developers and practitioners to discuss all science and technology aspects that are relevant to Internet and ICT Infrastructure for developing countries. We also expect that future AFRICOMM conferences will be as successful and stimulating as indicated by the contributions presented in this volume.

Glory O. Enaruvbe
Folasade Dahunsi
Ayodeji O. Oluwatope
Kalaivani Chellappan

Organization

Steering Committee

Roch H. Glitho	Concordia University, Canada

Organizing Committee

General Chair

Adesola Aderounmu	Obafemi Awolowo University, Nigeria

General Co-Chairs

Ayodeji Oluwatope	Obafemi Awolowo University, Nigeria
Kalaivani Chellappan	University Kebangsaan Malaysia, Malaysia

TPC Chair and Co-chairs

O. Osunade	University of Ibadan, Nigeria
Eric Tutu Tchao	Kwame Nkrumah University of Science and Technology, Ghana
Glory O. Enaruvbe	AFRIGIST, Obafemi Awolowo University, Nigeria
Emilio Paolini	Scuola Superiore Sant'Anna, Italy
Folashade Dahunsi	Federal University of Technology Akure, Nigeria

Local Chair

Ayodeji Oluwatope	Obafemi Awolowo University, Nigeria

Workshops Chair

Mike Awoleye	Obafemi Awolowo University, Nigeria

Publicity and Social Media Chair

Folake Ojo	Osun State University, Nigeria

Publications Chair

Folashade Dahunsi	Federal University of Technology Akure, Nigeria

Web Chair

Engr Opeyemi Akinwumi	Obafemi Awolowo University, Nigeria

Posters and PhD Track Chair

Sèmèvo Arnaud R. M. Ahouandjinou	Université d'Abomey-Calavi

Panels Chair

Pelagie Houngue	Université d'Abomey-Calavi , Benin

Technical Program Committee

Abdoulaye Sere	Bitplus, Burkina Faso
Arogundade Oluwasefunmi	Federal University of Agriculture Abeokuta, Nigeria
B. Akinyemi	Obafemi Awolowo University, Nigeria
Beman Kamagate	École Supérieure Africaine des Technologies de l'Information et de la Communication, Côte D'Ivoire
Eric Tutu Tchao	Kwame Nkrumah University of Science and Technology, Ghana

Contents

Emerging Networks

Implementation Steps of the SDN-CLOAK Architecture

Badolo Malikir[1(✉)] and Telesphore Tiendrebeogo[2]

[1] PhD student in computer science, Nazi BONI University (UNB), Bobo Dioulasso, Burkina Faso
malbadolo@gmail.com

[2] MC, Professor and Researcher in computer science, Nazi BONI University (UNB), Bobo-Dioulasso, Burkina Faso

Abstract. SDN (Software Defined Networking) is an architecture that has changed the way networks are designed and managed by separating the control plane from the data plane. However, in environments where multiple users share the same physical infrastructure, ensuring security becomes a major challenge. The DHT (Distributed Hash Table) CLOAK (Covering Layers Of Abstract Knowledge) is an architecture designed to address this issue. It enables the creation of secure overlay networks. This paper describes a model for integrating DHT CLOAK into the SDN architecture. In this paper, we will demonstrate how to couple the two technologies in order to achieve a modern, more robust, and scalable architecture. Our system will consist of replacing traditional NFV (Network Function Virtualization) components with CLOAK modules within the SDN architecture.

Our approach brings to the SDN architecture a new secure protocol with anonymization in the control plane, service continuity even if a controller is compromised, as well as churn management and scalability. It also integrates mechanisms such as fake traffic generation and the concealment of NFV locations to mislead potential attackers.

Keywords: SDN · CLOAK · Openflow · NFV · Orchestration · Opendaylight

1 Introduction

Technological advances have led to an increase in data usage. We are seeing enormous amounts of data traffic flowing through networks. Today, the internet has become an indispensable tool for large companies and billions of individuals. Initially, developers focused on facilitating communication between different applications and minimizing the security aspect of the network. As a result, we are seeing attacks such as Distributed Denial of Service (DDoS) attacks, which

A. Oluwatope et al. (Eds.): AFRICOMM 2025, LNICST 713, pp. 3–19, 2027.
https://doi.org/10.1007/978-3-032-38682-3_1

pose a major threat to mobile network operators and system administrators [1]. It is with this in mind that researchers have taken an interest in the topic of SDN/NFV.

Based on SDN architecture, we can define three types of architecture. We have pure SDN architecture, without NFV. NFV architecture without mentioning SDN [2],[3], and we have SDN-oriented NFV architecture [4]. In our case, we will focus on SDN/NFV architecture. For [5], this architecture allows the decision-making part (control plane) to be separated from the equipment and placed at one or more control points called the SDN control plane. Then, the networks equipments is programmed through APIs. With the arrival of NFV in SDN architecture, one of the concerns of operators is to minimize the cost of investigation expenses [6] and also to make network equipment (routers and switches) programmable [7]. For [8], Virtual Network Functions (VNFs) can be instantiated and scaled on demand without having to install new equipment. For him, SDN and NFV offer operators new opportunities to reduce costs, improve flexibility, and scale networks.

OpenFlow is a communication protocol in SDN architecture. In the literature, several papers dealing with SDN, such as [9], [10], and [11], have presented it as the most important communication protocol in SDN architecture and explained it in their paper.

CLOAK [13] is a DHT that allows the construction of an overlay network [42]. For [14] and [15], CLOAK is an architecture that allows the construction of overlay P2P networks that are autonomous and dynamic. A network node can join any peer already within the overlay by generally defining a transport layer connection such as TCP with that peer [44]. Its operation is based on a hyperbolic tree [17] and [18]. In Fig. 1 shows the CLOAK communication architecture, which was detailed in [19].

To continue improving the SDN architecture, we will use CLOAK as a virtual function. In this paper, we are interested in NFV in order to propose a mechanism for translation NFV by the CLOAK in the SDN architecture. The proposed model offers maximum security and also respects the principles of Capex and Opex. With recent advances in the field of SDN and work related to the DHT CLOAK, we have decided to add a security touch to this SDN architecture.

Which leads us to the following issue: How to propose and implement a CLOAK integration approach in SDN capable of optimizing flow management, ensuring security, and facilitating the communication of virtualized services ?

Our paper is structured as follows : in section II, we presented some existing work on SDN/NFV and CLOAK. What allowed us to identify these issues mentioned in paragraph six of this section. In Section III, we present our integration model. In this section, we first made a comparative analysis between CLOAK and NFV. Then, we presented the integration principle the our model. Finally, some translation algorithms, to finish with an explanatory diagram of our approach. In section IV, the article is concluded and some ideas for future research activities are listed in the future Works.

2 Related Work

According to [8] and [2] used SDN and NFV to improve network performance and significantly reduce network capital expenditure (CapEx) and operating expenditure (OpEx). According to [8], the aim was to combine SDN and NFV to achieve greater efficiency. For him, SDN and NFV have come to reduce investment losses and time as well. With an implementation based on the OpenDaylight (ODL) SDN controller with Mininet [20], the author demonstrated the feasibility of the approach and showed that technical implementation choices can have a significant impact on the time required to restore flows after a failure. The author proposed solutions such as optimal bandwidth protection and a scalable mathematical model using column generation. He proposed the ILP (Integer Linear Program) model using heuristic algorithms to address the energy saving problem [21].

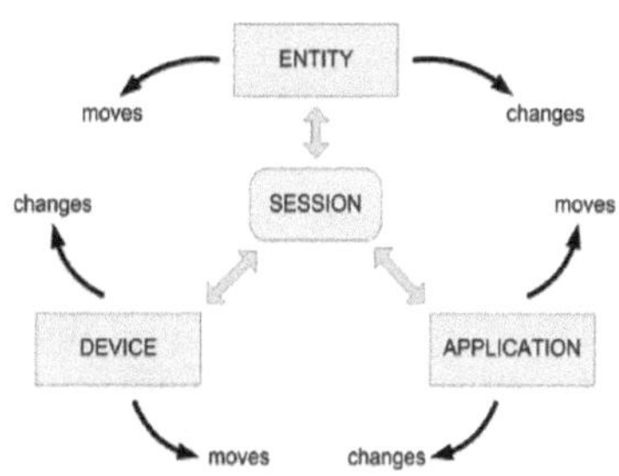

Fig. 1. CLOAK paradigm communication architecture [19].

For [6], he structured his work into two parts: the possibility of offering the Service Function Chain (SFC) as an Service (SFCaaS), and the problem of multi-domain network traffic, for which he provided a solution. He proposed a new multi-domain routing mechanism that is more economical in terms of time and resources. These contributions concern, on the one hand, the allocation of resources for SFCs and, on the other hand, the efficient management of traffic in multi-domain networks.

In his paper [22], the author provided a solution for optimizing computing resources in an NFV system in order to minimize the overall cost of deployment. He proposed three heuristic algorithms, namely Max-Min Resource, Path Selection, and Routing Before Placement (RBP). In his view, these proposed algorithms are more effective than Provision Traffic (PT) from [23].

According to [24], in his article, he studied different reconfiguration strategies. This reconfiguration made it possible to validate the various heuristic algorithms in the NFV framework, as well as the investment and energy costs.

In his paper [25], he studied and explored the NFV contribution to security in order to design effective solutions that mitigate several attack vectors on the one hand and protect SDN against these attacks on the other. Through this research, he contributed to the mitigation of denial-of-service attacks on two levels (intra-domain and extra-domain) using various algorithms.

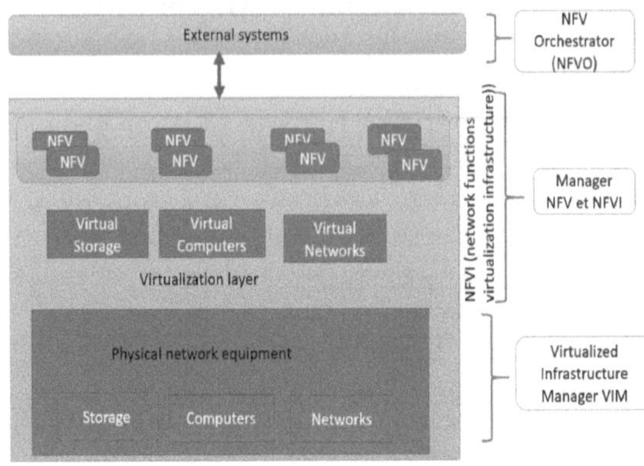

Fig. 2. Architecture NFV.

Several algorithms have proven their usefulness in the context of SDN oriented NFV security, such as in [28], [15], and [22]. It is within this framework that we will focus on algorithms to justify the relevance of our approach. [30], in his paper, presented algorithms for optimal placement in network function chains in order to integrate new functions. Quat in [31] proposed algorithms to extend the Transfer Graphs of Virtualized Network Functions (NFV-GT). He solved the problem of extending the service graph based on Integer Linear Programming (ILP) algorithms [31]. As for [32], it proposes an algorithm that is the most efficient in terms of acceptance rate, energy consumption, and execution time. The proposed algorithm enables the integration of VNF-FG into NFV infrastructures using a multi-agent mechanism. In [43], the author proposed a new Deep Reinforcement Learning (DRL) architecture based on Transformers, called TDRL (Transformer-based DRL), to solve the problem of dynamic placement of VNF-FG based on energy.

In [50] and [4], they explained the different components of NFV and demonstrated their importance in SDN architecture. [26], in his paper, examined several virtualization frameworks and the network support that can be provided to support resident network functions.

Security in DHT CLOAK is well detailed in [44]. He proposed a highly effective mechanism to facilitate information exchange. In his view, traffic confidentiality is ensured by highly effective algorithms.

In a similar vein, numerous researchers have taken an interest in 5G and SDN/NFV. It is in this sense that [33] and [35], proposed 5G with SDN and NFV. For them, these two technologies are involved together, but they are independent of each other. The introduction of 5G has optimized the use of network resources.

Also [36], proposes integrating 5G into SDN/NFV architecture offers several advantages. 5G has a significant impact on network infrastructure thanks to

SDN and NFV. For him, this approach must be treated with great care in order to take all necessary aspects into account.

For [34], he proposed a high-level architecture for 5G based on SDN and NFV. He explained the importance of this architecture for network administrators. Several authors, such as [37], [38], and [39], have proposed several solutions for integrating 5G into SDN/NFV. Together, they ensure a robust and scalable network infrastructure. For them, the arrival of 5G is a very significant innovation for SDN/NFV. We will draw on algorithms developed by various authors working on NFVs to propose an algorithm that takes security aspects into account in order to integrate CLOAK into the SDN architecture.

Based on our investigation of SDN/NFV and DHT CLOAK, substantial advancements have been achieved in both areas. However, critical challenges persist, especially with respect to security and economic efficiency. To the best of our knowledge, no prior work has explored a model for integrating DHT into SDN. To complicate the task of attackers, strengthen confidentiality and resilience, it is imperative to implement a mechanism for fake traffic or network camouflage. To address these insufficiencies, we have chosen to propose an integration model of the DHT CLOAK into the SDN. We are committed to using DHT CLOAK capability in the SDN architecture, which offers multiple advantages in terms of security and economy. The proposed architecture model is named SDN/CLOAK. Areas such as the military and mobile phone networks will be strongly interested in this architecture. With these principles of camouflage and anonymization, fake traffic and communication management, it will offer them a security advantage.

3 Contribution

This part will be devoted to the presentation of our contribution in SDN architecture using the CLOAK DHT. In Fig. 2 shows us the NFV architecture, which consists of three parts. NFVs are deployed on NFV Infrastructure (NFVI), the Virtualized Infrastructure Manager (VIM), and the NFV orchestrator [12], [4]. The authors explain how this virtual infrastructure works in their paper. We developed our NFV architecture based on the work of [4], [26], and [50] to propose this NFV architecture.

3.1 Comparative Analysis of NFV and CLOAK in SDN

To conduct a thorough analysis, it is crucial to understand how each element works. The operating principle of CLOAK is detailed in [17], [1], and [40], and that of NFV in [21], [37], and [41]. Table 1 presents a comparative study of NFV and CLOAK for SDN. Our analysis focused on some criteria that we selected during our review of the literature and which enabled us to draw up this table 1. In summary, we can say that the two technologies chosen, NFV and CLOAK, are excellent means of contributing to the creation of virtual networks. Each brings a touch of security, flexibility, and dynamism to the SDN architecture.

For example, NFV adds dynamism and elasticity to the SDN architecture. On the other hand, with CLOAK, we have guaranteed security, fake traffic, and resistance to analysis. Next, with regard to NFV functions in SDN, we can say that NFV provides virtual network functions. However, CLOAK conceals the actual operation of the network. This makes it possible to deceive the vigilance of stalkers. For good synergy with NFV, SFCs must be combined with SDN and NFV for better synergy. However, for better synergy in SDN, it is sufficient to use CLOAK in combination with SDN (multipair, overlay, fake traffic). This analysis clearly shows that their principles are fundamentally different in some areas such as security, routing, and flow processing. The results presented in this table are taken from several research papers, some of which we have cited: [50], [4] and other authors. We drew inspiration from these papers to produce this comparative table.

Table 1. Comparison between NFV components and CLOAK modules

Criteria	NFV	CLOAK
Main objective	Virtualize network functions (firewall, NAT) [37]	Obfuscate the network (fake traffic), camouflage traffic, and hide the topology [44]
Principle	Performs network functions on generic servers via VNEs [4]	Creation of an abstract virtual overlay to hide the reality of the network
Required compo-nents	VNFs, NFVI, MANO (NFVO, VNFM, VIM) [30]	Modules CLOAK, DHT overlay, random walk, fake traffic
Safety Principle	Indirect: isolation via virtualization, access control, flow segmentation	Direct: camouflage, anonymity, generation of false flows, non-traceability principle of information exchange [44]
Flexibility	Very high [44]	High (creation of dynamic virtual topologies) replication principle
Network visibility	Transparent and controllable (thanks to MANO and SDN) [4]	Intentionally non-transparent: Invisible, Cryptographic [44]
Typical deployment	In data centers	on intermediate nodes (overlay) [44]
Dynamism	Automated by MANO [4]	Periodic re-evaluation (e.g., restart random walk, camouflage if the path becomes predictable, or restart security module) [40]
Typical use case	5G, IoT, Cloud, telecom operators [37]	Military networks (in times of war), 5G and CLOUD in the future

Table 2 presents a comparative study of the different components that CLOAK can replace in NFV. After this analysis, we can say that CLOAK cannot typically replace NFV in SDN architecture, but rather part of NFV. This is because there are functions such as Nat (Network Address Translation), PDI (Deep Packet Inspection : technique of monitoring and analyzing network packets on the headers (IP, TCP/UDP) to examine the actual content of the packets), Transcoding, NFVI (Hypervisor and Datacenter), and orchestration systems NFVO that are complex business functions [4] and [37], which CLOAK cannot replace. In our paper, we will focus on CLOAK's contribution to security in SDN. The integration of CLOAK into the new SDN architecture should be able to replace security VNFs with CLOAK modules. Next, replace the load balancer and multipath routing VNF with CLOAK's random walk and DHT overlay. Finally, via the SDN controller, CLOAK can replace the VNF controller for routing obfuscation by defining and modifying obfuscated roads.

Table 2. Replaceability of NFV components with CLOAK modules

NFV component	Replaced	Justification / Details
Security VNFs (lightweight firewall based on masking, anonymous proxy, lightweight IDS) [37]	**Y**es	CLOAK modules offer: anonymization, address camouflage, fake traffic injection, rendering these VNFs partially useless.
Load balancer / multibath routing VNF	**Y**es	CLOAK's random walk + DHT overlay enables dynamic, non-deterministic routing, which replaces certain load balancing functions.
Anonymous proxy/gateway	**Y**es	CLOAK acts as a stealth proxy or anonymizing gateway by inserting cloaking modules between entities.
Basic IDS (passive obfuscation)	Partial	CLOAK does not detect attacks, but it prevents surveillance through concealment, which can reduce the need for certain IDS at the perimeter.
VNF controller for routing obfuscation	**Y**es	CLOAK can define and modify obfuscated routes via the SDN controller, without requiring a dedicated VNF for this purpose.
NFVI (Infrastructure) [37]	No	CLOAK does not provide hardware support or infrastructure virtualization. It relies on the existence of a programmable network (SDN).
MANO (NFV orchestrator) [37]	No	CLOAK does not replace management and orchestration (MANO), but it can interact with it via the SDN controller.

3.2 Principle of CLOAK Integration in SDN

After a comparative analysis of the two architectures, we can say that CLOAK can not typically replace NFVs in SDN architecture. However, it can replace some NFV components in SDN architecture. For our part, we will focus on the NFV components that CLOAK can replace in order to add a touch of security to the new SDN architecture. This allows us to change the way administrators configure networks. We have named this SDN-oriented CLOAK architecture (SDN/CLOAK). This new architecture must take into account all the security and configuration aspects (Capex and Opex) of traditional SDN architecture. With CLOAK's flexibility and dynamism in managing overlay networks, we have proposed integrating it into the SDN architecture to replace traditional network functions. The separation of the hardware layer from the software will rely on the existence of a programmable network SDN. The DHT CLOAK does not provide hardware support or infrastructure virtualization NFVI, it is based on SDN. It is a DHT that allows overlay networks to be built. Figure 3 shows The sequence diagram steps for integrating CLOAK into the SDN architecture.

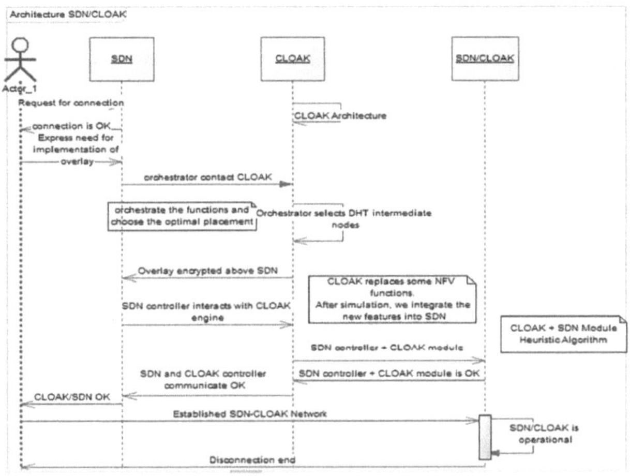

Fig. 3. Algorithm for integrating CLOAK into SDN architecture.

The final SDN/CLOAK architecture gives SDN architecture a more conceptual dimension. This combination makes the abstraction layer intelligent and adaptive to network functions. CLOAK integrates with SDN through APIs that interact with the SDN controller to obtain a view of the physical network. CLOAK programs the equipment via the SDN controller to isolate customer traffic, which is referred to as dynamic programming. Finally, the paths obtained are protected via encryption. Using the SDN architecture, we will implement the CLOAK module via the SDN controller. In the DHT CLOAK, applications can create their own overlay network through the SDN controller. This is a highly dynamic system, as the movement of pairs in the network has no impact on others. With the dynamism of CLOAK combined with various heuristic algorithms, we can add a touch of security to the SDN architecture. In terms of node management, CLOAK is an excellent DHT, even when the network is running. We have also taken the time to understand the place of the CLOAK system architecture in the OSI (Open Systems Interconnection) model. CLOAK in SDN architecture is a secure decentralized overlay that can replace same NFV components in SDN architecture. With Cloak, network functions (firewall, load balancing, etc.) are implemented in a distributed manner across DHT nodes.

We can conclude that our objective, which is to implement a secure management protocol in the SDN architecture, is welcome. Because with the dynamism of CLOAK combined with various heuristic algorithms, we will be able to add a touch of security to the SDN architecture. Figure 4 shows the SDN architecture with integrated CLOAK modules. This figure gives us an overview of our new architecture supporting CLOAK modules.

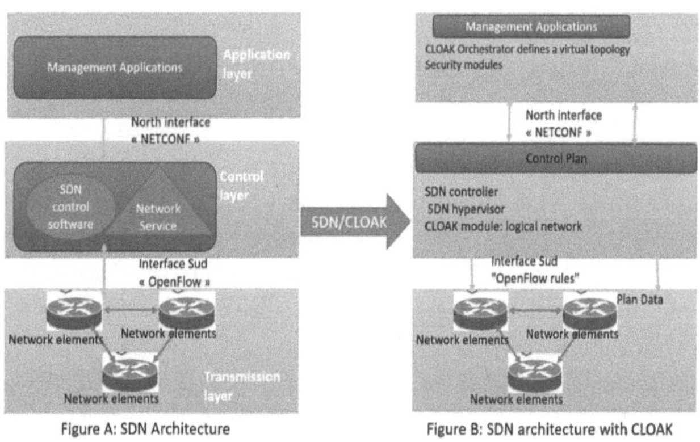

Fig. 4. SDN architecture with the CLOAK module.

Figure 5 below presents a CLOAK architecture with the necessary CLOAK functions for setting up a virtual network. In this architecture, we have three levels generally. The first level is called MANO (Management and Network Orchestration) space. In this part, we have the virtual function managers, the NFV orchestra and the virtualized infrastructure manager. The MANO space acts as the general coordinator between resources and functions. Then, the second level called CLOAK space, where all the CLOAK modules are (the NFV modules that CLOAK can replace). And finally the third level material space, which contains all that is physical material of the network. Our contribution will be based on the second level CLOAK space. We have introduced in the CLOAK space new features by replacing all the NFV components that CLOAK can support.

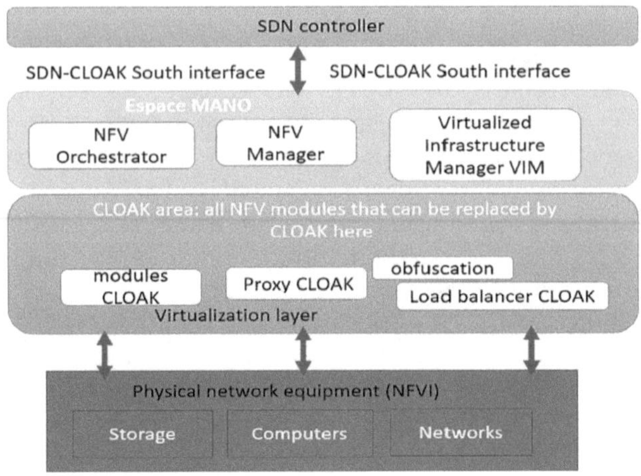

Fig. 5. Architecture CLOAK.

3.3 Comparative Analysis SDN Controllers

This section is devoted to the comparative study of the different SDN controllers that we will use in the case of our research. According to our research, there are several SDN controllers. All these controllers are excellent whether it is on the contribution plan or simulation. Several authors such as [45] and [46] have conducted a comparative study on OpenDaylight (ODL), Floodlight, and ONOS controllers. These authors have detailed the different controllers in their articles according to their efficiency that we can use as part of our SDN-CLOAK architecture. According to these analyses, we will use OpenDaylight as a controller for the development of our architecture. For the simulation of terminals and switches, we will use Mininet. There are several works on SDN controllers that we will not detail here.

For [47], the choice of different controllers is a function on one hand of the development languages. So it is an important factor in the implementation of the SDN-CLOAK controller. Table 1 of his article details all the SDN controllers. For more details, consult the articles [47] and [48].

This table 3 summarizes the three most used controllers in SDN. We can say that ONOS and Floodlight are very simple and easy to implement for a beginner. On the other hand, Opendaylight is very complex to implement because it is modular and has a higher latency. But Opendaylight is more complete in terms of protocol and integration of other protocols such as NFV and CLOAK. In view of all the advantages and disadvantages presented in these different articles, we will use the Opendaylight controller in the case of our study (facilitation of virtualization and integration with other technologies). The choice of this controller is due to the fact that it has APIs that facilitate the integration of other controllers. One of the difficulties of this controller lies in the complexity of its implementation and requires a good understanding of SDN and network protocols. In conclusion, given the complexity of our issue, which invites us to work on advanced scenarios, Opendaylight is more suitable.

4 Implementation Steps

In this part, we will present the implementation steps by steps. As a reminder, this architecture consists of integrating the DHT CLOAK into the SDN. We have

Table 3. Comparison of SDN Controllers: OpenDaylight, ONOS, and Floodlight

Criterion / Metric	OpenDaylight (ODL)	ONOS	Floodlight
Architecture	Centralized, modular (OSGi/Karaf) [46]	Distributed, multi-node cluster (HA) [53]	Centralized, monolithic (Java) [54]
Language / API	Java, RESTCONF, NETCONF, BGP, PCEP, OpenFlow [48]	Java, Intent framework, OpenFlow, P4, gNMI [52]	Java, OpenFlow 1.0/1.3, REST API [53]
Ecosystem / Use cases	Telco, NFV, ETSI integration, industrial projects [46]	Data centers, operators, scalable backbone [52]	Academic, rapid prototyping [54]
Response latency (CBench)	3–6 ms/flow-mod [54]	2–4 ms/flow-mod [53]	1–2 ms/flow-mod [52]
Maximum throughput (flows/s)	30k–50k [52]	40k–60k [53]	60k–80k [52]
Scalability	Good but limited (experimental cluster) [46]	Excellent (native clustering, fault tolerance) [53]	Limited (single-node) [54]
Memory consumption	High (heavy Karaf) [46]	Medium to high: distributed cluster [48]	Low [53]
Deployment complexity	High (multiple modules, heavy config) [46]	Medium/High (Zookeeper, Atomix) [48]	Low (a simple JAR) [54]
Protocol support	Very broad (OpenFlow, NETCONF, BGP, VPN, VXLAN) [46]	Broad (OpenFlow, SR, P4) [48]	Limited (OpenFlow 1.0/1.3) [53]
Academic usage	Less common (heavy) [54]	Medium (scalability research) [52]	Very common (Mininet + Floodlight) [53]
Typical results	Stability but high latency [54]	Good tradeoff scalability/latency [46]	Fast but less scalable [52]
Recommended domains	Telco, NFV orchestration, industrial [46]	Operators, ISP, distributed DC [53]	Research, education, testbeds [54]

an architecture of the DHT CLOAK that works on eclipse. Then, we have a functional SDN/NFV architecture with the Opendayligth controller. The implementation steps will consist of compiling all the CLOAK modules and integrating them into the Opendaylight Controller in order to have an SDN/CLOAK architecture. The following figure gives us an overview of the different implementation steps of our new architecture using the ODL controller.

The first step consists of preparing the project. It is in this part that the choice of the type of project must be made. Mono module or multi-module to facilitate the separation of layers such as core, API, implementation, features. What will facilitate maintenance and integration into the ODL (Fig. 6).

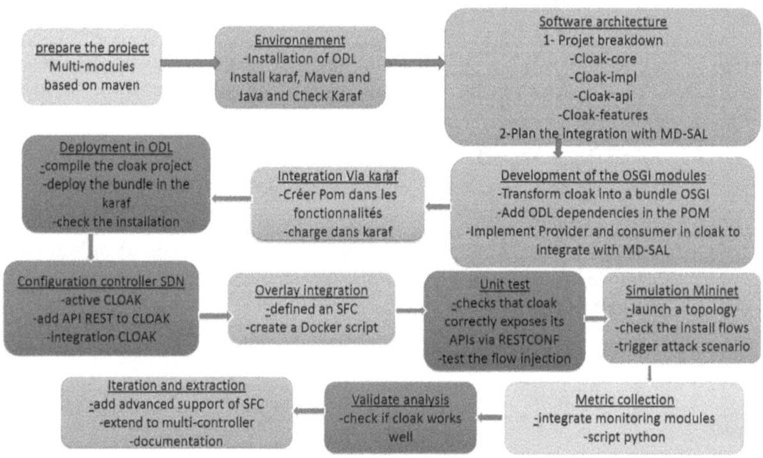

Fig. 6. Implementation steps of the SDN/CLOAK architecture with ODL.

The environmental step determines the implementation and installation of the different development tools. In this part, we will talk about the installation and configuration of ODL, Karaf, Maven, and Java compatible with our development system (Computer). Also make sure that DHT CLOAK works well on your system. In our case, we have the DHT CLOAK running well on Ubuntu 20.04. Also the ODL controller SDN works with the same system.

In the software architecture part, it is about presenting the structure of the future architecture. This part presents two main ideas, namely the splitting of the project and the integration of MD-SAL (Model-Driven Service Abstraction Layer). For the first idea, it is to break down the project into several modules (we talk about multi-modules). The following figure shows the breakdown of our project and the different sections. In the second part, plan the integration with MD-SAL. These modules will allow CLOAK to interact with the other services of the SDN controller.

Regarding the development of OSGI modules, it is about transforming CLOAK into a bundle compatible with OSGI. Which will allow CLOAK to compile in ODL as a feature. Then, add dependencies in the POMs. These pom are Maven configuration files. Finally the implementation of providers (provided services) and consumers (used services) for integration with MD-SAL.

For the integration part via Karaf, it is the step of compiling and integrating the modules obtained. In this part, you need to compile the entire project in order to have the necessary features. At this stage also, we will talk about the creation of the feature.xml files. The loading and activation of CLOAK bundles in Karaf via feature:install. Finally, at this level, it is necessary to verify if the bundles are active.

The next step is the deployment step in ODL. At this step, it is necessary to ensure that the project compiles correctly. Then, ensure that the deployment can be done in Karaf. This will lead you to use the feature installation commands in Karaf. As an example nature:install namDelaJar. If it goes well, it is possible to make a verification by accessing ODL using the identifiers for the connection.

The next step is the configuration of the SDN controller. At this integration stage, all modules must be ready to integrate into the SDN controller. This is the place to activate all CLOAK natures in ODL. Then external management such as securing flows, encryptions and many others. Finally configured the obtained CLOAK features to directly integrate ODL.

Afterwards, we will talk about integration in overlay networks. As a reminder, CLOAK is an excellent overlay network. We can cite SFC allowing to redirect certain flows via the security functions CLOAK, creation of other scripts. At this level, there is more scripting that can be injected into the network to help secure it.

The next step is the unit testing stage. The objective at this level is to verify that CLOAK indeed exposes its services via RESTCONF. Then, check the flow injection tests developed to ensure its proper functioning. The idea is to ensure that the CLOAK modules obtained and the test scripts developed work correctly.

After verifying that everything is working correctly in the ODL controller and that our SDN/CLOAK architecture runs well with ODL, the simulation step with mininet comes into play. Choose your topology to test the architecture. Then do pings and check the installed flows. Finally, trigger attack scenarios to check the robustness of our SDN/CLOAK architecture. Which allows us to know that our modules are robust.

After doing the simulations with Mininet, to perform a good analysis, you must first plan the collection of metrics. For this, the most mastered collection language can be used. Develop monitoring modules to observe network performance and security. For our case, we will use Python scripts to collect and analyze the metrics. As for the validation and analysis step, it consists of checking the output metrics. This allows to know if CLOAK is working correctly in ODL.

Finally, in the last step, plan an extension and make documentation. Give other possibilities to integrate other controllers, 5G, IoT and many others.

In conclusion, this diagram explains the implementation steps of our new architecture.

5 Conclusion and Future Work

5.1 Conclusion

Our contribution consisted in presenting a Implement steps of the SDN-CLOAK architecture. It was shown that it is possible to integrate the CLOAK into the SDN architecture. This model combining the CLOAK modules with some NFV components in order to strengthen security at the level of the SDN architecture. With this model, virtual networks are not only logically isolated, but also cryptograhically invisible. This contribution provides a high level of security in the SDN architecture. Our system does not completely replace NFV in the SDN architecture, but some components that can participate in strengthening the security of programmable networks. The proposed translation algorithms allow us to automate our approach while respecting the principles of NFV's. It is therefore a fertile ground for academic and industrial innovation.

5.2 Future Work

In the continuation of the work, we will implement this new architecture and integrate it into Opendaylight. In order to present our contribution, we plan to do simulations of our architecture model. In the future, we are considering on the one hand the integration of artificial intelligence into the new AI-oriented SDN/CLOAK architecture. Then, the integration of 5G in the SDN/CLOAK architecture, taking into account SDN, CLOAK and CLOUD and others. We are also planning an end-to-end implementation of our solution.

References

1. KREUTZ, Diego, RAMOS, Fernando MV, VERISSIMO, Paulo Esteves, et al.: Software-defined networking: A comprehensive survey. Proc. IEEE, **103** (1), p. 14-76 (2014)
2. PALKAR, Shoumik, LAN, Chang, HAN, Sangjin, et al. E2: A framework for NFV applications. In: Proceedings of the 25th Symposium on Operating Systems Principles, p. 121-136 (2015)
3. Sheoran, A., Sharma, P., Fahmy, S., et al.: Contain-ed: An NFV micro-service system for containing e2e latency. ACM SIGCOMM Comput. Commun. Rev., **47**(5), 54-60 (2017)
4. Rehman, A.U., Aguiar, R.L. and Barraca, J.P.: Network functions virtualization: the long road to commercial deployments. IEEE Access, **7**, 60439-60464 (2019)
5. Fouad, B., Mouad, M.: Etude des Performances des Architectures du Plan de Contrôle des Réseaux Software-Defined Networks (2017)
6. Moufakir, T., Zhani, M.F., Gherbi, A., Aloqaily, M. and Ghrada, N., et al.: SFCaaS: Service function chains as a service in NFV environments. arXiv preprint arXiv:2203.01098 (2022)
7. DURAND, J.: Le SDN pour les nuls. In: JRES (Journées réseaux de l'enseignement et de la recherche) (2015)

8. Tomassilli, A., Huin, N., Giroire, F. and Jaumard, B, et al.: Resource requirements for reliable service function chaining. In: 2018 IEEE International Conference on Communications (ICC), p. 1-7. IEEE (2018)
9. Youcef, M.: Intégration du Software-Defined Networking (SDN) dans les réseaux de véhicules (VANETs) (2019)
10. Choukri, I., Ouzzif, M. and Bouragba, K.: Software Defined Networking (SDN): Etat de L'art. In: Colloque sur les Objets et systèmes Connectés (2019)
11. Toufga, S., Abdellatif, S., Assouane, H.T., Owezarski, P., et al.: Towards dynamic controller placement in software defined vehicular networks. Sensors, **20**(6), 1701 (2020)
12. Gausseran, A., Tomassilli, A., Giroire, F., et al.: Don't interrupt me when you reconfigure my service function chains. Comput. Commun., **171**, 39-53 (2021)
13. Tiendrebeogo, T., Ahmat, D., Magoni, D., et al.: Virtual connections in P2P overlays with DHT-based name to address resolution. Int. J. Adv. Internet Technol. **5**(1), 11-25 (2012)
14. Tiendrebeogo, T., Ahmat, D. and Magoni, D.: Reliable and scalable distributed hash tables harnessing hyperbolic coordinates. In: 2012 5th International Conference on New Technologies, Mobility and Security (NTMS), p. 1-6. IEEE (2012)
15. Tiendrebeogo, T., Ahmat, D. and Magoni, D.: Évaluation de la fiabilité d'une table de hachage distribuée construite dans un plan hyperbolique. Revue des Sciences et Technologies de l'Information-Série TSI: Technique et Science Informatiques, **33**(4), 311-341 (2014)
16. Cassagnes, C., Tiendrebeogo, T., Bromberg, Y.D., et al.: DHT Basée sur la Géométrie Hyperbolique. Dans: 15èmes Colloque Francophone sur l'Ingénierie des Protocoles (2011)
17. DIARRA, Mamadou et TIENDREBEOGO, Telesphore. Cloak-Reduce Load Balancing Strategy for Mapreduce. Int. J. Comput. Sci. Inf. Technol. (IJCSIT). vol.13 (2021)
18. Tiendrebeogo, T.: A new spatial database management system using an hyperbolic tree. DBKDA 2015, p. 53 (2015)
19. Tiendrebeogo, T., Magoni, D. and Sié, O.: Virtual internet connections over dynamic peer-to-peer overlay networks. In: Proceedings of the 3rd International Conference on Evolving Internet, p. 58-65 (2011)
20. Di Lena, G., Tomassilli, A., Saucez, D., et al.: Mininet on steroids: exploiting the cloud for mininet performance. In : 2019 IEEE 8th International Conference on Cloud Networking (CloudNet). IEEE, pp. 1-3 (2019)
21. Tomassilli, A., Di Lena, G., Giroire, F.: Poster: design of survivable SDN, NFV-enabled networks with bandwidth-optimal failure recovery. In: IFIP Networking Conference (IFIP Networking). IEEE 2019, pp. 1–2 (2019)
22. NGUYEN, Thi-Minh, FDIDA, Serge, et PHAM, Tuan-Minh.: A comprehensive resource management and placement for network function virtualization. In: 2017 IEEE Conference on Network Softwarization (NetSoft). IEEE, pp. 1-9 (2017)
23. Bari, M.F., Chowdhury, S.R., Ahmed, R.: On orchestrating virtual network functions. In: 11th International Conference on Network and Service Management (CNSM). IEEE 2015, pp. 50–56 (2015)
24. Padhy, S. and Chou, J.: Reconfiguration aware orchestration for network function virtualization with time-varied workload in virtualized datacenters. IEEE Access, **9**, 48413-48428 (2021)
25. Abou El Houda, Z.: Renforcement de la sécurité à travers les réseaux programmables (2021)

26. Qi, S., Zeng, Z., Monis, L., et al.: MiddleNet: a unified, high-performance NFV and middlebox framework with eBPF and DPDK. IEEE Trans. Netw. Serv. Manage., **20**(4), 3950-3967 (2023)
27. Zhang, T., Qiu, H., Linguaglossa, L., et al.: NFV platforms: taxonomy, design choices and future challenges. IEEE Trans. Netw. Serv. Manage.,**18**, (1) 30-48 (2020)
28. Houidi, O., Soualah, O., Louati, W., et al.: Dynamic VNF forwarding graph extension algorithms. IEEE Trans. Netw. Serv. Manage., **17**(3), 1389-1402 (2020)
29. Gausseran, A., Tomassilli, A., Giroire, F.: Poster: Don't interrupt me when you reconfigure my service function chains. In: IFIP Networking Conference (IFIP Networking). IEEE 2019, pp. 1–2 (2019)
30. Houidi, O.: Algorithms for virtual network functions chaining. Ph. D. dissertation (2020)
31. Houidi, O., Soualah, O., Louati, W.: Virtualized network services extension algorithms. In: IEEE 17th International Symposium on Network Computing and Applications (NCA). IEEE 2018, pp. 1–5 (2018)
32. Houidi, O., Soualah, O., Houidi, I., et al.: Energy efficient VNF-FG embedding via attention-based deep reinforcement learning. In: 2023 19th International Conference on Network and Service Management (CNSM). IEEE, p. 1-7 (2023)
33. Wang, M.: Virtualization (SDN/NFV) in optical access networks: contributions for enhanced fixed-mobile convergence. Thèse de doctorat. Ecole nationale supérieure Mines-Télécom Atlantique (2022)
34. Zhang, J., Xie, W. and Yang, F.: An architecture for 5G mobile network based on SDN and NFV. In: 6th International Conference on Wireless, Mobile and Multi-Media (ICWMMN 2015). Stevenage UK : IET (2015)
35. Gausseran, A., Alliche, R.A., Lesfari, H.: Reconfiguring network slices at the best time with deep reinforcement learning. In: IEEE 11th International Conference on Cloud Networking (CloudNet). IEEE 2022, pp. 85–92 (2022)
36. Rajan, A.S. and Ramia, K.B.: Application of NFV and SDN to 5G infrastructure. Towards 5G: Applications, Requirements and Candidate Technologies, pp. 408-420 (2016)
37. Zaidi, Z., Friderikos, V., Yousaf, Z., et al.: Will SDN be part of 5G?. IEEE Commun. Surv. Tutorials, **20**(4) 3220-3258 (2018)
38. Bouras, C., Kollia, A. and Papazois, A.: SDN and NFV in 5G: advancements and challenges. In: 2017 20th Conference on Innovations in Clouds, Internet and Networks (ICIN). IEEE, pp. 107-111 (2017)
39. Hasneen, J. and Sadique, K.M.: A survey on 5G architecture and security scopes in SDN and NFV. In : Applied Information Processing Systems: Proceedings of ICCET 2021. Singapore : Springer Singapore, pp. 447-460 (2021)
40. Mamadou, D.,Telesphore, T.B.: Conception of a load balancing strategy for CLOAK-Reduce (2021)
41. Tantayakul, K., Dhaou, R. and Paillassa, B.: Mobility management with caching policy over SDN architecture. In: 2017 IEEE Conference on Network Function Virtualization and Software Defined Networks (NFV-SDN). IEEE, pp. 1-7 (2017)
42. Ahmat, D., Barka, M. and Magoni, D.: SEMOS: A Middleware for Providing Secure and Mobility-aware Sessions over a P2P Overlay Network. In: International Conference on e-Infrastructure and e-Services for Developing Countries. Cham : Springer International Publishing, pp. 111-121 (2016)
43. Sahraoui, R., Houidi, O. and Bannour, F.: Energy-Aware VNF-FG placement with transformer-based deep reinforcement learning. In: 2024 IEEE/IFIP Network Operations and Management Symposium (NOMS 2024) (2024)

44. Ahmat, D. and Magoni, D.: MUSeS: Mobile user secured session. In: IFIP Wireless Days. IEEE 2012, 1–6 (2012)
45. Mamushiane, L., Shozi, T.: A QoS-based evaluation of SDN controllers: ONOS and OpenDayLight. In: 2021 IST-Africa Conference, pp. 1–10. IEEE, IST-Africa (2021)
46. Singh, A., Kaur, N., Kaur, H.: Extensive performance analysis of OpenDayLight (ODL) and open network operating system (ONOS) SDN controllers. Microprocess. Microsyst. **95**, 104715 (2022)
47. Zhu, L., et al.: SDN controllers: a comprehensive analysis and performance evaluation study. ACM Comput. Surv. (CSUR) **53**(6), 1–40 (2020)
48. Sheikh, M.N.A., Hwang, I.S., Raza, M.S., Ab-Rahman, M.S.: A qualitative and comparative performance assessment of logically centralized SDN controllers via mininet emulator. Computers **13**(4), 85 (2024)
49. Costa-Perez, X., et al.: 5G-crosshaul: An SDN/NFV integrated fronthaul/backhaul transport network architecture. IEEE Wirel. Commun. 24(1), 38–45 (2017)
50. Zhang, T., Qiu, H., Linguaglossa, L., Cerroni, W., Giaccone, P.: NFV platforms: Taxonomy, design choices and future challenges. IEEE Trans. Netw. Serv. Manage. **18**(1), 30–48 (2020)
51. Zaidi, Z., Friderikos, V., Yousaf, Z., Fletcher, S., Dohler, M., Aghvami, H.: Will SDN be part of 5G?. IEEE Commun. Surv. Tutorials **20**(4), 3220–3258 (2018)
52. Zhu, L., Karim, M.M., Sharif, K., Li, F., Du, X., Guizani, M.: SDN controllers: Benchmarking performance evaluation. arXiv preprint arXiv:1902.04491 (2019)
53. Mamushiane, L., Lysko, A., Dlamini, S.: A comparative evaluation of the performance of popular SDN controllers. In: 2018 Wireless Days (WD), pp. 54–59. IEEE (2018)
54. Khattak, Z.K., Awais, M., Iqbal, A.: Performance evaluation of OpenDaylight SDN controller. In: 20th IEEE International Conference on Parallel and Distributed Systems (ICPADS), pp. 671–676. IEEE (2014)

MetricTest: A Client-Side Performance Measurement Tool for Wireless Community Networks in Rural Areas

Tonye Mandjel Justine Prudence[1], Fendji Kedieng Ebongue Jean Louis[1,2](✉), Yenke Blaise Omer[1], and Atemkeng Teufack Marcellin[3]

[1] University of Ngaoundere, P.O. Box 454, Ngaoundere, Cameroon
jl.fendji@egcim-univ-ndere.cm
[2] Stellenbosch Institute for Advanced Study (STIAS), Stellenbosch, South Africa
[3] Rhodes University, P.O. Box 6140, Grahamstown, South Africa
m.atemkeng@ru.ac.za

Abstract. Wireless community networks offer a promising solution for connecting underserved rural areas, yet assessing their performance from the end-user perspective remains a significant challenge. Existing network measurement tools often lack critical features such as client-side geolocation, automatic measurement scheduling, and shared performance data, thus limiting their utility for effective community network administration and optimization. This paper introduces MetricTest, a mobile application specifically designed to address these limitations in African contexts, where digital divides persist and connectivity resources are often constrained. MetricTest empowers end-users to precisely measure key network metrics, including latency, packet loss, jitter, and both upload and download speeds, directly from their mobile devices. Crucially, it incorporates geolocation capabilities, enables automatic and scheduled testing, and facilitates the sharing of performance data among users and with network administrators. A comparative analysis, utilizing real-world data from deployments in Cameroon, demonstrates MetricTest's significant advantage in data efficiency compared to other tools. This minimal data footprint is a critical feature for resource-limited community networks. Beyond its primary focus, MetricTest also proves effective in evaluating the Quality of Service (QoS) offered by commercial mobile telecommunication operators, potentially aiding advocacy for improved services.

Keywords: Community networks · QoS · Client-side measurement · Mobile application · Network performance · MetricTest

1 Introduction

Internet access has become an indispensable part of daily life for many, with the UN Human Rights Council recognizing it as a fundamental right. According to ITU, 2.6 billion people are still offline [1]. This figure shows significant digital disparities, particularly in rural areas that remain underserved. To address this, initiatives like the

A. Oluwatope et al. (Eds.): AFRICOMM 2025, LNICST 713, pp. 20–30, 2027.
https://doi.org/10.1007/978-3-032-38682-3_2

African Community Networks Summit, organized by the Internet Society, have promoted wireless community networks as a viable solution.

Wireless Community networks are telecommunication infrastructures built and managed by citizens for the benefit of their local communities [2]. These self-sustaining, shared wireless computer networks offer a democratically controlled and cost-effective solution to internet access challenges, especially in regions where traditional telecommunication operators find it unprofitable to invest due to a lack of guaranteed return on investment [3].

However, wireless community networks face inherent challenges. They can be fragile and subject to link attenuation [4], with equipment prone to failure, leading to reduced coverage, especially in case of bad planning [3, 5]. Furthermore, a common issue is the lack of qualified personnel within these communities to manage and measure network performance effectively [6]. Crucially, there is often a limited understanding of the quality of service (QoS) experienced by the end-user. Unlike mobile telecommunication networks offering broad coverage, community network nodes have a short range, and their placement doesn't always guarantee optimal user coverage [7, 8]. The geographic distribution of future users is difficult to predict, leading to situations where some nodes are underutilized while others are overloaded. Without accurate client-side QoS data, administrators struggle to make informed decisions for network improvement.

Existing network analysis tools, while numerous, have limitations when applied to community networks. Desktop tools are often unsuitable as users primarily access the internet via smartphones. Mobile solutions like Fing, nPerf, Speedtest, Netflow, and OONI Probe fall short by not offering geolocation of client-side performance measurements, automatic test scheduling, or easy sharing of results between users and with administrators.

This paper addresses these limitations by proposing MetricTest, a mobile application designed to provide comprehensive network performance measurements from the user's perspective. The primary goal is to empower users and administrators with the ability to assess network quality at any given location. MetricTest specifically aims to:

- Determine jitter, latency, packet loss, upload speed, and download speed.
- Provide an overview of measurements taken in a specific geographical area.
- Perform scheduled as well as instant tests.

The remainder of this paper is organized as follows: Sect. 2 provides a background on community network and related work on tools for network performance measurements. Section 3 presents the design and implementation of the proposed tool. Section 4 presents and discusses the results. Finally, Sect. 5 presents the results of various tests conducted with the proposed tool and discusses future perspectives.

2 Background and Related Work

2.1 Community Networks in Africa

Community networks are autonomous, shared wireless computer networks managed by local communities [9]. They are characterized by local control, cost-effectiveness, and adaptability to specific community needs. Examples in Africa include Zenzeleni

Networks in South Africa, Mesh Bukavu in DRC, and Pamoja Net on Idjwi Island, DRC [10]. In Cameroon, initiatives like the Télécentre Communautaires Polyvalents (TCP) project, supported by GIZ, aim to transform telecenters into community networks in regions like Bibemi and Mayo-Oulo/Mandama.

Despite their contribution in connecting the unconnected, community networks are facing numerous challenges including:

- Network Fragility: Equipment failures and limited robustness can lead to reduced coverage and degraded performance. The failure of a single node can significantly impact the entire network's throughput.
- Lack of Skilled Personnel: Network managers in CNs often lack the technical expertise or appropriate tools to effectively measure and diagnose network performance issues at various locations.
- Lack of User-Side QoS Appreciation: Unlike commercial mobile networks with wide coverage, CN nodes have limited range. Predicting user distribution during planning is difficult, leading to potential imbalances where some nodes are overloaded while others are underutilized. Without client-side QoS data, administrators struggle to make informed decisions for network optimization.

2.2 Existing Network Performance Measurement Tools

Network performance measurement involves continuously monitoring network devices and services. Various tools exist, catering to developers, researchers, and network operators.

Table 1 highlights common shortcomings of existing network performance tools. This includes:

- Limited Data Access and Transparency: Most tools do not allow users to view measurements from others, hindering a holistic understanding of network quality in a given area.
- Lack of Automatic Scheduling: The inability to program recurring measurements means users must manually initiate tests, limiting the collection of continuous performance data.
- No Coverage Area Delimitation: Visualizing measurements within a user-defined radius is often not supported.
- High Data Consumption: Many tools consume significant amounts of data during tests, which is a critical concern in bandwidth-scarce environments.
- Administrator Insight Gap: Existing tools primarily focus on individual user experience, providing limited aggregated data or geographical insights for network administrators to identify problem areas and plan improvements.

These limitations underscore the need for a more comprehensive, participatory approach to network performance measurement, particularly for community networks where client-side data and collaborative insights are paramount.

Table 1. Comparative summary of existing network performance measurement tools

Tool	Latency	Jitter	Upload	Download	Packet Loss	Geolocation	Automatic Scheduling	Data Sharing
FCC Speed Test	✓	✓	✓	✓	✓	✓	X	X
WinRider	X	X	✓	✓	X	X	X	X
MySpeedTest	✓	✓	✓	✓	✓	X	X	X
MobiPerf	✓	X	✓	✓	✓	X	X	X
Ookla SpeedTest	✓	✓	✓	✓	✓	X	X	X
OpenSignal	✓	X	✓	✓	X	X	X	X
nPerf	X	X	✓	✓	X	X	X	X
Fing	X	X	✓	✓	X	X	X	X

https://www.fcc.gov/BroadbandData/speed-test-app
https://users.cs.northwestern.edu/~ict992/mobile.htm
https://speedtestapp.net/
https://mobiperf.com/
https://www.speedtest.net/
https://www.opensignal.com/apps
https://www.nperf.com/en/
https://help.fing.com/hc/en-us/articles/4418449575186-Internet-Speed-Test

3 MetricTest: Design and Implementation

3.1 System Architecture

MetricTest is designed as a client-server application, leveraging a NoSQL database (Firebase Cloud Firestore) for data storage and various APIs for functionality.

The application operates as follows:

1. Client-Side Data Recovery: The application initiates by obtaining the user's connection operator and geographical location. This is achieved using the getNetworkOperatorName() function and the Android Location API.
2. Server Selection: Before any measurement, MetricTest identifies the nearest and most available server. It approximates the user's location using a GeoIP database and then pings up to five nearby servers. The server with the lowest Round-Trip Time (RTT) is selected for the performance tests, ensuring the most accurate results based on network proximity.
3. Execution of Tasks: Once a server is selected, MetricTest performs a series of active measurements to quantify network performance metrics.
4. Data Storage: All collected measurements, along with their associated metadata (timestamp, location, operator), are stored in Firebase Cloud Firestore.
5. Visualization and Reporting: Measurements are visualized on a map using the Google Maps API and GeoFire, allowing users to view performance data within a specified

radius. The application also aggregates and displays average QoS values per operator within defined zones.

3.2 Metric Recovery and Calculation

MetricTest calculates the following performance metrics:

Latency (Round-Trip Time-RTT): RTT is measured as the time taken for a packet to travel from the client to the server and back. MetricTest performs 20 iterations of sending requests and receiving responses, with the smallest RTT value determining the final result (in milliseconds). This process ensures robustness against transient network conditions.

Algorithm 1: Latency

1. ***Input:*** *Server Address*
2. ***Output:*** *Latency in milliseconds*
3. *Initialize RTT_values array.*
4. ***While*** *number of requests less than 20* ***do****:*
    Send a request and note the start time t0.
    Receive the response and note the end time t1.
    Calculate RTT = $t_1 - t_0$.
    Add RTT to RTT_values.
5. ***End While***
6. *Min_RTT = Minimum value in RTT_values.*
7. ***Display*** *Min_RTT.*

Download Speed: This metric quantifies how fast the internet connection can retrieve data from the server. MetricTest employs an algorithm similar to popular speed test tools:

Algorithm 2: Download Speed

1. ***Output:*** *Download speed in Mbps*
2. *Download small binary files from the web server to the client to estimate connection speed.*
3. *Select an appropriate file size for the actual download test.*
4. *Add a random string to each download to prevent cache effects.*
5. *Utilize up to 8 parallel HTTP threads for testing.*
6. *Receive up to 30 traffic samples per second.*
7. *Divide samples into 20 slices (each representing 5% of the total sample).*
8. *Eliminate the fastest 10% and slowest 30% of slices to remove outliers.*
9. *Calculate the average of the remaining slices to determine the final result.*
10. ***Display*** *Download Speed.*

Upload Speed: This measures how quickly data can be sent from the client's device to the internet.

Algorithm 3: Upload Speed

1. ***Output:*** *Upload speed in Mbps*
2. *Generate a small quantity of random data on the client side and send it to the web server to estimate connection speed.*
3. *Select a set of randomly generated data of appropriate size for uploading.*
4. *Perform an upload test (via POST to a server-side script) with a configurable block size.*
5. *Utilize up to 8 parallel HTTP threads for testing.*
6. *Sort the data pieces by speed, and calculate the average of the fastest half to eliminate anomalies and determine the result.*
7. ***Display*** *Upload Speed.*

Jitter: It describes the inconsistency in delay between data packets over a network. It is measured in milliseconds (ms) and calculated as the average time difference between consecutive packet sequences.

Algorithm 4: Jitter

1. ***Input:*** *Latency values L1,...,Ln*
2. ***Output:*** *Jitter in milliseconds*
3. *Initialize Jitter = 0.*
4. ***For*** *i from 1 to n-1* ***do:***
   $Jitter = Jitter + |L_{i+1} - L_i| / (n-1)$
5. ***End For***
6. ***Display*** *Jitter.*

Packet Loss: It refers to the number of data packets lost during transmission. The packet loss rate is the ratio of lost packets to the total packets sent.

Algorithm 5: Packet Loss

1. ***Input:*** *Total number of packets sent n*
2. ***Output:*** *Total number of lost packets*
3. *Calculate PL = ((Number of packets sent - Number of packets received) / Number of packets sent) * 100.*
4. ***Display*** *PL (packet loss percentage).*

Operator Identification: MetricTest uses the Android getNetworkOperatorName() function to identify the mobile network operator. If connected to Wi-Fi, it also identifies the Wi-Fi network's SSID. The application also records the precise date, time, longitude, latitude, and connection type (2G, 3G, 4G) for each measurement.

3.3 APIs and Features

MetricTest integrates several key APIs and features to enhance its functionality:

- GeoFire: This open-source Android library facilitates storing and querying data based on geographical location. It enables real-time queries for data within a specified region, making it ideal for visualizing measurements taken by different users in a given vicinity. For example, it allows the application to show performance data points within a 5 km radius, enhancing the community-driven aspect of performance monitoring.

- Google Maps API: Used for integrating and customizing maps, displaying geolocated measurements, and allowing users to zoom and filter results visually.
- Android Location API: Essential for precisely locating the device performing the measurement (latitude and longitude).
- Automatic Measurement Scheduling: MetricTest offers two methods for automated testing:

• Single Shot: Users can set a specific end date and time for a test to be automatically initiated. For example, the app can be configured to run a test daily at 12:00 PM until a chosen date.
• By Frequency: In addition to an end date, users can specify a frequency (e.g., every 1, 2, or 3 h) for tests to run throughout the day. This provides a more granular view of network performance fluctuations.

- QoS Estimation within a Zone: To provide a comprehensive view of QoS, MetricTest allows users to define a search radius. The application then aggregates all measurements taken within that radius by different users and calculates the average values for latency, upload, download, jitter, and packet loss for each operator (or Wi-Fi). This aggregated data offers valuable insights into network quality in specific areas. The mean for each metric is calculated by summing the individual metric values for a given operator within the selected zone and dividing by the number of measurements (snapshot.size) for that operator in that zone.

4 Results and Discussion

MetricTest provides an intuitive interface for users to perform tests and visualize results. The application's main interface displays current speed and other metrics, while a dedicated map interface allows geographical visualization of measurements.

4.1 Interface Presentation

MetricTest offers a series of user-friendly interfaces inspired by the other measurement tools.

- Home Interface: Fig. 1.a displays the real-time speed dial and initial values for jitter, packet loss, ping, download, and upload. Users tap the play button to initiate an instant test.

- Instant Test Results: Fig. 1.b shows the detailed results of an instant test, including download and upload speeds, ping, jitter, and packet loss, along with the identified network operator.

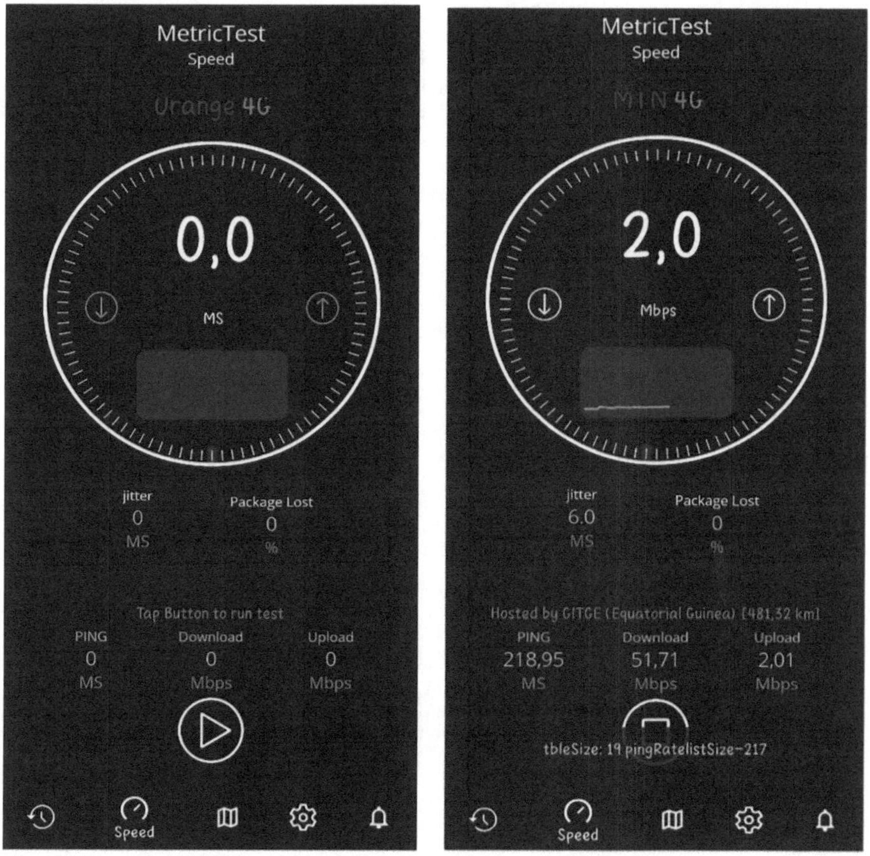

(a) (b)

Fig. 1. (a) User interface of MetricTest. (b) Instant test results

- Measurement Type Localization on Map: The map interface visually represents different connection types (2G, 3G, 4G) for measurements taken by various users in a selected area.

- QoS within a Radius: Users can select a radius (e.g., 5 km) on the map (Fig. 2.a), and MetricTest displays aggregated average QoS values for Wi-Fi and different mobile operators, as shown in Fig. 2.b. This feature provides a crucial aggregated view for administrators.

4.2 Data Consumption Comparison

A key advantage of MetricTest is its low data consumption. Table 2 summarizes a comparative analysis with existing tools.

MetricTest consistently consumes significantly less data (50.4 MB) per test compared to OpenSignal (97 MB), Speedtest (122.33 MB), and OONI Probe (181 MB).

(a) (b)

Fig. 2. (a) Selection of a radius on the map for the average measurements. (b) Display of the results

Table 2. Comparative summary of MetricTest vs. other tools

Tool	Latency	Download	Upload	Jitter	Packet Loss	**Data Used**
MetricTest	225.304 ms	27.69 Mbps	3.51 Mbps	41.6 ms	0	**50.4 MB**
Speedtest	36.67 ms	62.37 Mbps	20.37 Mbps	8 ms	0	122.33 MB
OONI probe	–	49.9 Mbps	15.85 Mbps	–	–	181 MB
Opensignal	182 ms	50.5 Mbps	16.6 Mbps	–	–	97 MB

This efficiency is critical for community networks where bandwidth is often a scarce and costly resource. While MetricTest's raw performance numbers (e.g., lower download/upload speeds than some tools) might vary due to different underlying measurement methodologies or chosen servers, its ability to provide comprehensive metrics with minimal data overhead is its primary strength for its target environment. The results confirm that MetricTest provides measurements comparable to existing tools while offering a substantial advantage in data efficiency.

5 Conclusion

Assessing client-side QoS in community networks is vital for their sustainable development. This paper presented MetricTest, a mobile application designed to empower end-users with tools to measure and geolocate network performance. MetricTest accurately measures critical metrics such as latency, packet loss, jitter, and network throughput. Its unique features, including automatic measurement scheduling and the ability to visualize aggregated QoS data within specific geographical zones, make it an invaluable tool for both community members and network administrators.

A comparative analysis demonstrated that MetricTest maintains comparable measurement accuracy while significantly reducing data consumption, which is a key benefit in bandwidth-constrained environments. Beyond community networks, MetricTest's capabilities extend to evaluating the QoS provided by mobile telecommunication operators, potentially supporting advocacy for service improvements.

For future work, we plan to develop an administrator-side visualization tool to provide a centralized overview of user-reported QoS data, facilitating proactive network planning and optimization. Integrating alert thresholds for performance degradation would further enhance its utility. Furthermore, to address scenarios where internet connectivity is minimal or non-existent, exploring completely offline measurement approaches would be a valuable next step, potentially allowing data collection and local aggregation before opportunistic synchronization.

References

1. ITU: Facts and Figures 2024-Internet use. https://www.itu.int/itu-d/reports/statistics/2024/11/10/ff24-internet-use/. Accessed 10 Aug 2025
2. Gwaka, L.T., May, J., Tucker, W.: Towards low-cost community networks in rural communities: the impact of context using the case study of Beitbridge, Zimbabwe. E. J. Info. Sys. Dev. Countries. **84**, e12029 (2018). https://doi.org/10.1002/isd2.12029
3. Ebongue, J.L.F.K.: Rethinking network connectivity in rural communities in cameroon. arXiv preprint (2015). https://arxiv.org/abs/1505.04449
4. Fendji, J.L.E.K., Mafai, N.M., Nlong, J.M.: Slope-based empirical path loss prediction models for rural networks at 2.4 GHz. Trans. Netw. Commun. **7**, 84–84 (2019) https://doi.org/10.14738/tnc.71.6162
5. Fendji, J.L.E.K., Nlong, J.M.: Rural wireless mesh network: A design methodology. arXiv preprint (2015). https://arxiv.org/abs/1504.08213
6. Gemmi, G., Cerdà-Alabern, L., Navarro, L., Maccari, L.: Toward smart community networks. IEEE Netw. **37**, 128–134 (2023)
7. Fendji, J.L.K.E., Thron, C.: A simulated annealing based Centre of mass (SAC) approach for mesh routers placement in rural areas. Int. J. Oper. Res. Inf. Syst. (IJORIS). **11**, 37–65 (2020)
8. Fendji, J.L.E.K., Thron, C., Förster, A.: A multi-objective approach for wireless heterogeneous router placement in rural wireless mesh networks. In: Zitouni, R., Phokeer, A., Chavula, J., Elmokashfi, A., Gueye, A., Benamar, N. (eds.) Towards New e-Infrastructure and e-Services for Developing Countries, pp. 43–55. Springer International Publishing, Cham (2021). https://doi.org/10.1007/978-3-030-70572-5_3

9. Gwaka, L., Haseki, M., Yoo, C.S.: Community networks as models to address connectivity gaps in underserved communities. Inf. Dev. **39**, 524–538 (2023). https://doi.org/10.1177/02666669221089658
10. Rey-Moreno, C., Graaf, M.: Map of the community network initiatives in Africa. L. Belli, Community connectivity: building the internet from scratch 149–169 (2016)

Traffic-Aware Dynamic Pricing in LTE: Deep Learning Approach

Temitope Oluseun Efuwape[1,2](✉), Olusegun Ayodeji Ojesanmi[2], Oluwasefunmi Tale Arogundade[2], and Emmanuel Oyeyemi Adeleke[2]

[1] Bells University of Technology, Ota, Nigeria
toefuwape@bellsuniversity.edu.ng
[2] Federal University of Agriculture, Abeokuta, Nigeria
{ojesanmioa,arogundadeot,adelekeeo}@funaab.edu.ng

Abstract. The increasing growth of mobile subscribers and multimedia applications has intensified the demand for reliable and efficient communication networks. Long Term Evolution (LTE), the dominant 4G standard, is widely adopted for its high throughput, low latency, and spectral efficiency. However, sustaining Quality of Service (QoS) under fluctuating traffic demand and limited spectrum remains a critical challenge. This study introduces a dynamic pricing framework integrated with predictive modelling of LTE traffic load to address these issues. Using the CRISP-DM methodology, historical downlink traffic dataset was analysed with deep learning (DL) models. Three architectures, vanilla LSTM, stacked LSTM, and bidirectional LSTM were employed, and performance was evaluated using R^2, MSE, MAE, and RMSE. Additionally, a range of loss functions, including MSLE, Huber Loss, Quantile, and Smooth L1 were tested, all proving effective for model optimisation and training convergence in their own respect. Results indicate that vanilla LSTM achieved the highest predictive accuracy (R^2 = 0.8644), while stacked LSTM outperformed others in dynamic pricing implementation (R^2 = 0.7544). Comparative benchmarking against flat-rate pricing confirmed improvements in bandwidth utilisation and daily user cost. This demonstrates that integrating DL models and efficient loss function optimisation with dynamic pricing enables adaptive, resilient LTE networks, offering both economic and technical benefits.

Keywords: LTE · dynamic pricing · traffic prediction

1 Introduction

Cellular networks have become a cornerstone of modern communication, enabling reliable, high-bandwidth, and low-latency connectivity through technologies ranging from Wi-Fi to long term evolution (LTE) and beyond (Wu et

A. Oluwatope et al. (Eds.): AFRICOMM 2025, LNICST 713, pp. 31–47, 2027.
https://doi.org/10.1007/978-3-032-38682-3_3

al., 2023). The widespread adoption of mobile services has fueled rapid growth in data-intensive applications across education, media, banking, transportation, and manufacturing. According to industry reports (Ericsson,2023), global mobile data traffic reached nearly 90 EB per month in 2022 and is projected to exceed 115 EB per month by 2028. Likewise, the number of wireless data devices is expected to grow from 7.3 billion in 2022 to more than 9.2 billion by 2028. This explosive growth presents a pressing challenge for mobile operators in sustaining Quality of Service (QoS) while efficiently managing limited spectrum and infrastructure resources.Expanding network capacity through the deployment of additional base stations offers a straightforward solution but comes with significant capital(CAPEX) and operational expenditures (OPEX); thus, attention has shifted toward demand-side mechanisms such as dynamic pricing, which adjusts tariffs based on real-time or predicted network conditions (Masli et al., 2022). By incentivizing users to shift or reduce consumption during peak hours, dynamic pricing can mitigate congestion, improve user experience, and enhance revenue for service providers.

While these advantages are evident, existing pricing schemes often lack accurate traffic forecasting, which are essential for proactive and effective tariff adjustments. To address this gap, this paper proposes a traffic-aware dynamic pricing framework for LTE, leveraging deep learning methods to predict traffic load patterns. The proposed framework integrates traffic prediction with adaptive pricing scheme to balance network load, maintain QoS, and support scalable next-generation networks. This study addresses these limitations by introducing a traffic-aware dynamic pricing framework driven by deep learning traffic prediction. The proposed framework forecasts cellular traffic load patterns using LSTM networks and dynamically adjusts tariffs to mitigate congestion while ensuring fairness.

The contributions of this study are threefold:

1. A deep learning framework for accurate LTE traffic forecasting at the cell level.
2. A dynamic pricing engine that integrates predictive insights into tariff adjustment policies.
3. An extensive evaluation using real LTE traffic traces, demonstrating improvements in cost efficiency, congestion mitigation, and bandwidth utilization.

2 Related Work

The Long Term Evolution (LTE), introduced by the Third Generation Partnership Project (3GPP), was designed to enhance the efficiency and flexibility of cellular network architectures. LTE operates by partitioning a geographical area into smaller cells, each managed by an evolved NodeB (eNodeB) base station. These eNodeBs interconnect with one another and the core network, thereby enabling seamless data and voice communication services for end users (Nisar and Baseer, 2021). An LTE system consists of three fundamental components: user equipment (UE), the access network, and the core network (Jaffry, 2020).

UEs are equipped with LTE-compatible modems and antennas, facilitating wireless connectivity with the eNodeB over the access network. At the core, the evolved packet core (EPC) functions as the central hub and comprises multiple logical entities, these elements collectively manage mobility, session control, and data routing across heterogeneous environments. The deployment of LTE has brought notable improvements over earlier cellular technologies, offering higher data rates, lower latency, and enhanced spectral efficiency. These features support a wide range of bandwidth-intensive applications and services, such as HD video streaming, cloud services, and online gaming. Owing to these advantages, LTE has become the dominant global standard for mobile broadband services. Successive advancements namely LTE-Advanced and LTE-Advanced Pro have introduced capabilities such as carrier aggregation and improved multi-antenna support, further extending LTE's performance and ensuring its relevance in the transition toward 5G networks and beyond.

Recent studies have explored diverse approaches to dynamic pricing in cellular networks. Puspita et al. (2022) proposed a heuristic priority-based dynamic pricing algorithm with multiple service levels, enabling efficient control of radio resource usage and improved alignment of pricing plans with user requirements. Chounos et al.(2020) introduced a novel framework for dynamic policy and charging rules in multi-tenancy environments. Their framework focused on adaptive pricing under resource scarcity, supporting negotiations between mobile operators and infrastructure providers (InPs) through service-level agreements (SLAs). The authors validated their approach with analytical modeling, collaboration mechanisms, and testbed trials, highlighting its capacity to handle increasing traffic demands. Other works have applied game-theoretic formulations to pricing. Zhou et al. (2020) extended the Stackelberg game approach to spectrum sharing in 5G vehicular ad–hoc networks (VANETs), introducing dynamic access pricing and distributed mode selection for vehicle users (VUEs). Simulation results showed significant throughput improvements. Xiong et al. (2020) proposed a sequential pricing policy in which mobile users were repeatedly offered adaptive prices across multiple periods. This strategy improved both operator revenue and user utility relative to static pricing, while promoting social fairness.Although these contributions demonstrate the potential of dynamic pricing, most approaches do not incorporate predictive intelligence of user behavior and traffic load.

Artificial Intelligence (AI) has emerged as an area of interest in cellular network management, providing new opportunities for improving QoS, traffic prediction, and optimising resource utilisation. By analysing large-scale datasets, AI techniques can uncover hidden patterns and generate predictive insights, thereby supporting data-driven decision-making for network providers (Goiz et al., 2024). A wide range of studies has demonstrated the effectiveness of traditional, machine learning (ML), and deep learning (DL) approaches for cellular network management. DL methods such as Long Short-Term Memory (LSTM) networks have demonstrated considerable promise in overcoming the limitations of traditional statistical modeling. These techniques leverage on data-driven algorithms that can efficiently handle large, complex datasets, and capture non-linear and temporal relationships in cellular network traffic. They can provide robust predictive outcomes even in data-limited conditions (Wu et al., 2023). For example, Alsaade and Al-Adhaileh (2021) employed statistical time-series models such as single exponential smoothing (SES) and autoregressive integrated moving average (ARIMA) to model and forecast LTE traffic volumes, achieving strong predictive accuracy. Extending beyond classical approaches, Gijon et al. (2021) investigated congestion prediction in LTE networks through user perception analysis, applying multiple supervised learning models. Their study demonstrated that the k-Nearest Neighbor algorithm provided superior accuracy compared to traditional statistical approaches. These contributions highlight the increasing relevance of ML and DL techniques, which not only outperform traditional techniques but also offer greater scalability and adaptability for dynamic LTE network environments. Aouedi et al.(2025) provide complete surveys of artificial intelligence applications in network management. Their analyses highlight traffic prediction as a critical capability for future mobile networks, with the potential to guarantee QoS while at the same time reducing operational (OPEX) and capital expenses (CAPEX). In addition, their findings indicate that machine learning approaches consistently outperform traditional statistical methods in terms of prediction accuracy, scalability, and adaptability, underscoring their suitability for large-scale, data-driven network environments.

3 Conceptual Framework

This section introduces the conceptual framework that reinforces the proposed traffic-aware dynamic pricing framework for LTE shown in Fig. 1. The framework is composed of multiple interdependent modules, each playing a critical role in the dynamic pricing process. The predictive modeling module forecasts traffic load patterns using machine learning, ensuring accurate anticipation of network congestion. The decision-making engine translates these predictions into adaptive pricing strategies, adjusting tariffs in near real-time. The user communication interface disseminates pricing updates to subscribers, encouraging behavioral shifts that reduce peak-hour congestion. The traffic-aware dynamic pricing framework operates on user-specific parameters and predicted traffic demand, enabling adaptive rate determination in real-time network conditions. The algorithm leverages traffic demand predictions to adjust pricing dynamically, ensuring efficient bandwidth utilization and fairness across users. The process is detailed in Algorithm 1. This study embraces a theoretical-descriptive approach, focusing on the systematic analysis of LTE network challenges and the formulation of a structured response and, designed to enhance service quality by aligning user demand with available network resources through a data-driven pricing mechanism. Both quantitative (traffic load, prediction accuracy, pricing efficiency) and qualitative (user behavior, service satisfaction) dimensions are considered, ensuring a comprehensive evaluation of the proposed framework.

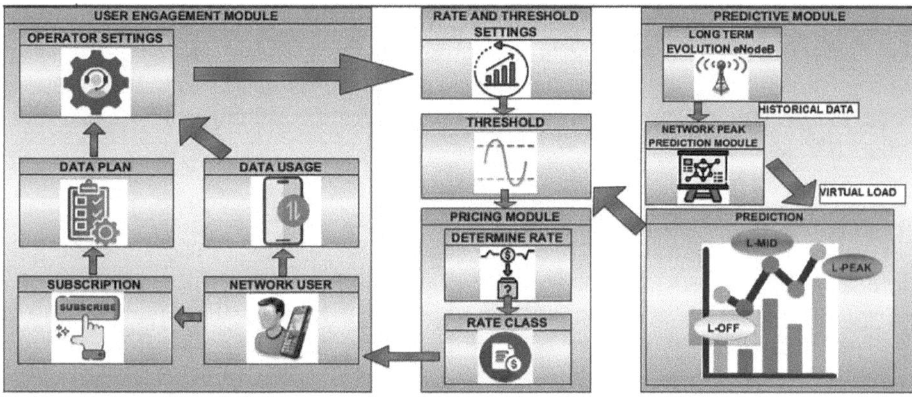

Fig. 1. Traffic-Aware Dynamic Pricing Framework. Historical LTE traffic is predicted using LSTM models, and the dynamic pricing engine adjusts tariffs based on predicted traffic .

4 Methodology

To implement the proposed traffic-aware dynamic pricing framework in LTE networks, the methodology follows a structured pipeline consisting of data preprocessing, traffic prediction, dynamic pricing formulation, and evaluation. Each stage is described below.

4.1 Dataset and Preprocessing

In this study, we employ an anonymized dataset obtained from LTE networks operated by a major telecommunications service provider in sub-Saharan Africa. The dataset serves as the primary source of key performance indicators (KPIs) for each LTE site, as collected through the Huawei U2020 monitoring and statistical server. Each observation contains essential attributes, including the eNodeB identification (eNodeB ID), date, timestamp, geographical coordinates (latitude and longitude), cluster information, CellID, local cell ID, uplink (UL) and downlink (DL) traffic volumes, as well as the utilization of physical resource blocks (PRBs) in both UL and DL directions.

The methodological framework follows the Cross-Industry Standard Process for Data Mining (CRISP-DM) (Vos, 2024) which provides six iterative phases to guide data understanding, preparation, modeling, and evaluation. To capture temporal variations in network traffic behavior, the dataset was aggregated along dimensions of CellID, Hour, and Seconds, thereby generating representative metrics for different time intervals and reflecting typical network conditions.

Subsequently, since raw traffic logs are often noisy and irregular, preprocessing is performed to handle missing values, normalize feature scales, and align temporal sequences. A normalization process was applied to prevent scale imbalances across features from biasing the learning performance of the predictive model. Specifically, a sequence-based scaling function was employed to ensure that all features contributed proportionately to the training process. Finally, a Min-Max Scaler was adopted to transform the features into a common range of [0,1], thereby enhancing convergence stability and optimizing the performance of the LSTM models.

4.2 Traffic Load Prediction

Three Long Short-Term Memory (LSTM) architectures were considered: vanilla LSTM, stacked LSTM, and bidirectional LSTM (bi-LSTM). These architectures were chosen for their ability to capture long-term dependencies and nonlinear behaviors inherent in mobile traffic.

Vanilla LSTM The Long Short-Term Memory (LSTM), a deep recurrent neural network (DRNN), is designed to model sequential data and capture long-term temporal dependencies (Escriche et al., 2023). First introduced to address the limitations of conventional RNNs, the model was later extended with the vanilla LSTM, which effectively mitigates vanishing and exploding gradient problems while retaining essential information over extended periods. The incorporation of gating mechanisms enables LSTMs to learn from long-term dependencies, making them highly suitable for time-series prediction tasks where past behavioural patterns significantly influence future outcomes.

Concept of Vanilla LSTM Let's assume the number of hidden units is h_t, and given input $x_t \in \mathbb{R}^{n \times m}$ with n samples and m inputs at a time step, along with the previous time step hidden state $h_{t-1} \in \mathbb{R}^{n \times \mathcal{H}}$, forget gate $f_t \in \mathbb{R}^{n \times \mathcal{H}}$, input gate $i_t \in \mathbb{R}^{n \times \mathcal{H}}$, and output gate $o_t \in \mathbb{R}^{n \times \mathcal{H}}$. The cell state C_{t-1} acts as a memory that carries information across all cell components. The model is mathematically expressed in Equations (1– 8), while the activation functions is given in Equations (9– 10)

Forget Gate

$$f_t = \sigma\left((W_f[h_{t-1}, x_t] + b_f\right) \tag{1}$$

Input Gate

$$i_{1_t} = \sigma\left(W_i[h_{t-1}, x_t] + b_i\right) \tag{2}$$

$$i_{2_t} = \tanh\left(W_i[h_{t-1}, x_t] + b_i\right) \tag{3}$$

$$i_t = i_{1_t} \odot i_{2_t} \tag{4}$$

Cell State

$$\tilde{C}_t = \tanh\left(W_c[h_{t-1}, x_t] + b_c\right) \tag{5}$$
$$C_t = f_t \odot C_{t-1} + i_t \odot \tilde{C}_t \tag{6}$$

Output Gate

$$o_t = \sigma\left(W_o[h_{t-1}, x_t] + b_o\right) \tag{7}$$
$$h_t = o_t \odot \tanh(C_t) \tag{8}$$

Activation Functions

$$\sigma(x_t) = \frac{1}{1 + e^{-x_t}} \tag{9}$$
$$\tanh(x_t) = \frac{2}{1 + e^{-2x_t}} - 1 \tag{10}$$

Stacked LSTM The stacked LSTM extends the vanilla LSTM by incorporating multiple hidden layers, thereby enhancing model depth and expressive power. This improves predictive accuracy, supports the capture of long-term dependencies, and reduces the risk of overfitting, making it well-suited for cellular traffic prediction (Kumar et al., 2025). The output layer h_T^n serves as the input for the fully connected layer. Equation (11) details the weight matrix W and the bias term b connection between the fully connected layer and the output layer of the vanilla LSTM .

$$\tilde{h}_T = W h_T^n + b \tag{11}$$

Bidirectional LSTM The bidirectional LSTM (bi-LSTM) extends the vanilla LSTM by integrating forward and backward process layers into a unified output. This dual-directional structure enables the model to capture both past and future dependencies, thereby enhancing contextual learning and predictive accuracy. The threshold calculations follow the vanilla LSTM formulations for both forward is defined in Equations (1)– (8)and reverse processing layers is defined in Equations (12– 17) (Zhang et al., 2025).

Backward Process of Bi-LSTM The backward LSTM processes the input in reverse. The equations for the backward hidden state ($\overleftarrow{h}_t$) are defined as:

$$f_t = \sigma\left(W_f[\overleftarrow{h}_{t+1}, x_t] + b_f\right) \tag{12}$$

$$i_t = \sigma\left(W_i[\overleftarrow{h}_{t+1}, x_t] + b_i\right) \tag{13}$$

$$\tilde{C}_t = \tanh\left(W_c[\overleftarrow{h}_{t+1}, x_t] + b_c\right) \tag{14}$$

$$C_t = f_t \circ C_{t+1} + i_t \circ \tilde{C}_t \tag{15}$$

$$o_t = \sigma\left(W_o[\overleftarrow{h}_{t+1}, x_t] + b_o\right) \tag{16}$$

$$\overleftarrow{h}_t = o_t \circ \tanh(C_t) \tag{17}$$

Final Output Combination of Bi-LSTM The outcome of bi-LSTM includes both forward and backward hidden states. They are combined linearly, and the combined process is presented as in Equation (18):

$$h_t = W_{fw} \cdot \overrightarrow{h}_t + W_{bw} \cdot \overleftarrow{h}_t + b \tag{18}$$

Training is performed in an unsupervised manner, where historical traffic values are mapped to subsequent load values. The optimization objective is to minimize prediction errors, evaluated through metrics in Equations (24–27). This predictive capability serves as the foundation of the framework, providing reliable inputs to the dynamic pricing engine, which adjusts tariffs in response to predicted network conditions.

4.3 Dynamic Pricing Formulation

Based on the predicted traffic load L_t, a dynamic pricing engine computes tariffs that balance network utilization and user satisfaction. The pricing function is designed to *increase tariffs during high-demand periods* and *decrease tariffs during low-demand periods*, thereby incentivizing users to shift their usage patterns while ensuring efficient resource allocation.This scheme incentivizes users to shift non-critical data consumption away from peak times, thus smoothing network demand. The dynamic pricing model for $P_{\text{off}(t)}$, mid $P_{\text{mid}(t)}$, and peak $P_{\text{peak}(t)}$ is given in Equations (19–21).

The pricing for off-peak $P_{\text{off}(t)}$, mid $P_{\text{mid}(t)}$, and peak $P_{\text{peak}(t)}$ is calculated based on the predicted traffic demand and user data consumption. The total data consumed by a user is tracked against their subscription data plan limit; the user will be disconnected if they exceed their limit.

Definition of the Following Variables:

- L_t: predicted LTE traffic demand load at time t, where $0 \leq L_t \leq L_{\max}$
- D_t: user data consumption at time step t
- S: user's subscription data plan limit
- α is a pricing sensitivity coefficient controlling the strength of price variation,
- p_t: dynamic pricing at time step t
- δ: demand load threshold

- T_{off}: temporal window for off-peak period
- T_{mid}: temporal window for mid-peak period
- T_{peak}: temporal window for peak period

Based on the predicted traffic demand load, The dynamic pricing model is defined in Equations (19)– (21).

$$P_{\text{off}(t)} = \sum_{t \in T_{\text{off}}} R_{\text{off}}(L_t) \cdot D_t \quad \text{for } L_t \leq \delta_{\text{off}} \tag{19}$$

$$P_{\text{mid}(t)} = \sum_{t \in T_{\text{mid}}} R_{\text{mid}}(L_t) \cdot D_t \quad \text{for } \delta_{\text{off}} < L_t < \delta_{\text{peak}} \tag{20}$$

$$P_{\text{peak}(t)} = \sum_{t \in T_{\text{peak}}} R_{\text{peak}}(L_t) \cdot D_t \quad \text{for } L_t \geq \delta_{\text{peak}} \tag{21}$$

The total data consumed by the user is given in Eqs. 22:

$$D_{\text{total}} = \sum_t D_t \tag{22}$$

The condition for disconnection is expressed in Eqs. 23:

$$\text{If } D_{\text{total}} \geq S, \text{ then disconnect the user from the network} \tag{23}$$

where the rate functions $R_{\text{off}}(L_t)$, $R_{\text{mid}}(L_t)$, and $R_{\text{peak}}(L_t)$ determine the pricing function based on predicted traffic demand.

This integration of predicted traffic demand with dynamic pricing enables demand regulation across time, discourages excessive usage during peak periods, and supports equitable resource allocation while preserving Quality of Service (QoS).

Load-Dependent Pricing Functions The load-dependent pricing functions is given in the expression from Equations (24)– (26).

The off-peak pricing function is defined as

$$R_{\text{off}}(L_t) = P_0 \left(1 + \alpha_{\text{off}} \frac{L_t}{L_{\max}}\right), \quad L_t \leq \delta_{\text{off}}, \tag{24}$$

where $\alpha_{\text{off}} \geq 0$ controls price sensitivity during off-peak periods.

For mid-peak operation, the pricing function is given by

$$R_{\text{mid}}(L_t) = P_0 \left(1 + \alpha_{\text{mid}} \frac{L_t}{L_{\max}}\right), \quad \delta_{\text{off}} < L_t < \delta_{\text{peak}}, \tag{25}$$

where $\alpha_{\text{mid}} > \alpha_{\text{off}}$ reflects increased congestion risk.

During peak traffic conditions, a stronger penalty is applied:

$$R_{\text{peak}}(L_t) = P_0 \left(1 + \alpha_{\text{peak}} \frac{L_t}{L_{\max}}\right), \quad L_t \geq \delta_{\text{peak}}, \tag{26}$$

with $\alpha_{\text{peak}} > \alpha_{\text{mid}}$ to discourage excessive demand under high congestion.

These functions ensure a smooth and progressive increase in pricing as predicted traffic load approaches network capacity.

4.4 Evaluation Metrics

The prediction accuracy of the framework is measured using Mean Squared Error (MSE), Root Mean Squared Error (RMSE), Mean Absolute Error (MAE), and Coefficient of Determination (R-squared). Equations (27– 30) evaluate and

Algorithm 1. Dynamic Pricing for Each User

```
Inputs:
    user_data_subscription_plan:
        data_limit (MB/GB), base_plan_price
    traffic_demand_predictions
    user_data_usage: (time_stamp, data_usage_mb, location_id)
Output: total_price  dynamic price charged for user's usage
Action: continue_browsing(), activate_FUP(), or disconnect()
Initialization:
    total_price ← 0; total_data_used ← 0
    data_tuples ← [ ]
for each usage in user_data_usage do
    Extract (time_stamp, data_usage_mb, location_id)
    Predict demand from traffic_demand_predictions(time_stamp,
    location_id)
    if demand > 80% then
        peak_rate ← 5.5 × base_rate {Peak load period}
    else
        peak_rate ← base_rate {Normal load period}
    end if
    consumption_rate ← adjusted based on load curve
    duration ← 1
    Append (peak_rate, data_usage_mb, duration) to data_tuples
end for
for each (peak_rate, usage_mb, duration) in data_tuples do
    total_price ← total_price + (peak_rate × usage_mb × duration)
    total_data_used ← total_data_used + (usage_mb × duration)
end for
if total_price ≤ base_plan_price and total_data_used ≤ data_limit then
    continue_browsing()
else if total_price ≤ base_plan_price and total_data_used > data_limit then
    activate_FUP() {Throttle speed or apply moderate charge}
else
    disconnect() {Redirect to top-up portal}
end if
return total_price
```

compare the performance of the implemented techniques. The dynamic pricing efficiency is measured by average user cost, and bandwidth utilization

$$\mathrm{MSE} = \{\frac{1}{n}\sum_{t=1}^{n}(x_t - \hat{f}_t)^2\} \tag{27}$$

$$\mathrm{RMSE} = \sqrt{\frac{1}{n}\sum_{t=1}^{n}(x_t - \hat{f}_t)^2} \tag{28}$$

$$\mathrm{MAE} = \{\frac{1}{n}\sum_{t=1}^{n}\left|x_t - \hat{f}_t\right|\} \tag{29}$$

$$R^2 = 1 - \frac{\sum_{t=1}^{n}(x_t - \hat{f}_t)^2}{\sum_{t=1}^{n}(x_t - \bar{x})^2} \tag{30}$$

In the equations, x_t represents the actual value, $\hat{f}_t$ represents the predicted value corresponding to the actual value, and $\bar{x}_t$ is the mean of all the actual values.

5 Experimental Setup

The LSTM models in this study were implemented in Python 3.9.13, a versatile, open-source programming language widely adopted for artificial intelligence, machine learning and data analytics applications (Robeson et al., 2023). The experiments were conducted using Visual Studio Code as the Integrated Development Environment(IDE), with TensorFlow 2.3.1, Scikit-learn, and additional Python libraries providing the computational framework. Visualization of results was carried out using the Matplotlib library.

The training pipeline followed a structured process to ensure robust model performance. Each model was trained with a batch size of 32 over 100 epochs, utilizing 26,879 trainable parameters. The learning rate was initialized at 0.0001 and updated at fixed intervals of 30 steps. For non-linear transformations, the models employed both the hyperbolic tangent (tanh) and sigmoid activation functions. Weight updates were optimized using the Adaptive Moment Estimation (Adam) algorithm, while performance evaluation considered multiple loss functions to assess model sensitivity and robustness. Table 1 summarizes the key experimental parameters.

Table 1. Experimental Setup Parameters

Hyperparameter	Value
Programming Language	Python 3.9.13
Framework	TensorFlow 2.3.1
Batch Size	32
Epochs	100
Trainable Parameters	26,879
Learning Rate	0.0001
Optimizer	Adam
Activation Functions	Sigmoid, Tanh
Loss Functions	MSE, RMSE, MAE, MSLE, Quantile Loss, Smooth_L1, Huber Loss, Log-Cosh

6 Results and Discussion

Figures (2– 4) present the graphical comparison of the prediction outcomes generated by the vanilla LSTM, bidirectional LSTM, and stacked LSTM models on the testing traffic load dataset. The blue line denotes the actual traffic values, while the remaining lines represent the predictions from the respective models. This visualization provides an intuitive understanding of how effectively each model approximates the ground truth values. By comparing the predicted trajectories with the actual traffic pattern, it becomes evident that all three DL models are capable of capturing the temporal dynamics of traffic load, though with varying degrees of accuracy. The vanilla and stacked LSTM exhibit closer alignment with the actual traffic curve, demonstrating their superior ability to extract long-term dependencies and complex patterns compared to the bidirectional LSTM (Fig. 3).

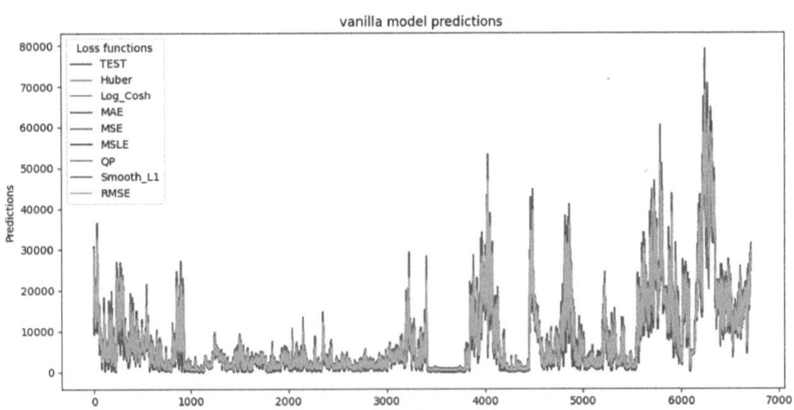

Fig. 2. vanilla LSTM prediction results.

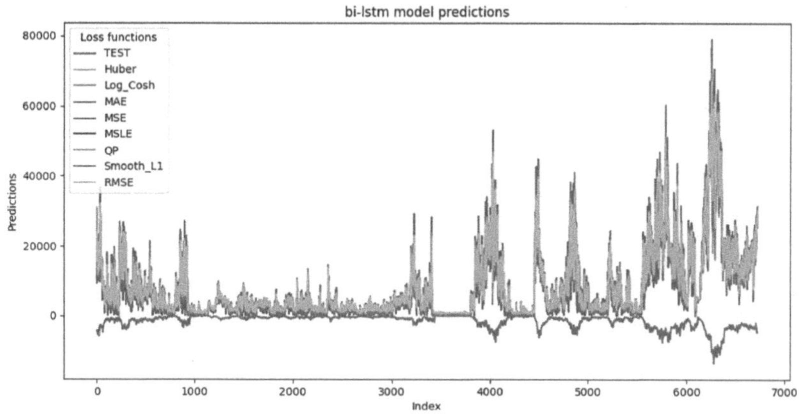

Fig. 3. bi-LSTM prediction results.

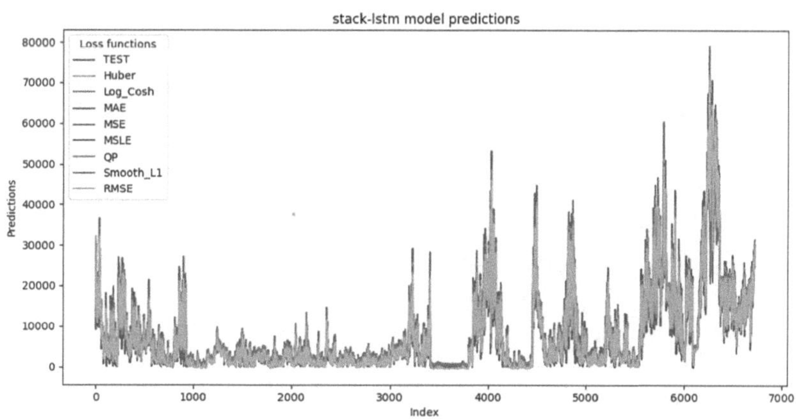

Fig. 4. stacked LSTM prediction results.

Tables (2–4) compare the performance results of vanilla LSTM, stacked LSTM and bidirectional LSTM under different loss functions. The vanilla LSTM with MSE loss achieved the best result, with an accuracy of 86.44%, slightly higher than the stacked LSTM with Quantile (QP)loss (86.35%). The bidirectional LSTM reached 85.43% with Smooth L1 but performed poorly with MAE loss, yielding a negative predictive performance score (41.11). These experimental results demonstrate that while all three architectures are capable of predicting daily LTE traffic load, their predictive effectiveness is highly dependent on the choice of loss function and optimization algorithm employed.

Fig (5)shows the visualization of average total user cost per day for flat-rate and dynamic pricing over a 13-day period. Here the red dashed line represent the fixed cost under flat-rate pricing at N35,000 per day while the green line with dots tells us how dynamic pricing varies with the predicted traffic load. Notably, traffic-aware dynamic pricing framework reflects lower costs during off-peak and mid-peak days. Fig (6) shows dynamic pricing bandwidth utilization (orange

Table 2. Performance Results for vanilla LSTM

	MSE	**RMSE**	**MAE**	$\mathbf{R}^2$
Huber	0.002674	0.051709	0.030902	0.838073
Log_Cosh	0.003412	0.058413	0.034658	0.793362
MAE	0.004229	0.047314	0.027527	0.743885
MSE	**0.002239**	0.065031	0.038950	**0.864430**
MSLE	0.002268	0.047620	0.028071	0.862667
Quantile	0.002655	0.051524	0.030067	0.839229
Smooth_L1	0.002586	0.050853	0.030371	0.843389
RMSE	0.002262	0.047564	0.027766	0.862994

Table 3. Performance Results for bi-LSTM

	MSE	**RMSE**	**MAE**	$\mathbf{R}^2$
Huber	0.002925	0.054084	0.032077	0.822856
Log_Cosh	0.002562	0.050619	0.030372	0.844827
MAE	0.695326	0.833862	0.807992	-41.1095
MSE	0.002760	0.052539	0.031270	0.832832
MSLE	0.002871	0.053581	0.031553	0.826138
Quantile	0.002759	0.049046	0.028933	0.832923
Smooth_L1	**0.002456**	0.052525	0.031311	**0.854319**
RMSE	0.002554	0.050534	0.030036	0.845347

Table 4. Performance Results for stacked LSTM

	MSE	**RMSE**	**MAE**	$\mathbf{R}^2$
Huber	0.003234	0.056872	0.033976	0.804122
Log_Cosh	0.002491	0.049908	0.029347	0.849156
MAE	0.002406	0.049051	0.029269	0.854290
MSE	0.002385	0.048834	0.028997	0.855578
MSLE	0.002388	0.048862	0.028762	0.855410
Quantile	**0.002254**	0.047476	0.027472	**0.863497**
Smooth_L1	0.003015	0.054910	0.032257	0.817400
RMSE	0.002297	0.047928	0.028332	0.860888

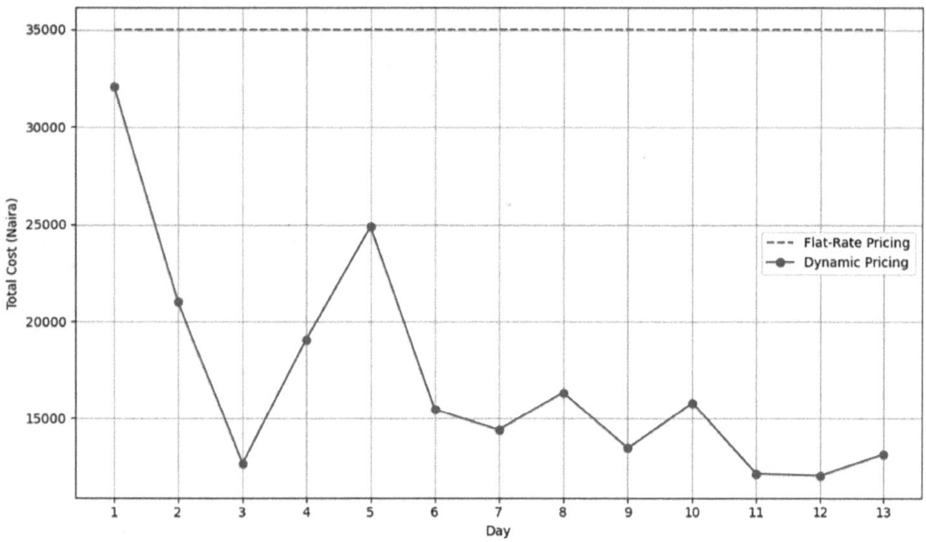

Fig. 5. Average User Cost: Traffic-Aware Dynamic Pricing and Flat-rate Pricing.

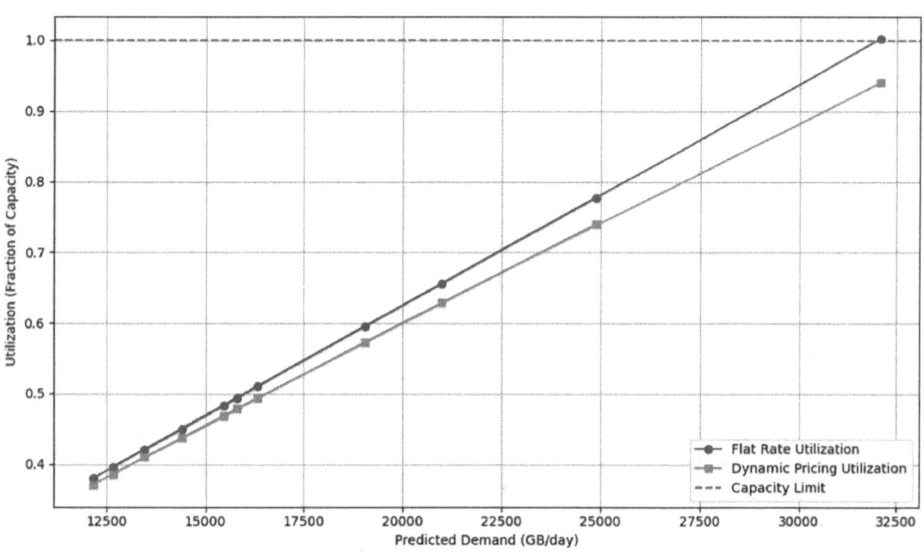

Fig. 6. Bandwidth Utilization: Traffic-Aware Dynamic Pricing and Flat-rate Pricing.

line) keeps user demand regulated in response to higher prices, reducing over utilization of resources and mitigate congestion on high-demand days

7 Conclusion and Future Work

This study presented a traffic-aware dynamic pricing framework for LTE networks, integrating deep learning-based prediction with adaptive tariff design. Results demonstrate significant benefits in congestion management, average user cost, and bandwidth utilization. The domain of intelligent network management remains a dynamic and evolving research frontier, continually challenging the boundaries of existing knowledge and opening new avenues for exploration.

While the present work demonstrates the potential of LSTM-based models in enabling traffic-aware dynamic pricing for LTE networks, several promising directions warrant further investigation. Future directions include extending the model to 5G/6G network slicing environments, integrating reinforcement learning for adaptive pricing policy optimization, and conducting large-scale field deployments using real datasets from telecom operators.

References

1. Alsaade, F.W., Al-Adhaileh, M.H.: Cellular traffic prediction based on an intelligent model. Mob. Inf. Syst. **1**(6050627), 1–15 (2021). https://doi.org/10.1155/2021/6050627
2. Aouedi, O., Le, V.A., Piamrat, K., Ji, Y.: Deep learning on network traffic prediction: Recent advances, analysis, and future directions. ACM Comput. Surv. **57**, 1–37 (2025). https://doi.org/10.1145/3703447
3. Chounos, K., Apostolaras, A., Korakis, T.: A dynamic pricing and leasing module for 5G networks. In: IEEE 3rd 5G World Forum (5GWF), pp. 343–348. IEEE, New York (2020). https://doi.org/10.1109/5GWF49715.2020.9221096
4. Ericsson Mobility Report: Mobile data traffic outlook. https://www.ericsson.com/reports-and-papers/mobility-report/data-forecasts/mobile-traffic-forecast Accessed 30 June 2023
5. Gijón, C., Toril, M., Luna-Ramírez, S., Marí-Altozano, M.L., Ruiz-Aviles, J.M.: Long-term data traffic forecasting for network dimensioning in LTE with short time series. Electronics **10**(10), 1151 (2021). https://doi.org/10.3390/electronics10101151
6. Goiz, G., de Farias, C.M., Delicato, F.C.: SNSM – Dynamic Resource Allocation for Network Slices with LSTM, GRU and Random Forest. In: Proceedings of the IEEE International Conference on Cloud Networking (CloudNet), pp. 1–9. IEEE (2024). https://doi.org/10.1109/cloudnet62863.2024.10815784
7. Jaffry, S.: Cellular traffic prediction with recurrent neural network. arXiv preprint abs/2003.02807 (2020). https://arxiv.org/abs/2003.02807
8. Kumar, P., Kushwaha, C., Sethi, D., Ghosh, D., Gupta, P., Vidyarthi, A.: Investigating the performance of multivariate LSTM models to predict the occurrence of Distributed Denial of Service (DDoS) attack. PLoS ONE **20**, e0313930 (2025). https://doi.org/10.1371/journal.pone.0313930

9. Masli, A.A., Ahmed, F.Y.H., Mansoor, A.M.: QoS-aware scheduling algorithm enabling video services in LTE networks. Computers **11**(5), 77 (2021). https://doi.org/10.3390/computers11050077
10. Nisar, F., Baseer, S.: A comprehensive survey on mobile communication generation. In: 4th International Conference on Innovative Computing (ICIC), vol. 2, p. 16. IEEE, New York (2021). https://doi.org/10.1109/ICIC53490.2021.9692972
11. Puspita, F.M., Arda, S., Sitepu, R., Yunita, Y., Yuliza, E., Oktarina, S., Yahdin, S.: Validation of improved dynamic spectrum and traffic management models of internet pricing of fair DSL-LTE multiple QoS network. Sci. Technol. Indones. **7**(1), 49–57 (2022). https://doi.org/10.26554/sti.2022.7.1.49-57
12. Robeson, S.M., Willmott, C.J.: Decomposition of the mean absolute error (MAE) into systematic and unsystematic components. PLoS ONE **18**(2), e0279774 (2023). https://doi.org/10.1371/journal.pone.0279774
13. Santos Escriche, E., Vassaki, S., Peters, G.: A comparative study of cellular traffic prediction mechanisms. Wireless Netw. **29**, 2371–2389 (2023). https://doi.org/10.1007/s11276-023-0331
14. Vos, P.: Rethinking Mean Square Error: Why Information is a Superior Assessment of Estimators. arXiv preprint https://arxiv.org/abs/2412.08475 (2024)
15. Wu, D., Li, J., Ferini, A., Xu, Y., et al.: Reinforcement learning for communication load balancing approaches and challenges. Front. Comp. Sci. **5**, 1156064 (2023). https://doi.org/10.3389/fcomp.2023.1156064
16. Zhang, Y., Li, X., Wang, J.: An optimized bidirectional long short-term memory model based on hyperspectral analysis of protein content in milk powder. Food Sci. Nutr. **13**(4), 1929–1935 (2025). https://doi.org/10.1002/fsn3.4556
17. Zhou, H., Qian, B., Ma, T., Xu, Y., Yu, K., Shen, X., Hou, F.: Leveraging dynamic Stackelberg pricing game for multi-mode spectrum sharing in 5G-VANET. IEEE Trans. Veh. Technol. **69**(6), 6374–6387 (2020). https://doi.org/10.1109/TVT.2020.2987014

Cybersecurity

On the Security of Pre-installed Android Apps in Low-Cost Devices

Alioune Diallo[1(✉)], Anta Diop[2], Abdoul Kader Kabore[1], Aleksandr Pilgun[1], Jordan Samhi[1], Tegawendé F. Bissyande[1], and Jacques Klein[1]

[1] SnT/TruX, University of Luxembourg, Esch-sur-Alzette, Luxembourg
{alioune.diallo,abdoulkader.kabore,aleksandr.pilgun,jordan.samhi,
tegawende.bissyande,jacques.klein}@uni.lu

[2] ESP, Université Cheikh Anta Diop de Dakar, Dakar, Senegal
antadiop1@esp.sn

Abstract. Pre-installed system and vendor applications on low-cost Android devices can run with elevated privileges yet receive little independent scrutiny. In this work, we present ***PiPLAnD***, a pipeline that extracts APKs from physical devices and applies static analysis to detect sensitive-data leaks, manifest misconfigurations, and suspicious behaviors in pre-installed apps. Using ***PiPLAnD***, we analyzed 1544 pre-installed APKs collected from seven devices (Infinix, itel, Tecno). Our findings show that 145 apps (9%) leak sensitive information, 249 apps (16%) export sensitive components without adequate protection, and numerous apps exhibit risky behaviors (226 execute dangerous commands, 79 access/send/delete SMS, 33 perform silent installation actions). We also identified a vendor-shipped package that appears to exfiltrate device identifiers and location to a third-party vendor. These results indicate that pre-installed software on widely distributed, low-cost devices can pose real privacy and security risks to end users.

Keywords: pre-installed apps · sensitive data · Android · static analysis · low-cost devices · Africa

1 Introduction

The Android operating system has enabled affordable smartphones for millions of people worldwide. Devices typically ship with manufacturer- or vendor-installed systems and third-party apps, which can become a distribution vector for malware and privacy-invasive functionality, especially in developing regions [24]. Low-cost smartphones remain widely used across Africa [36] and have helped reduce the digital divide by expanding access to services [15,31]. For example, roughly 20–22 million people in South Africa use smartphones, accounting for one third of the population [36]. Feature phones and inexpensive devices are still popular in Africa, which preserves the market opportunity for the expansion of low-cost Android devices. Although low-cost Android initiatives have

A. Oluwatope et al. (Eds.): AFRICOMM 2025, LNICST 713, pp. 51–68, 2027.
https://doi.org/10.1007/978-3-032-38682-3_4

improved device accessibility [3], the pre-installation process can be abused to embed harmful apps that reach large user populations.

Multiple reports document dangerous apps shipped with devices [4,7,25,27, 34,38]. These apps have been observed exfiltrating personal data to remote servers [7], harvesting financial credentials via clipboard monitoring [27], performing silent installations [38], or enrolling users in paid services without consent [4]. Several of the reported apps appear specifically on low-cost devices, including phones sold in Africa [4,7].

A few studies collected firmware images from vendor websites and online forums, extracting pre-installed apps for analysis [11,21,33,38]. The extracted apps are then examined for suspicious permissions, misconfigurations in manifest files [21,33,38], malware [38], and data leaks [6,11,14]. Other studies have directly extracted pre-installed apps from physical devices [6,14], allowing for a more comprehensive assessment across various Android brands. Yet, research on pre-installed applications remains limited since Android device manufacturers are expected to strictly follow compliance guidelines enforced by Google [20]. Unlike globally known brands, Android devices sold in African markets are often very low-priced. This raises concerns about the trade-offs manufacturers make between cost and security.

We studied seven low-cost device models from Infinix, Tecno, and itel brands—all produced by TRANSSION and together accounting for 51% of the African smartphone market in 2023 [8]. We extracted a dataset of 1544 pre-installed APKs for analysis. Pre-installed apps on these devices have received little systematic analysis despite their prevalence. The most notable work is by Elsabagh et al. [11] who examined pre-installed apps from Infinix and Tecno, focusing on privilege escalation. To the best of our knowledge, no prior work has systematically analyzed pre-installed apps across these low-cost Android devices commonly sold in Africa. To explore this gap, we developed ***PiPLAnD***, a pipeline that extracts APKs from physical devices and applies taint-based leak detection, pattern-driven behavior scanning, and manifest/component inspection to find data leaks, insecurely exported components, and suspicious behaviors. Our study builds upon existing work by taking a more in-depth approach. For instance, previous studies identified exported components by analyzing only the application manifests. In contrast, we extended this analysis by examining the corresponding code to detect components that provide access to sensitive data. Moreover, while prior research on data leaks has mainly focused on those occurring through Android or Java API methods, our analysis also considers leaks introduced via third-party libraries.

Our analysis uncovered multiple suspicious pre-installed apps across the tested devices. A substantial fraction of these apps leak sensitive information (for example, IMEI, IMSI, location) and exhibit manifest misconfigurations that expose components without adequate protection. In a notable case, ***PiPLAnD*** identified the package *com.transsion.statisticalsales*, which was not flagged by VirusTotal. These findings underscore the need for independent audits of pre-installed software on low-cost devices in developing regions.

Below, we summarize our main contributions:

① We present ***PiPLAnD***, a pipeline to systematically inspect pre-installed apps from Android devices.
② We collected a dataset of 1544 pre-installed APKs from seven low-cost device models (Infinix, Tecno, itel).
③ We identify manifest misconfigurations: 249 app versions (16%) export sensitive components without adequate protection.
④ We quantify sensitive-data leakage: 145 apps (9%) leak identifiers or location data.
⑤ We document widespread suspicious behaviors in pre-installed apps.

2 Background

This short background defines terms used in the paper and clarifies our measurement scope.

Android Firmware and Pre-installed Apps. Firmware boots device hardware and the Android OS[1]. Devices ship with *system apps* and *manufacturer-supplied* pre-installed apps [23]. *System apps* can run with elevated privileges or reside in privileged locations (e.g., `/system/priv-app`). Some devices in our dataset use Android Go, a lightweight Android configuration for entry-level hardware. Android Go was designed to optimize its running on low-end devices; however, the security implications of this optimization are not fully understood [17].

Exported Components and Misconfigurations. Apps declare components in AndroidManifest.xml. A component is "exported" if other apps can start or bind to it (via `android:exported` or an `intent-filter`). Exported components without proper permissions or access checks form an attack surface and are treated here as security misconfigurations [18].

PII, Sources, Sinks, and Leaks. PII includes identifiers and user data (IMEI, IMSI, phone number, location) [26]. A SOURCE is a method that reads sensitive data (e.g., `getLastKnownLocation()`); a SINK is a method that can exfiltrate data (network send, SMS, world-readable storage). When an app allows to get this data and send it outside the app itself, in this case, we talk about data leakage (or data leak). Static taint analysis tools like FlowDroid are well known to detect leaks in Android apps [2].

Low-Cost Device. In this study, we often use the terms "low-cost", "low-end", "cheap", and "affordable" when talking about devices that are not expensive but affordable, specifically targeting devices primarily used in Africa.

[1] https://www.androidpolice.com/what-is-firmware/.

3 Related Work

To the best of our knowledge, this study is the first one that focuses on analyzing Android apps pre-installed on the devices primarily used in Africa. However, there are some existing works about the analysis of pre-installed apps in Android devices.

Indeed, Zheng et al. [38] presented a tool named DroidRay that extracts statically and dynamically pre-installed apps from 250 firmware downloaded from forums and websites. The static extraction consists of extracting pre-installed apps directly from the firmware images. They also flashed the image into a device and then dynamically extracted the pre-installed apps using ADB commands. DroidRay performs pre-installed app analysis and system analysis by extracting the "SharedUserId" attribute from the AndroidManifest.xml and the signature information from the RSA file before comparing them with the default signatures they found from the AOSP. They also analyzed the apps in VirusTotal to detect potential malware. It performs static and dynamic analysis of the Android firmware by doing a system signature vulnerability detection, a network security analysis, and a privilege escalation vulnerability detection. In our proposed pipeline, we leveraged the technique of dynamic extraction to directly extract pre-installed apps from a physical device using ADB commands rather than collecting firmware and flashing it into a device.

Mitchell et al. [30] designed DexDiff, a system for assessing the security impacts of vendor customization to the official Android system. DexDiff helps the security analyst, who first retrieves the pre-installed apps and libraries from the phone and then builds their corresponding base binaries from the release branch in AOSP on which the phone is based. DexDiff compares each pair of these binaries obtained and evaluates the security impacts of individual modifications. The only similarity between this study and our approach is that it extracts pre-installed apps from the phone. However, the proposed tool did not automate this process. The apps are supposed to be extracted before using DexDiff. Contrary to our approach, PiPLAnD automated the process of extraction and analysis.

Elsabagh et al. [11] proposed a static analysis tool named FIRMSCOPE to identify unwanted functionality in pre-installed apps by analyzing the Android firmware. FIRMSCOPE extracts pre-installed apps from the firmware and then performs a taint analysis with context-sensitive, flow-sensitive, field-sensitive, and partially object-sensitive. Specifically, it focuses exclusively on identifying the increase in privileges.

Gamba et al. [14] presented a large-scale study of Android pre-installed using crowd-sourcing methods. In this study, the authors built an Android app, Firmware Scanner, that looks for and extracts pre-installed apps when installed on a device. This study performs permission analysis using Androguard, static analysis leveraging existing tools such as Androwarn, FlowDroid, and Amandroid, as well as apktool and Androguard frameworks to identify unwanted behaviors, and traffic analysis using the crowd-sourced Lumen mobile traffic dataset to see app real-world behaviors. Compared to this work, we did the same by extracting pre-installed apps from the physical device, but using ADB commands rather than an installed app. We also performed a taint analysis using FlowDroid, but by considering third-party libraries as well.

Blázquez et al. [6] proposed FOTA (Firmware-Over-The-Air) Finder to automatically classify a given APK as FOTA or not based on Androguard, using the dataset of pre-installed apps from Firmware Scanner [14]. Then, they performed behavior analysis relying on FlowDroid and Amandroid for a taint analysis and a modification of Androwarn to analyze the use of API calls. This part of the work is a bit similar to our data leak detection using FlowDroid. However, we considered all the pre-installed apps extracted from devices, and also performed malware detection.

Hou et al. [21] performed a study in which they collected firmware images from vendors, official websites, and open source repositories, and CVE data to link them with pre-installed apps. In this study, they proposed a tool named AndScanner that automates the extraction of pre-installed apps from firmware images before analyzing them. AndScanner proposes an analysis of the security patches of the firmware to know if it has been patched in time and if the security issues have been fixed. It also performs app analysis by analyzing the pre-installed apps using Androguard to identify misconfiguration in the manifest file and CryptoGuard to detect cryptography misuse. Our study is different since we did not only focus on analyzing the manifest files, but also analyzed the cryptography misuse. However, we leveraged on Androguard framework in our pipeline.

More recently, Sutter and Tellenbach [33] proposed FirmwareDroid, an automated static analysis tool for pre-installed apps. This tool automates the process of extracting pre-installed apps from firmware images and their analysis using existing tools, including Androgurad and Exodus. The study identifies the advertising tracker libraries used with Exodus and the permissions pre-installed apps inherited with Androguard. The authors have integrated 8 open source static analysis tools in FirmwareDroid, which could be used for further analysis.

Almost all of these studies are a bit similar since they follow almost the same approach, such as collecting firmware from the Internet, extracting the pre-installed apps, and analyzing them. Our approach allows the extraction of pre-installed apps from physical devices, the detection of apps having suspicious behaviors, the detection of data leakage, and security misconfiguration on the Manifest files. Furthermore, our approach is particularly tested on low-cost devices sold in Africa. However, with this approach, every brand and every Android device can be inspected and analyzed. Consequently, we do not have a limitation related to missing some brands or firmware.

4 Low-Cost Android Devices in Africa

Upon careful investigation of the African mobile device market, we identified three popular brands shipping Android devices under 100 US dollars price – Infinix, itel, and Tecno. All these devices run Android Go Edition. We acquired 7 devices in total from these brands for our study.

4.1 Android Go Edition

Android Go Edition is a lightweight configuration of standard Android designed for entry-level devices with limited memory (≤ 2 GB) and storage [17]. Android Go ships with resource-optimized "Go" versions of Google apps, but users can still install apps from the Play Store. Android Go may receive updates less frequently than standard Android [17,32]. To reduce resource consumption, Android Go disables several features by default [17]:

- Picture-in-picture support;
- `SYSTEM_ALERT_WINDOW` permission (display over other apps);
- Split-screen/multi-window;
- Live wallpapers;
- Multi-display;
- Launcher shortcuts (deep shortcuts);
- Reduced maximum width/height for images in remote views;
- VR mode.

Android Go is not necessarily less secure than standard Android. In fact, users may gain security benefits from the removal of the `SYSTEM_ALERT_WINDOW` permission, which has often been abused by malicious apps [13]. We did not find literature that evaluates the security implications of the other optimizations introduced in Android Go. However, Android Go devices typically receive fewer updates and have a shorter support lifecycle, which can leave users without critical security patches [1].

Many pre-installed apps on some device brands are not available on Google Play. They may come from unverified third-party vendors that may potentially distribute malicious apps to the end users.

4.2 Devices and Pre-installed Apps

From our seven devices (Infinix, itel, and Tecno) we extracted 1544 pre-installed APK files, including both system and third-party apps, which form the dataset used in this study. Most of the pre-installed apps extracted cannot be found in the Google Play Store, as shown in Fig. 1. Several brands provide their own app stores. In particular, the Palm Store is reported to be the official app distribution platform for Infinix, Tecno, and itel[2]. Palm Store is preinstalled on the devices we examined and allows users to install, uninstall, and update apps. According to the provider, the store performs automated and manual security checks, compatibility testing, and content-compliance monitoring.

System apps are signed by multiple different certificate authorities, and the dominant signer varies by device. For example, Table 1 shows that on the Infinix SMART8, 68% of system apps are signed by Infinix; 20% by Google; 4% by Transsion; 2% by Tecno; 1% by Facebook; 1% with the default AOSP certificate; and 4% by other authorities. System apps are usually found on */system/app*

[2] Palmstore: https://www.palmplaystore.com/.

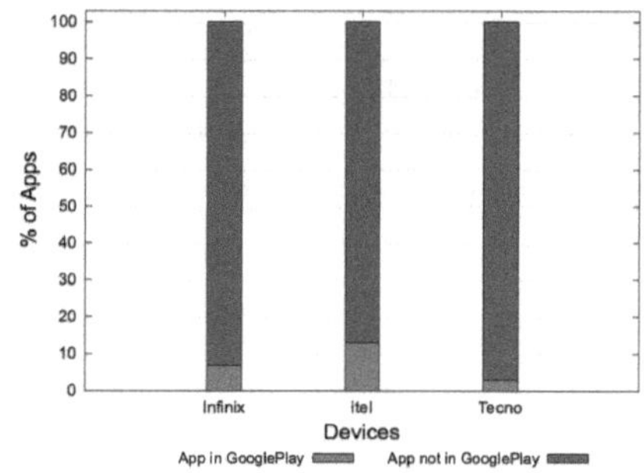

Fig. 1. App present in Google Play vs. App not present in Google Play.

Table 1. System apps grouped by certificate authority for some devices.

Signed by	*Infinix SMART8*	*itel A50*	*Tecno POP8*
Infinix	68%	0%	0%
itel	0%	71%	0%
Tecno	2%	1%	68%
Transsion	4%	2%	3%
Google	20%	22%	21%
Facebook	1%	1%	2%
Default	1%	1%	1%
SW	0%	0%	2%
Others	4%	2%	3%

and */system/priv-app* folders. However, when extracting the APK files, we have found that the apps have been distributed not only in these two folders, but in several others as well. Figure 2 shows an example of the folders on Infinix. Many apps for some brands have been pre-installed based on the regional needs. For

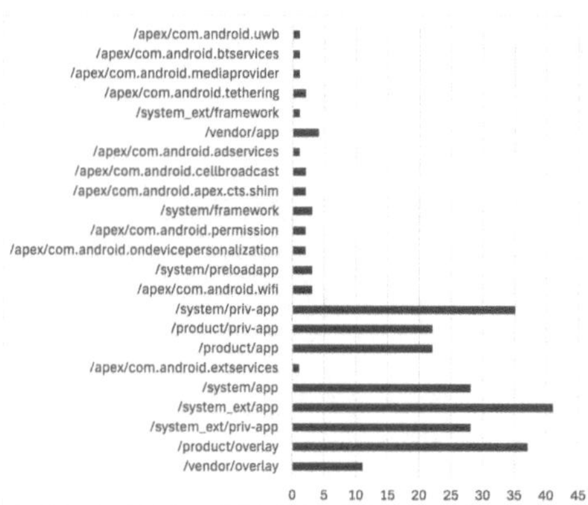

Fig. 2. Location folders of the system apps in Infinix.

example, the supply chain of Transsion devices suggests that Transsion works with partners in Africa, which could pre-install apps and services tailored for the regional needs [22]. Since many steps exist to pre-install apps, this could be an entry point for introducing malicious apps on these devices [37].

5 Methodology

5.1 Research Questions

Understanding the potential risks of pre-installed apps is essential. To guide our research, we have established the following key questions.

RQ1: To what extent do pre-installed apps leak sensitive data on low-cost devices? This question focuses on checking whether pre-installed apps perform activities, such as leaking sensitive data via the Internet or using other ways. This helps us to understand not just if these apps pose risks, but also how they do so.

RQ2: To what extent do pre-installed apps exhibit suspicious behaviors on low-cost devices? The aim of this question is to determine how widespread suspicious pre-installed apps are on affordable devices. Although previous research has shown that some of these apps may contain harmful code [38], a more comprehensive assessment is needed to quantify the extent of the problem in different manufacturers and regions. Through this question, we will explore the devices to identify apps having suspicious behaviors (including malware) as well as those using malicious URLs.

RQ3: How prevalent are security misconfigurations in the manifest files of pre-installed apps on low-cost devices? Through this question, we explore apps to identify those exposing sensitive data across the exported components.

By addressing these research questions, our study provides a clearer picture of the security landscape around pre-installed apps on low-cost mobile devices and highlights potential areas where better security measures are needed.

5.2 PiPLAnD Design

This section outlines the workflow of ***PiPLAnD***, a pipeline designed to inspect pre-installed apps using static analysis approaches. Figure 3 gives an overview of the pipeline. The source code of ***PiPLAnD*** is available on our GitHub repository[3]. We present the details of the workflow of each module in the following sections.

Data Collection. We have used seven (7) low-cost Android devices in this study. ***PiPLAnD*** first automatically extracts the pre-installed apps from a physical device using ADB commands when we plug the device into the computer. After

[3] PiPLAnD source code: https://github.com/liounea/PiPLAnD.

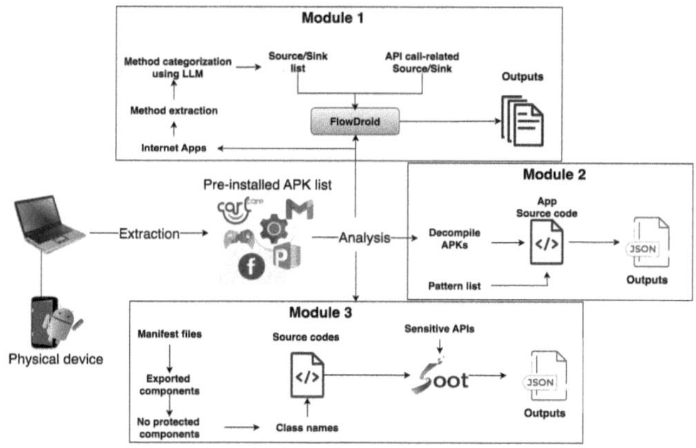

Fig. 3. Overview of ***PiPLAnD***'s workflow.

extraction, we got a dataset of 1544 APK files from the overall devices. This dataset includes system and third-party apps.

Module 1: Data leak detection.
We integrate FlowDroid into ***PiPLAnD*** to identify pre-installed apps that leak sensitive data. FlowDroid is based on a list of sources and sinks for the detection. This list contains Android API calls and Java methods. Thus, by default, it cannot detect data leaked from methods other than Android API calls and Java methods. During our study, we have noticed that there are pre-installed apps that use custom methods from third-party libraries to send data over the Internet. Because of that, we have identified apps that access to Internet by looking for *android.permission.INTERNET* permission on their manifest files. For these apps, we extracted all their methods that we have given to LLMs for source and sink categorization. The resulting list is used, in combination with the default list of sources and sinks, to identify Internet apps leaking sensitive data over the Internet. The default Source and Sink list is also used for detecting other types of data leakage in other apps.

Module 2: Behavior analysis.
The behavior analysis focuses on pattern detection. More specifically, we looked for patterns such as *"pm install"*, *"installPackage"*, etc., to detect installation behaviors, *"logcat"* for apps collecting log data, *"content://sms"*, *"delete"*, *"sendTextMessage"*, *"Telephony.SMS_RECEIVED"* for accessing SMS, deleting, sending, and listening to received SMS, etc. Table 2 shows the full list of the patterns we used. ***PiPLAnD*** helps with this analysis by decompiling the APK file using the Androguard framework and by checking for patterns that match our list in the app code. We only consider these patterns since they are the most obvious and are based on the existing literature, as well. Then, it reports the findings in a JSON file. This file is used for a manual analysis to confirm the behavior of the app based on the patterns detected in its code.

Table 2. The list of patterns

Behaviors	Patterns
Access/Delete/Send SMS	content://sms delete sendTextMessage Telephony.SMS_RECEIVED Telephony.Sms
Dangerous commands	"am start" "chmod" "su" "sudo" "rm -rf"
Log collection	logcat
Installation indicators	"pm install" installPackage

Module 3: Security misconfigurations on Manifest files.
This module allows for the identification of security misconfigurations in the Android manifest files. In this study, we only focus on identifying components exported that allow access to sensitive information. Android allows restricting access to an exported component by using permissions. We first extracted exported components from the manifest files for each app. Then, we filter out and keep those who did not have permission to protect and restrict their access. This gives us a list of class names with their full path in the app code. Besides that, we have constructed a list of sensitive API calls based on the source and sink list from FlowDroid, and from the Androwarn study [10], in which authors look for sensitive data accessed. We explored the list containing the classes of the exported components, and for each class, we analyzed it using the SOOT framework [28]. For the analysis with SOOT, we used the sensitive API list and looked for each of them in the code of the corresponding class to know whether this component allows access to sensitive data. If we did not find the presence of a sensitive API in the code, our analysis program constructs a call graph (CG) of the corresponding class to search whether the sensitive API is used in a method called in the code of the exported component. The results are put into a JSON file, in which we have the corresponding class, the sensitive API, and the method where we found this API.

6 Analysis Results

In this section, we present the findings from seven (7) identified affordable devices that are primarily used in Africa. The main goal of this study is to evaluate the security of the pre-installed apps and to investigate the prevalence of suspicious ones on low-cost devices. Our analysis has revealed interesting findings. Table 3 summarizes these findings. This section shows the results of the analysis by answering the different research questions.

Table 3. Summary of the results.

Analysis Modules	Behaviors	# of apps (%)
Exported sensitive components	Components that allow to access sensitive data	249 (16%)
Leak of sensitive data	Leak of sensitive data	145 (9%)
Suspicious behaviors	Dangerous commands	226 (15%)
	Log collection	10 (0.7%)
	Silent installation behaviors	33 (2%)
	Access/Send/Delete SMS	79 (5%)

6.1 Apps Leaking Sensitive Data

Mobile apps often handle sensitive data on the device. With the privileges that pre-installed apps have, they can perform harmful activities, including leaking this data. Our analysis, consisting of identifying apps that leak sensitive data, has identified several pre-installed apps on seven 7 different devices leaking data, such as Mobile Country Code (MCC), user location (longitude and latitude), device info, International Mobile Subscriber Identity (IMSI), IMEI (International Mobile Equipment Identity), etc. Sensitive data is leaked in different ways, such as in SharedPreferences, in logs, in Intents, as well as on the network. Overall, we have found around 9% of the pre-installed apps on the devices leaking sensitive data, which represent 145 pre-installed apps. As an example, the app (*com.transsion.statisticalsales*) sends sensitive information to a remote host by using third-party libraries with customized methods. As illustrated in Listing 1, the app collects location info, IMSI, IMEI, phone version, etc., and sends them to a remote server. Pre-installed apps also leak data using other ways, such as SharedPreferences storage, device logs, etc. These practices expose the user to many security and privacy problems.

Answer to RQ1

The results show that several pre-installed apps on the three devices exhibit harmful activities such as leaking sensitive data, exposing the users to severe risks.

```
[...]
public class SSHttpClient {
    public static final String BASE_URLFLAG = "PCHttpClient";
    private static final String DEFAULT_BASE_SERVER = "https://asv.transsion.com:443/SaleStatistics/sendsale/sendSale";
    private static final String DEFAULT_INDIA_SERVER = "https://asvin.transsion.com:8080/SaleStatistics/sendsale/sendSale";
    protected static final String TAG = "SSHttpClient_";
    [...]
    public void RegisterInformation(final HttpCallback<HttprequestResult> httpCallback, boolean z) {
        RequestParams requestParams = new RequestParams();
        requestParams.put("ua", this.requestInfo.getUa());
        requestParams.put("screen", this.requestInfo.getScreen());
        requestParams.put("imsi", this.requestInfo.getImsi());
        requestParams.put("imei", this.requestInfo.getImei());
        requestParams.put("phone_version", this.requestInfo.getPhone_version());
        requestParams.put("platform", this.requestInfo.getPlatform());
        requestParams.put("device", this.requestInfo.getDevice());
        requestParams.put("lang", this.requestInfo.getLang());
        requestParams.put("timeStamp", this.requestInfo.getTimeStamp());
        requestParams.put("auth", this.requestInfo.getAuth());
        requestParams.put("lat", this.requestInfo.getLat());
        requestParams.put("lng", this.requestInfo.getLng());
        requestParams.put("client_type", this.requestInfo.getClient_type());
        requestParams.put("phone", this.requestInfo.getPhone());
        requestParams.put("client_version", this.requestInfo.getClient_version());
        requestParams.put("lac", this.requestInfo.getCELL_LAC());
        requestParams.put("cid", this.requestInfo.getCELL_CID());
        mClient.post(z ? DEFAULT_INDIA_SERVER : DEFAULT_BASE_SERVER, requestParams, new AsyncHttpResponseHandler() {
            [...]
        });
    }
}
```

Listing 1: App sending sensitive data to a remote server

6.2 Suspicious Behaviors on Pre-installed Apps

Since mobile devices come with pre-installed apps, these may contain harmful code that can compromise the security of users [38]. We have looked for apps having suspicious behaviors. Several pre-installed malware have been identified to have silent installation behaviors [38]. Others steal sensitive data using different ways [9,35,38]. To identify these kinds of malware, we focus the analysis on detecting patterns. When a pre-installed app declares the *INSTALL_PACKAGES* permission, it has the ability to install an app without the user's knowledge. It can use *android.content.pm.PackageManager.installPackage()* or *Runtime.exec('pm install')* to silently install the app [38]. Our analysis has revealed 33 pre-installed apps having this silent installation behavior on the overall devices. Several pre-installed apps have access to the SMS provider *content://sms*. Some of them delete SMS or declare the *SEND_SMS* and *RECEIVE_SMS* permissions with the broadcast action *Telephony.SMS_RECEIVED*, allowing them to listen and send messages. We have found around 79 apps pre-installed on these low-cost devices, sending, deleting, and/or reading SMS contents. Furthermore, at least 10 pre-installed apps can access and collect the logcat content. Since they have déclared the *READ_LOGS* permission, they can access the overall logcat content, including logs from other applications. In addition to this, we have found several apps that execute dangerous commands (226 apps).

Answer to RQ2

Low-cost Android devices ship pre-installed apps with suspicious behaviors, including sending/deleting/reading SMS, executing dangerous commands, accessing overall logcat memory, and having silent installation behaviors.

6.3 Security Misconfigurations on the Manifest Files

Exported Sensitive Components. Android apps often export components, such as activities, services, receivers, and providers, explicitly by setting *android:exported="true"* or implicitly by declaring an *intent-filter* in the manifest file. When it is the case, the app allows other apps to launch the component [18]. The access to exported components is often restricted using permissions [19]. If there is permission for an exported component, the app that wants to launch it should declare this permission. If an app exports a component without properly enforcing permission, any app could launch it or access sensitive data it contains[4]. When a component allows access to sensitive data, we call it a sensitive component. Our analysis has revealed that several pre-installed apps have sensitive components exported. As illustrated in Table 3, we have found around 16% of the pre-installed apps, representing 249 different app versions, that have exported sensitive components on the low-cost devices, without any restriction or protection mechanism. It means that these devices embed apps that allow other apps to potentially access sensitive information, exposing the user to security and privacy problems. For example, we have found a pre-installed app (*com.transsion.carlcare*) having this method (Listing 2), from an exported activity (*com.transsion.carlcare.WarrantyCardActivity*). This method allows access to location information (lines 13 and 14). In the Android manifest file of the app, this component is clearly exported; however, it is protected by no mechanism, facilitating its easy access and its potential exploitation. Another example shows an exported ContentProvider (*com.sprd.providers.photos.SpecialTypesProvider*) found in the app (*com.sprd.providers.photos*) that allows access to media files, contained in an external storage, from a URI (Listing 3, line 10). This exported component does not have a mechanism that restricts its access by other apps.

[4] CWE-926: https://cwe.mitre.org/data/definitions/926.html.

Answer to RQ3

The results have revealed several pre-installed apps exporting sensitive components, including activities, services, content providers, and receivers, on low-cost devices. This potentially puts users at risk, as their data could be accessed by third parties.

```
public void R1() {
    [...]
    HashMap<String, String> map = new HashMap<>();
    if (TextUtils.isEmpty(this.f15263g0)) {
        map.put("imei", listA.get(0));
    } else {
        map.put("imei", this.f15263g0);
    }
    map.put("imsi", wd.c.g());
    map.put("lang", getResources().getConfiguration().locale.
                                    toString());
    if (this.f15282z0 != null) {
        map.put("lat", this.f15282z0.getLatitude() + "");
        map.put("lng", this.f15282z0.getLongitude() + "");
    }
    map.put("phone_version", a2());
    map.put("screen", getResources().getDisplayMetrics().widthPixels + "*" +
    ↪ getResources().getDisplayMetrics().heightPixels);
    map.put("ua", Build.BRAND + "-" + Build.MODEL);
    [...]
}
```

Listing 2: Exported activity accessing sensitive information

7 Discussion

In this section, we discuss the results from the analysis of the devices.

Sensitive Data Leakage. During our analysis, we have found several pre-installed apps leaking sensitive data. Several of them send the data to a remote host by using Android API calls. Others use third-party libraries that use customized methods to avoid existing detection (e.g., *com.transsion.statisticalsales*). We have considered these customized methods and added them to FlowDroid, and we have detected apps sending sensitive data over the Internet with these methods. Considered as malware by some blog posts [7], the app (*com.transsion.statisticalsales*) is not detectable by malware scanners such as VirusTotal. It silently collects data (phone version, IMSI, user location, CID (Cell Tower ID), LAC (Location Area Code), etc.) and sends it to a remote host. This suspicious behavior compromises users' security and privacy. Several other apps get and store sensitive data in internal storage, such as SharedPreferences, or log it in the logcat memory. These leaked data can be used by malicious actors for user profiling, user tracking [5], or accessed by other apps since pre-installed apps can share each other's data when they have the same *sharedUserId* and have signed with the same certificate [38].

```java
[...]
public final class SpecialTypesProvider extends ContentProvider {
    [...]
    private static final Uri EXTERNAL_CONTENT_URI = MediaStore.Files.getContentUri("external");
    private static final String[] SPECIAL_TYPE_PROJECTION = {"_data", "owner_package_name"};
    [...]
    private int getCameraType(long j) {
        Log.d(TAG, "mediaStoreId = " + j);
        boolean z = true;
        Cursor cursorQuery = getContext().getContentResolver().query( EXTERNAL_CONTENT_URI, SPECIAL_TYPE_PROJECTION,
↪   "_id=?", new String[]{String.valueOf(j)}, null);
        if (cursorQuery != null) {
            try {
                if (cursorQuery.moveToFirst()) {
                    String string = cursorQuery.getString(0);
                    Log.d(TAG, "mediaPath = " + string);
                    String string2 = cursorQuery.getString(1);
                    if (!GOOGLE_PHOTOS_PACKAGE_NAME.equals( string2) && !GOOGLE_GALLERY_PACKAGE_NAME.equals( string2)) {
                        z = false;
                    }
                    Log.d(TAG, "ownerPackageName = " + string2 + ", isGoogleCreatedImage = " + z);
                    try {
                        ExifInterface exifInterface = new ExifInterface();
                        exifInterface.readExif(string);
                        iIntValue = z ? 0 : exifInterface.getTagIntValue( ExifInterface.TAG_CAMERATYPE_IFD). intValue();
                        Log.d(TAG, "getCameraType cameraType = " + iIntValue);
                    } catch (Exception e) {
                        Log.d(TAG, "Exception occurs, mediaPath = " + string + ". ex = " + e);
                    }
                }
            } finally {
                if (cursorQuery != null) {
                    cursorQuery.close();
                }
            }
        }
        return iIntValue;
    }
    [...]
}
```

Listing 3: Exported ContentProvider accessing external storage files

Suspicious Behaviors. We have found several pre-installed apps having suspicious behaviors, including silent installation behavior, sending/deleting SMS, etc. These are done without the user's knowledge and may have negative consequences. Indeed, when an app is able to install another app silently, it may install a malicious app from a malicious remote server or via dynamic code loading. This technique is often used by malicious actors to infect Android devices and avoid detection [38]. This is possible only with system apps, since non-system apps cannot declare the required permission. When a pre-installed app has the ability to send and delete messages without the user's interaction, this can lead to the theft of sensitive data. Several malware are known to use this technique. For instance, a variant of the Triada malware has been found pre-installed in Android devices [35]. This malware performs several actions, among which we have enabling premium SMS services, intercepting, sending, and deleting messages.

Security Misconfiguration. Our analysis has revealed several apps exporting components that allow other apps to potentially access sensitive data, without any protection. The Android framework proposes permission levels, including normal, dangerous, and signature, to protect and restrict access to components [16]. The absence of protecting exported components is a known vulnerability from the community [16]. When an app exports a component without any restriction, it allows other apps to access it. From this, a malicious app may access sensitive resources, as mentioned in the Common Weakness Enumeration (CWE - 926). The app can be victim to an attack named confused deputy attack [12,14], as well as a malicious app can abuse the privileges that these components have to gain unauthorized access to these resources [16,29].

8 Conclusion

This study investigates and analyzes Android pre-installed apps, in particular, those shipped with phones sold in Africa. For this purpose, we have proposed a pipeline that allows the extraction of APK files from a physical device and inspects them to look for different suspicious behaviors, including pre-installed malware, apps exposing sensitive data, and apps sending personal data to remote hosts. The pipeline is tested by inspecting three different low-cost Android devices bought in Africa. The results show interesting findings, such as (1) the leak of sensitive data, (2) sensitive data exposure through exported components, and (3) apps having suspicious behaviors. As future research, we planned to go deeper into these pre-installed apps by analyzing the URLs they use to identify malicious ones, the native libraries used, and by looking for further suspicious behaviors. Our future study will extend the number of low-cost devices and compare the results from the analysis of pre-installed apps with those from European devices, as well. In addition, we planned to perform a dynamic analysis by implementing a solution that monitors the system log and detects suspicious behaviors using AI models.

References

1. Acar, A., Tuncay, G.S., Luques, E., Oz, H., Aris, A., Uluagac, S.: 50 shades of support: a device-centric analysis of android security updates. In: Network and Distributed System Security Symposium, San Diego, CA, USA (2024)
2. Arzt, S., et al.: Flowdroid: precise context, flow, field, object-sensitive and lifecycle-aware taint analysis for android apps. In: Proceedings of the 35th ACM SIGPLAN Conference on Programming Language Design and Implementation, PLDI 2014, pp. 259–269. Association for Computing Machinery, New York, NY, USA (2014). https://doi.org/10.1145/2594291.2594299
3. Barton, J.: Orange releasing android-powered ultra-low cost smartphone for Africa (2020). https://developingtelecoms.com/telecom-technology/telecom-devices-platforms/10053-orange-releasing-android-powered-ultra-low-cost-smartphone-for-africa.html
4. BBC: Chinese phones with built-in malware sold in Africa (2020). https://www.bbc.com/news/technology-53903436
5. Becenti, M.: Leaky apps: how they're stealing your data without you knowing (2024). https://www.quokka.io/blog/leaky-apps-security-risks
6. Blázquez, E., et al.: Trouble over-the-air: an analysis of fota apps in the android ecosystem. In: 2021 IEEE Symposium on Security and Privacy (SP), pp. 1606–1622 (2021). https://doi.org/10.1109/SP40001.2021.00095
7. Bobe, B.: Statisticalsales — the malware pre-installed on your phone (2024). https://medium.com/@threatspotlight/episode-5-statisticalsales-417a14e0f75a

8. Canalys: African smartphone market surges 24% in q4 2023, despite macro headwinds (2024). https://www.canalys.com/newsroom/africa-smartphone-market-Q4-2023
9. Cimpanu, C.: Triada trojan found in firmware of low-cost android smartphones (2017). https://www.bleepingcomputer.com/news/security/triada-trojan-found-in-firmware-of-low-cost-android-smartphones/
10. Debize, T.: Androwarn: Yet another static code analyzer for malicious android applications (2012). https://github.com/maaaaz/androwarn
11. Elsabagh, M., Johnson, R., Stavrou, A., Zuo, C., Zhao, Q., Lin, Z.: FIRMSCOPE: automatic uncovering of privilege-escalation vulnerabilities in pre-installed apps in android firmware. In: 29th USENIX Security Symposium (USENIX Security 2020), pp. 2379–2396. USENIX Association (2020). https://www.usenix.org/conference/usenixsecurity20/presentation/elsabagh
12. Felt, A.P., Wang, H.J., Moshchuk, A., Hanna, S., Chin, E.: Permission re-delegation: attacks and defenses. In: SEC 2011, p. 22. USENIX Association, USA (2011)
13. Fratantonio, Y., Qian, C., Chung, S.P., Lee, W.: Cloak and dagger: from two permissions to complete control of the UI feedback loop. In: 2017 IEEE Symposium on Security and Privacy (SP), pp. 1041–1057. IEEE (2017)
14. Gamba, J., Rashed, M., Razaghpanah, A., Tapiador, J., Vallina-Rodriguez, N.: An analysis of pre-installed android software. In: 2020 IEEE Symposium on Security and Privacy (SP), pp. 1039–1055 (2020). https://doi.org/10.1109/SP40000.2020.00013
15. Goodin, D.: Potentially millions of android TVS and phones come with malware preinstalled (2023). https://arstechnica.com/information-technology/2023/05/potentially-millions-of-android-tvs-and-phones-come-with-malware-preinstalled/
16. Google: Permission-based access control to exported components (2024). https://developer.android.com/privacy-and-security/risks/access-control-to-exported-components
17. Google: Android (Go edition) (2025). https://developer.android.com/guide/topics/androidgo
18. Google: android: exported (2025). https://developer.android.com/privacy-and-security/risks/android-exported
19. Google: App components (2025). https://developer.android.com/guide/topics/manifest/manifest-intro#components
20. Google: Play Protect Certified Android devices: safe and secure (2025). https://www.android.com/certified/
21. Hou, Q., et al.: Large-scale security measurements on the android firmware ecosystem. In: 2022 IEEE/ACM 44th International Conference on Software Engineering (ICSE), pp. 1257–1268 (2022). https://doi.org/10.1145/3510003.3510072
22. Hu, A.: From mobile king in Africa to e-scooter giant? Transsion's next big move (2025). https://www.exportsemi.com/company-post/from-africa-phone-king-to-e-bikes-can-transsion-work-another-miracle/
23. Hutchinson, R.: How to delete pre-installed android apps from your smartphone (2024). https://www.geeky-gadgets.com/how-to-delete-pre-installed-android-apps-from-your-smartphone/
24. kaspersky: Malware attacks in Africa are increasing, reaching 85 million in only 6 months (2021). https://kaspersky.africa-newsroom.com/press/malware-attacks-in-africa-are-increasing-reaching-85-million-in-only-6-months?lang=en

25. Kurt Knutsson, C.R.: FBI warns over 1 million android devices hijacked by malware (2025). https://www.foxnews.com/tech/fbi-warns-over-1-million-android-devices-hijacked-malware.amp
26. U.S. Department of Labor: Guidance on the protection of personally identifiable information (PII). https://www.dol.gov/general/ppii
27. Lakshmanan, R.: Chinese android phones shipped with fake whatsapp, telegram apps targeting crypto users (2025). https://thehackernews.com/2025/04/chinese-android-phones-shipped-with.html
28. Lam, P., Bodden, E., Lhoták, O., Hendren, L.: The soot framework for java program analysis: a retrospective. In: Cetus Users and Compiler Infastructure Workshop (CETUS 2011), vol. 15 (2011)
29. Maqsood, H.M.A., Qureshi, K.N., Bashir, F., Islam, N.U.: Privacy leakage through exploitation of vulnerable inter-app communication on android. In: 2019 13th International Conference on Open Source Systems and Technologies (ICOSST), pp. 1–6 (2019). https://doi.org/10.1109/ICOSST48232.2019.9043935
30. Mitchell, M., Tian, G., Wang, Z.: Systematic audit of third-party android phones. In: Proceedings of the 4th ACM Conference on Data and Application Security and Privacy, CODASPY 2014, pp. 175–186. Association for Computing Machinery, New York, NY, USA (2014). https://doi.org/10.1145/2557547.2557557
31. Ng, A.: Android malware that comes preinstalled is a massive threat (2019). https://www.cnet.com/tech/mobile/android-malware-that-comes-preinstalled-are-a-massive-threat/
32. Sharma, S.: Android go vs regular android – which is right for your business app? (2025). https://www.appventurez.com/blog/android-go-apps-vs-regular-apps
33. Sutter, T., Tellenbach, B.: Firmwaredroid: towards automated static analysis of pre-installed android apps. In: 2023 IEEE/ACM 10th International Conference on Mobile Software Engineering and Systems (MOBILESoft), pp. 12–22 (2023). https://doi.org/10.1109/MOBILSoft59058.2023.00009
34. TIMESOFINDIA: These android phones come with dangerous pre-installed apps (2019). https://timesofindia.indiatimes.com/gadgets-news/these-android-phones-come-with-dangerous-pre-installed-apps/articleshow/72110567.cms
35. Toulas, B.: Counterfeit android devices found preloaded with triada malware (2025). https://www.bleepingcomputer.com/news/security/counterfeit-android-devices-found-preloaded-with-triada-malware/
36. TRUSTONIC: Closing the digital divide with android smartphones in Africa (2021). https://www.trustonic.com/opinion/closing-the-digital-divide-with-android-smartphones-in-africa/
37. upstream: xhelper/triada malware pre-installed on thousands of low cost Chinese android devices in emerging markets (2020). https://www.upstreamsystems.com/press/press-releases/xhelper-triada-malware-pre-installed-on-thousands-of-low-cost-chinese-android-devices-in-emerging-markets/
38. Zheng, M., Sun, M., Lui, J.C.: Droidray: a security evaluation system for customized android firmwares. In: Proceedings of the 9th ACM Symposium on Information, Computer and Communications Security, ASIA CCS 2014, pp. 471–482. Association for Computing Machinery, New York, NY, USA (2014). https://doi.org/10.1145/2590296.2590313

Towards Innovative Intelligent Cyber Defense Approach Based on Deceptive Security and Deep Learning Techniques

Saoudata Bougma, Didier Bassole(✉), Pegdwindé Justin kouraogo, and Sidwendluian Romaric Nana

Laboratoire de Mathématiques et d'Informatique, Université Joseph Ki-Zerbo, Ouagadougou, Burkina Faso
dbassole@gmail.com

Abstract. In this paper, we propose a critical analysis of recent advances in cybersecurity, particularly the application of deep learning, cyber threat intelligence, and deceptive security. Building on this analysis, we introduce an integrated and innovative approach that combines the collection of attacker traces through deception systems (honeypots) with deep learning techniques, in order to enhance the resilience of cyber defense strategies. Our methodology is structured around three components: (1) constructing a labeled dataset from the traces collected on the T-Pot deception platform, based on the MITRE ATT&CK framework; (2) developing a deep learning model capable of identifying attacker profiles in real time; and (3) integrating an automated incident response mechanism that can trigger countermeasures tailored to the identified profile. This approach seeks to overcome the limitations of current solutions by providing an adaptive, intelligent and automated cyber defense system.

Keywords: Cybersecurity · Deceptive Security · Deep Learning · Real Time

1 Introduction

Artificial intelligence (AI)-based intrusion detection systems (IDS) face a major challenge: the lack of real-world data on cyber threats. This limitation reduces their ability to effectively detect attacks and adapt to the evolving tactics of cyber adversaries. Deceptive security has emerged as a compensatory strategy by providing a means to collect real data on attacker behaviors through decoy systems (honeypots, honeynets). These mechanisms make it possible to observe

https://www.ujkz.bf/.

A. Oluwatope et al. (Eds.): AFRICOMM 2025, LNICST 713, pp. 69–87, 2027.
https://doi.org/10.1007/978-3-032-38682-3_5

the tactics, techniques, and procedures (TTPs) used by attackers, thereby offering the potential to enrich the datasets used to train IDS.

However, the exploitation of these raw data to improve the actual security of the systems remains limited. Existing research often focuses on descriptive analysis of attacks or profiling restricted to specific attacker categories, without integrating this information into an adaptive and operational framework for system defense. After conducting a critical review of the literature on deep learning applied to cybersecurity, deceptive security, and attacker profiling, we propose an integrated methodological approach that combines deceptive security with deep learning to strengthen cyber defense. We introduce a mechanism based on the analysis of traces left by attackers on deception systems (honeypots), with the aim of automatically profiling their behavior and adapting defense systems according to the detected profile. Our primary objective is to design an intelligent and innovative approach that merges deception-based security with deep learning techniques to improve cyber defense strategies.

The remainder of this article is organized as follows. Section 2 presents a review of the literature on the application of deep learning to cybersecurity, deceptive security, cyber threat intelligence, attacker profiling, and automated incident response. In this section, we discuss existing approaches and analyze their limitations in order to position our contribution. Section 3 provides a detailed description of our methodological approach. Finally, Sect. 4 summarizes the results and outlines future research directions.

2 Related Work

Recent research in cybersecurity shows a growing interest in leveraging deep learning, deceptive security, and cyber threat intelligence to strengthen defense mechanisms. This section provides a synthesis of existing studies along five main axes: 2.1 the application of deep learning to cybersecurity, 2.2 deceptive security, 2.3 cyber threat intelligence (CTI), 2.4 attacker profiling, and 2.5 automated incident response.

2.1 Deep Learning Applied to Cybersecurity

The emergence of deep learning has profoundly transformed several domains, including cybersecurity, by enabling the automated analysis of large volumes of data and facilitating the advanced detection of threats such as SQL injections, ransomware, DDoS attacks, zero-day exploits, and phishing. Numerous studies have demonstrated the effectiveness of deep learning in detecting, analyzing, and reconstructing malicious actions.

The work of Uhongora et al. [1], Salah Fathi et al. [2], and D. Kumar et al. [3] shows that deep learning models (LSTM, BERT, Transformers) achieve very high performance levels ($F_1 > 0.95$) in intrusion detection. Similarly, Miranda-Garca et al. [4] confirm their effectiveness in various domains (spam, malware, deepfakes). These results highlight the potential of deep learning to automatically identify attack patterns.

However, several studies (Ring and al. [5]; Cremer et al. [6]) point to a major limitation: the reliance on artificial or outdated datasets, which are often far removed from operational environments. The effectiveness of the models therefore depends heavily on the quality and representativeness of the data, which justifies the search for more realistic sources, such as those provided by deceptive security.

2.2 Deceptive Security

Rather than merely focusing on blocking cyberattacks, cybersecurity research is increasingly shifting toward a more proactive stance, aiming to understand the tactics, techniques, and procedures (TTPs) of adversaries.

Wael Ahmad AlZoubia and Maen T. Alrashdan [7] evaluated the impact of integrating honeypots into defense mechanisms. Their findings indicate that these tools make it possible to gather relevant information about attackers while increasing the complexity of their task. However, a significant limitation is that honeypots capture only attacks explicitly directed at them. They therefore appear as complementary tools, effective when combined with other security mechanisms. In a broader analysis, Kalpin Erlangga Silaen et al. [8] reviewed 38 articles addressing the contribution of honeypots to data security. Their study highlights several key roles: attack detection, deterrence, forensic investigation support, and enhancement of defensive strategies.

The benefits of deceptive security are also emphasized by Zlatan Morić, Vedran Dakić, and Damir Regvart [9] in their article Advancing Cybersecurity with Honeypots and Deception Strategies. The authors confirm that honeypots enrich the understanding of threats and support forensic investigations.

From an optimization perspective, Md Ali Reza Al Amin [10] proposed a Dynamic Deception System (DDS), capable of evaluating attackers based on criteria such as aggressiveness, stealth, or technical expertise. This system allows defensive resources to be prioritized according to the detected threat, thereby optimizing monitoring and analysis efforts. Similarly, Walid Bin Shahid et al. [11] introduced a customized deception system, reinforced with deep learning techniques, to counter web application attacks. Their detection module achieved a remarkable accuracy of 99.94%, illustrating the power of AI applied to proactive cyber defense. Nivedhaa [12] explores the role of deep learning in deception techniques for network defense. According to the author, artificial intelligence enables the development of more effective deception strategies, capable of disrupting even the most sophisticated attackers.

Far from replacing traditional detection (IDS, Intrusion Detection System) and prevention (IPS, Intrusion Prevention System) mechanisms, honeypots serve as reinforcements. Muhammet Baykara and Resul Daş [13] highlighted their complementarity to traditional IDS / IPS. Honeypots provide an additional layer of security by luring and identifying attackers, thereby strengthening the overall defensive posture. Ammar Boulache et al. [14] proposed a probabilistic approach that combined n-grams and Markov models integrated into a honeypot. Their system anticipates certain attacks before their full execution, although its effectiveness is heavily dependent on the diversity and quality of the collected data. A particularly innovative approach was developed by Araujo and al. at the University of Texas [15], with their concept of DECeption Digging. By integrating honeypots into a semi-supervised learning system, they transform attackers into involuntary penetration testers. The data collected dynamically enriches the detection databases, continuously improving the IDS performance.

2.3 Cyber Threat Intelligence (CTI)

In a context where cyber threats are becoming increasingly complex, persistent, and targeted, the ability to trace, understand, and anticipate attacks has become a major strategic lever for cybersecurity. Cyber Threat Intelligence (CTI) thus emerges as an essential discipline, centered on the collection, analysis, and exploitation of threat-related information to improve the defensive posture of organizations [16].

Several models have been developed to facilitate attack analysis and understanding of adversarial behaviors. Odarchenko et al. [17] provide a comparative analysis of the main cyber threat intelligence frameworks such as the Diamond Model, the Cyber Kill Chain (CKC), the Unified Kill Chain (UKC), and MITRE ATT&CK, highlighting their respective strengths and limitations. A comparative summary of these frameworks is presented in The table 1:

Each model addresses specific needs:

- Diamond Model is ideal for identifying attackers and understanding their motivations.
- MITRE ATT&CK is better suited for detecting and classifying adversarial techniques.
- Cyber Kill Chain is useful for retracing classical attack scenarios.

These frameworks have been used by many researchers to propose innovative defense approaches: for example, Zambiancoa et al. [18] propose a proactive decoy selection scheme based on the MITRE ATT&CK framework, designed to dynamically adapt deception according to adversarial tactics and techniques. This approach highlights the value of coupling cyber deception with CTI to anticipate malicious behaviors but remains essentially conceptual, with no empirical validation or exploitation of deception data for attacker profiling. Our approach seeks to overcome this limitation by leveraging traces collected in deception environments to feed a deep learning process, thereby enabling the identification of attacker behavioral profiles and reinforcing adaptive cyber defense.

A notable contribution is that of Shuqin Zhang et al. [19] with DeepOP, a hybrid framework combining a cybersecurity ontology and a causal attention Transformer model to predict MITRE ATT&CK attack sequences. This approach significantly improves prediction performance compared to existing models and demonstrates robustness in the presence of incomplete data.

Table 1. Comparaison: Diamond / Extended Diamond, Cyber Kill Chain / Unified Kill Chain et MITRE ATT&CK

Characteristic	Diamond / Extended Diamond	Cyber Kill Chain / Unified Kill Chain	MITRE ATT&CK
Focus / Objective	Focuses on attacker motivations and capabilities	Emphasizes the stages of an attack	Focuses on attack stages, techniques, sub-techniques, and TTPs
Granularity	Provides a broader perspective	More specific	Very detailed, with fine-grained coverage of TTPs
Primary Application	Incident response oriented	Understanding threat actor behavior by documenting TTPs of past attacks	Threat hunting and research; direct support from MITRE and the cybersecurity community
Maintenance / Update	Users must feed the model themselves	Uses the MITRE ATT&CK matrix for updates	Maintained directly by MITRE and indirectly by the community
Attack Stage Coverage	Partial; requires complementary analysis	CKC: 7 stages; UKC: 18 stages	Very broad, with comprehensive coverage of stages, tactics, techniques, and tools used
Added Value / Strengths	Provides deep understanding of infrastructure, victim capabilities, and adversary capabilities	Offers a structured view of attack stages and their sequence	Provides a comprehensive and detailed view of TTPs for precise attacker profiling and analysis

Aimad Berady [19] proposes an in-depth modeling of TTPs. He also contributes to the field by publishing a dataset derived from experiments in a professional environment. Building on Berady's dataset, Rodríguez et al. [20] combine process mining and MITRE ATT&CK to reconstruct attack sequences.

Finally, Lingzi Li et al. [21] propose a framework based on the analysis of textual data extracted from security audit reports, relying on two multi-label classifiers based on DistilBERT. The proposed approach automatically identifies the tactics and techniques contained in security logs according to the MITRE ATT&CK framework.

2.4 Attacker Profiling

Far from being a homogeneous group, cyber attackers exhibit a wide variety of profiles, each with its own methods and objectives. Attacker profiling has been addressed in previous research, with some studies focusing on psychological traits and others on behavioral analysis.

Psychological Profiling

Sanders et al. [22] and Hani et al. [23] explore personality traits (Dark Triad, sensation seeking) to distinguish three types of cyber attackers: White Hats, Grey Hats, and Black Hats. Tshimula and al. [24] go further by leveraging large language models (LLMs) to automatically detect psycholinguistic traits in attackers' textual outputs. These studies enrich the understanding of attacker motivations but remain detached from technical traces.

Behavioral Profiling and TTPs

Torres and García [25] focused on identifying the perpetrator of a given attack using Transformers. Their method allows classification of network alert sequences and associates them with a specific attacker with near-perfect accuracy (≈99%), significantly outperforming classical approaches such as multilayer perceptrons. Kotenko et al. [26] introduce a two-level attacker profiling model (opportunistic vs. advanced) by linking low-level attributes (e.g., Bash command histories, event logs) to high-level attributes that characterize adversarial behaviors. Their experiments demonstrate that activity logs can be leveraged with machine learning, notably LSTM networks, to differentiate attacker or team profiles.

2.5 Automated Incident Response

Automated incident response encompasses the technologies and processes implemented to detect, analyze, and neutralize cybersecurity threats without immediate human intervention. It relies on artificial intelligence (AI) to identify suspicious patterns, classify security alerts, and execute predefined defensive actions, such as isolating a compromised device, blocking malicious access, or launching additional security scans.

Several studies have proposed mechanisms for automating response, either integrated into or independent from SOAR (Security Orchestration, Automation, and Response) platforms. Ren et al. [27] propose a deep reinforcement learning approach (ARCS) to dynamically optimize response actions. Tested on a corpus of 20,000 real incidents, their solution significantly reduces processing time (-27.3%) and false positive rate (-42.8%), while increasing overall process effectiveness (+31.2%). Despite these promising results, this method is limited by high computational resource requirements and the need for high-quality labeled data. Nguyen et al. [28] focus on automating the selection of SOAR playbooks using similarity learning, integrated into the Shuffle platform. This mechanism enables the dynamic generation of response action plans for common attacks (e.g., SSH brute-force), thereby reducing reaction times. However, their method shows rigidity when confronted with unknown threats or low-quality historical data.

In the article A Logical Ontology for Structuring Incident Response Processes in SOCs, Kuznetsov [29] proposes a logical ontology to structure incident response processes in Security Operations Centers (SOCs). The goal is to unify and formalize the way incidents are detected, categorized, and handled, by defining a common language based on logic and conceptual relationships. A comparison of existing approaches has been made in the table 2:

Table 2. Comparison of Existing Approaches and Their Limitations in Cybersecurity

Axis	Existing Approaches	Identified Limitations
Deep Learning in Cybersecurity	Used for intrusion and anomaly detection based on public datasets (KDD'99, CICIDS2017, UNSW-NB15, etc.)	Dependence on artificial or outdated data; focus on detection without profiling or response
Deceptive Security (honeypots, honeytokens)	Enables collection of real and behavioral traces of attackers (e.g., Cowrie, Dionaea, Conpot)	Raw, noisy, and heterogeneous data; limited use for post-incident analysis only
Cyber Threat Intelligence (CTI)	Frameworks such as MITRE ATT&CK, used for attack modeling and threat information sharing	Manual analysis requiring advanced expertise; low automation; underused in integrated systems
Attacker Profiling	Psychological approaches or TTP-based analysis; often binary (e.g., opportunistic vs advanced)	Profiling focused on psychological traits, neglecting observable technical and behavioral aspects; generally limited to simplified or binary classification
Incident Response	AI-based approaches with alerts and basic correlations	Requires high-quality labeled data

2.6 Limitations and Perspectives of Related Work

Based on the reviewed studies, several major observations emerge. First, advances in deep learning applied to cybersecurity have demonstrated strong effectiveness in detecting complex attack patterns and identifying anomalous behaviors from large datasets. However, deep learning models remain dependent on artificial or outdated datasets.

Deceptive security, through mechanisms such as honeypots and honeytokens, has proven particularly effective for collecting behavioral data. It provides a proactive view of cyber threats and enables real-time monitoring of the tactics and tools used by attackers. Nevertheless, the collected data is often raw and heterogeneous, requiring sophisticated analytical processing to extract actionable patterns.

Cyber Threat Intelligence (CTI) constitutes a strategic lever for understanding the threat ecosystem, identifying malicious actors, their objectives, and operational methods. When combined with deceptive security, CTI enables a shift from reactive cybersecurity to predictive, adversary-oriented cybersecurity. However, existing frameworks require expertise for in-depth threat analysis and understanding. The operational exploitation of CTI frameworks (such as MITRE ATT&CK) still demands advanced expertise and remains underutilized in integrated and automated approaches.

Regarding attacker profiling, psychological approaches remain focused on personality traits, neglecting observable technical and behavioral aspects. Deep learningbased methods and TTP analysis allow attribution of an attack to a specific actor but are generally limited to simplified or binary profile classifications (e.g., opportunistic vs. advanced), failing to capture the richness and diversity of attacker behaviors. Moreover, few studies exploit data collected through honeypots to enhance profiling models and trigger adaptive responses.

Our work builds on these studies and aims to address these limitations. It demonstrates that data from deception systems is sufficiently rich and can be leveraged by deep learning algorithms to create a dynamic defense mechanism. Our contribution is twofold: first, to valorize data from deceptive security by constructing a dataset usable by a deep learning model to accurately identify a cybercriminal from traces left on decoy systems; second, to automate the adaptation of countermeasures according to the attacker's profile.

Thus, unlike existing approaches, which often focus solely on detection or post-incident analysis, our solution aims to close the cybersecurity defense loop, namely: observe, analyze, identify, and respond dynamically and automatically.

3 Methodological Approach

We propose an innovative methodology that combines deep learning and deceptive security with the objective of profiling attackers and dynamically adapting defense mechanisms according to their behaviors. Figure 1 illustrates our methodological workflow. We begin with a comparative study to identify the most appropriate tools. Once these tools are selected, we proceed with the implementation of a data collection mechanism, enabling us to build a dataset suitable for attacker profiling. After obtaining the dataset, we implement an attacker classification algorithm based on behavioral profiles. The model is then evaluated:

- If the results are satisfactory, we move forward with the integration of an automated incident response system.
- If the results are unsatisfactory, the model is refined and retrained before continuing.

Finally, after integrating the automated incident response system, we conduct a global evaluation of the entire system to assess its effectiveness and robustness, as summarized in Fig. 1.

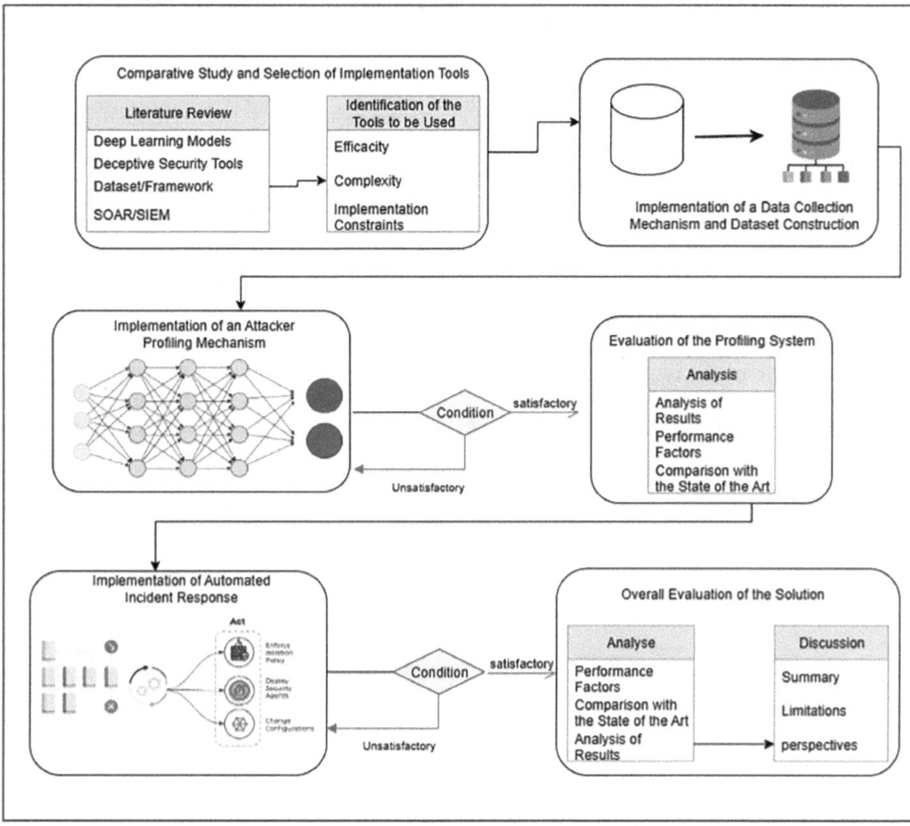

Fig. 1. Methodological Workflow.

The architecture of our solution is based on four key stages:

1. Data collection via deception techniques;
2. Construction of a labeled dataset from the collected traces;
3. Attacker profiling using a deep learning model;
4. Triggering countermeasures according to the detected profile.

3.1 Data Collection

This stage consists of deploying a controlled deception environment that enables the generation of realistic traces of attacker behavior. To this end, we deploy a virtualized T-Pot platform on VMware, which aggregates around fifteen honeypots covering various critical services (e.g., Cowrie for SSH/Telnet, Dionaea for SMB/FTP/HTTP, Conpot for SCADA, Elasticpot for vulnerable Elasticsearch instances).

The rationale for this choice is twofold: diversity of attack vectors and realism of interactions. Indeed, T-Pot's honeypots, such as Cowrie, capture diverse interactive sessions (commands, file transfers, scripts), which allows analysis not only of the presence of an attack but also of the attacker's behavioral logic.

To generate controlled attacks, we use the Atomic Red Team (ART) framework from a Kali Linux machine. Each test corresponds to a scenario aligned with MITRE ATT&CK and reproduces specific tactics/techniques (e.g., Privilege Escalation, Persistence, Exfiltration). These scenarios enrich the collected data with known, labeled attacks while complementing opportunistic attacks resulting from real intrusions captured by T-Pot.

All produced logs are centralized via the ELK stack (Elasticsearch, Logstash, Kibana), which is natively integrated into T-Pot. This component ensures:

- aggregation and normalization of logs originating from multiple honeypots;
- temporal traceability of events;
- secure storage and preservation of raw data for subsequent labeling and training phases.

A schematic of the data generation and collection pipeline is shown in Fig. 2.

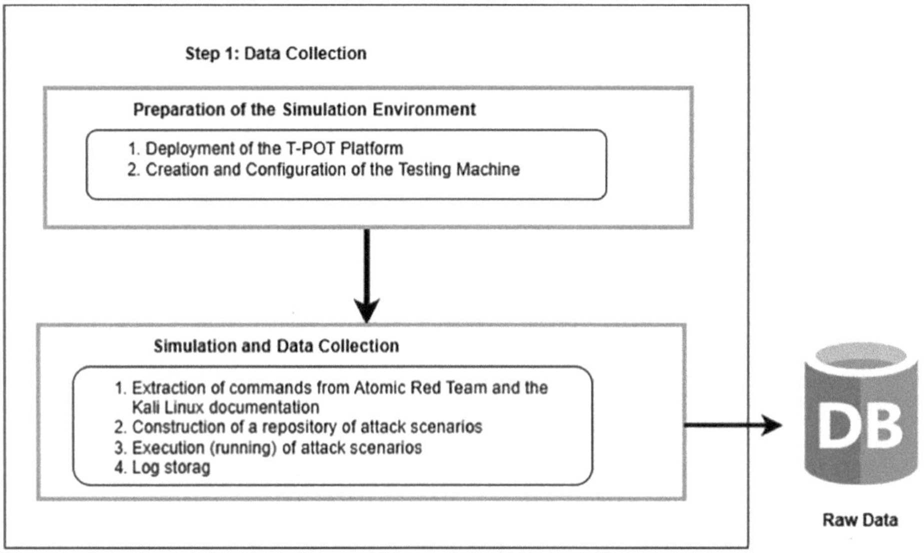

Fig. 2. Data Collection Process.

Description of the Data Collection Setup

The most comprehensive open-source deception platform available, T-Pot, is a Linux image that comes with numerous preinstalled honeypots and built-in log monitoring through the ELK stack, developed and maintained by Deutsche Telekom AG. The platform aggregates multiple low- and high-interaction honeypots, facilitating the collection of diverse telemetry (network flows, protocol exchanges, payloads and shell sessions) that are essential for attacker profiling and model training. Table 3 provides an overview of the main honeypots available in a standard T-Pot installation (examples).

Table 3. Summary of honeypots integrated into T-Pot

Honeypot	Objective	Simulated Services	Collected Data
`adbhoney`	Target Android attacks via ADB	ADB port (5555)	Issued commands, file transfers
`ciscoasa`	Simulate Cisco ASA firewall	SSH, Telnet, SFTP	Authentication logs, transfers
`conpot`	Emulate industrial SCADA systems	Modbus, SNMP, BACnet	ICS commands, SCADA scans
`cowrie`	Attract SSH/Telnet attacks	SSH, Telnet (ports 22, 23)	Shell sessions, transferred files, commands
`dionaea`	Capture malware and exploits	SMB, FTP, HTTP, SIP, MSSQL	Malware binaries, shellcodes
`elasticpot`	Simulate vulnerable Elasticsearch server	Elasticsearch API	RCE requests, payloads
`glastopf`	Attract automated web attacks	HTTP	Vulnerable requests, injections
`glutton`	Capture all TCP/UDP traffic on open ports	Multi-port (MITM proxy)	TCP sessions, raw traffic
`heralding`	Collect credentials over various protocols	FTP, SSH, RDP, HTTP	Credentials, login failures
`honeypy`	Modular honeypot in Python	Customizable TCP/UDP services	Interactive custom logs
`honeytrap`	Dynamic deployment of fake services	Dynamic TCP/UDP	Incoming connections, payloads
`mailoney`	Simulate vulnerable SMTP server	SMTP (port 25)	Received emails, spam, malware
`medpot`	Simulate connected health systems	HL7, FHIR	Simulated medical accesses
`rdpy`	Simulate vulnerable RDP server	RDP (port 3389)	RDP connection attempts
`snare`	Collect logs via remote protocols	Syslog, audit log	Remote system logs
`tanner`	Simulate low-interaction diverse services	TCP, HTTP	Connections, basic requests

The architecture is illustrated in Fig. 3.

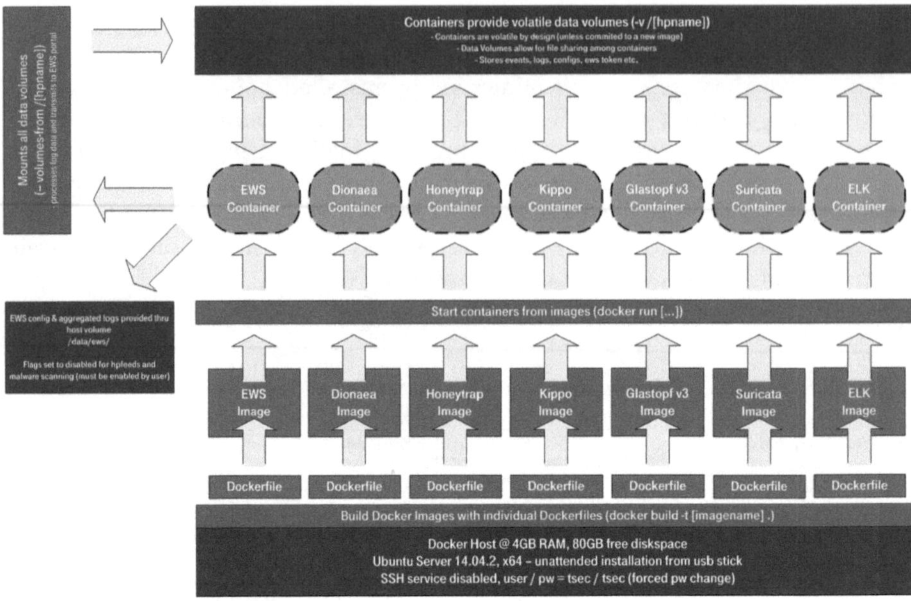

Fig. 3. Architecture of the T-Pot Platform [26].

3.2 Construction of a Labeled Dataset

The raw data collected by honeypots is often noisy (redundancies, false positives, system errors). An initial cleaning phase is therefore performed: removal of incomplete entries, filtering out system packets with no analytical value, and normalization of timestamp formats. Next, we carry out an automatic labeling of events based on the MITRE ATT&CK framework by associating each action with tactics, techniques, and procedures (TTPs). This step involves:

1. Mapping each command or sequence of actions to an ATT&CK technique (e.g., net user → T1087: Account Discovery).
2. Associating that technique with a tactic (e.g., Discovery).
3. Linking the whole to a hypothetical attacker profile (e.g., systematic reconnaissance → advanced attacker; opportunistic scans → script kiddie).

To automate this mapping, we build a semantic dictionary that links:

- keywords/commands ↔ MITRE techniques,
- attack sequences ↔ behavioral profiles.

The final dataset therefore contains instances represented as sequences of labeled events (e.g., [Initial Access → Discovery → Persistence]), which can be used directly by sequential deep learning models. Figure 4 summarizes the whole pipeline from raw logs to a labelled dataset.

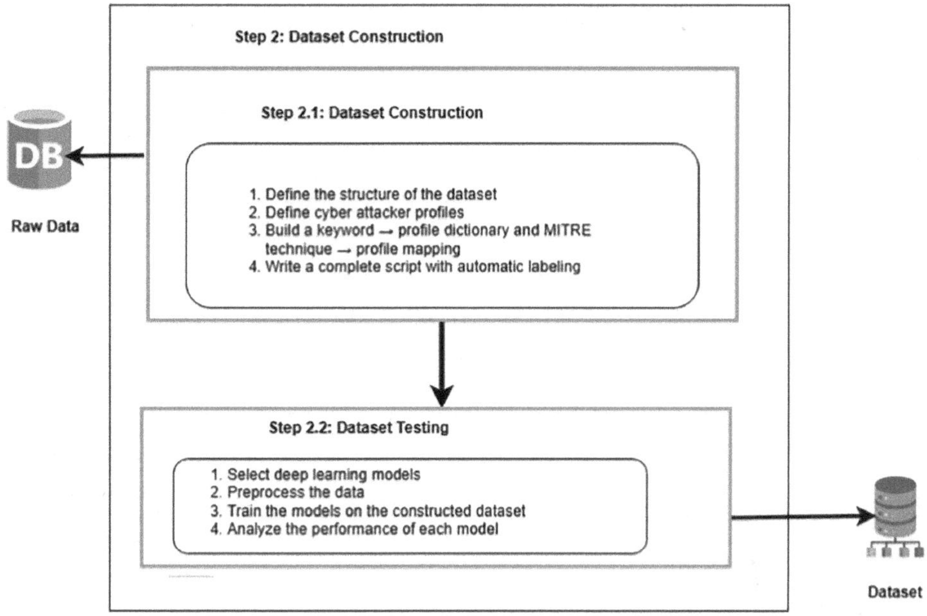

Fig. 4. Dataset Construction Process.

3.3 Attacker Profiling with Deep Learning

The labeled dataset serves as the foundation for training a deep learning model designed to:

1. Analyze temporal attack sequences (not just isolated events).
2. Classify attackers according to their profile (e.g., opportunistic, cybercriminal, APT, destructive, etc.).

We consider three families of models:

- LSTM (Long Short-Term Memory): effective for sequential data and detecting temporal dependencies.
- Transformers: suitable for contextual analysis of long and varied sequences.
- Hybrid CNN-LSTM models: combining local pattern detection with global dependencies.

The process follows four main stages:

1. Preprocessing: vectorization of events (e.g., command embeddings), sequence normalization, and padding for variable-length sequences.
2. Training: supervised learning with cross-validation, in order to reduce bias related to class imbalance.

3. Evaluation: we compute accuracy, recall, and F1-score, as well as profiling-specific metrics (false attribution rate, inter-profile confusion).
4. Real-time recognition: integration of an engine that compares new attack sequences with those previously learned and dynamically assigns an attacker profile.

Fig. 5 illustrates the deep learning-based attacker profiling workflow.

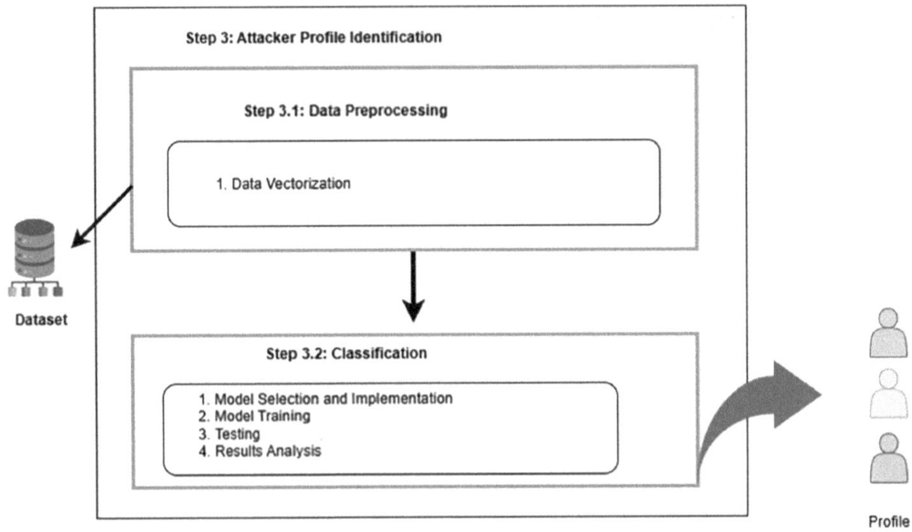

Fig. 5. Attacker Profile Identification Process.

3.4 Integration with a Security Information and Event Management (SIEM) for Adaptive Response

The final stage of our work aims to connect the automated profiling engine to an active response system. To achieve this, we couple our classification engine with an automated incident response system. The engine provides, in real time, the attacker's profile based on observed behaviors within the honeynet or the network. The SIEM receives this information as enriched events, which feed correlation rules and automated response workflows. The logic is as follows:

1. Definition of correlation rules: For each attacker profile, we define specific correlation rules to determine the most appropriate reaction. For example:
   - If profile = opportunistic, then apply simple countermeasures (IP blocking, session termination).
   - If profile = APT/persistent, then apply reinforced countermeasures (network segmentation, host isolation, administrator alerts).
2. Automation of reaction: Countermeasures are triggered in real time without human intervention, thereby reducing reaction time and minimizing the exposure surface.

This integration provides the system with proactive self-defense capabilities, where each attack contributes to improving both the accuracy of the model and the relevance of the countermeasures (Fig. 6)).

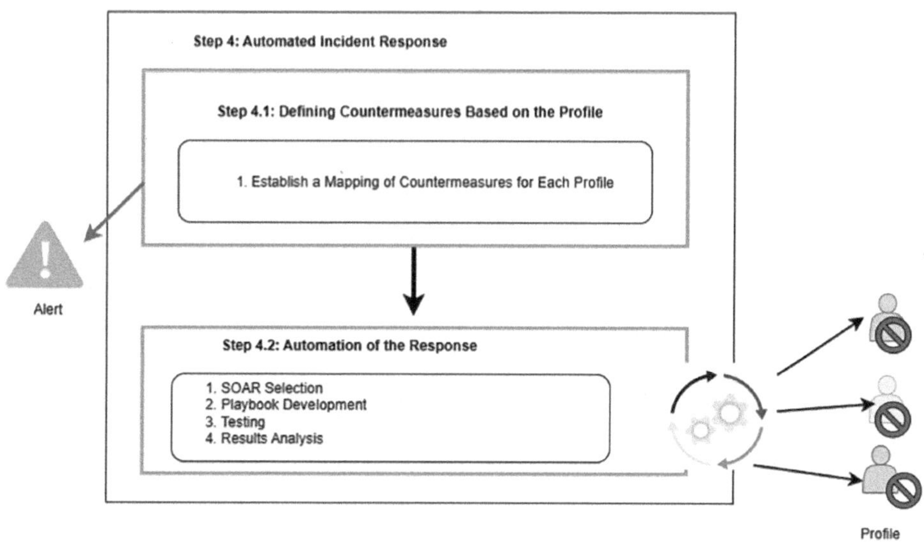

Fig. 6. Automated Incident Response Process.

The overall architecture of the solution is presented in Fig. 7:

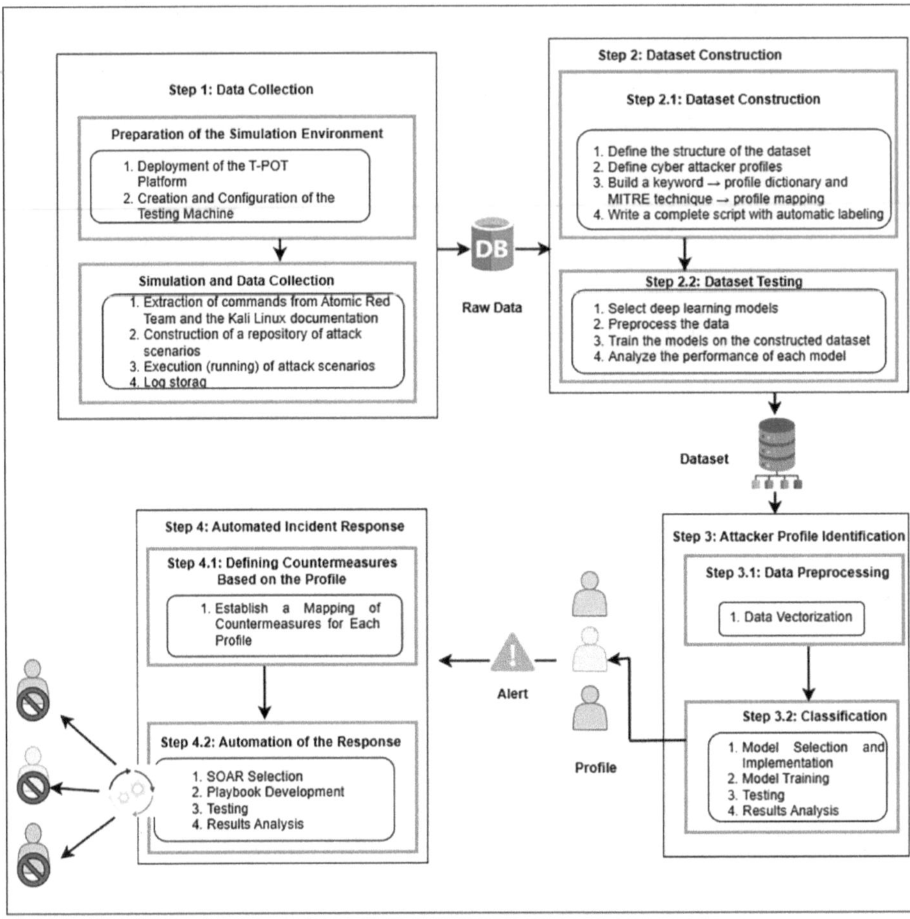

Fig. 7. Overall Architecture.

4 Conclusion and Future Work

In this article, we first conducted a review of the research related to deep learning applied to cybersecurity, deceptive security, and cyber threat intelligence. This analysis enabled us to identify both the potential and limitations of these approaches when used in isolation. In particular, deceptive security has proven effective for capturing, in real time, the tactics, techniques, and tools used by attackers, providing rich behavioral data. However, this raw information requires in-depth analytical processing to extract actionable patterns.

Meanwhile, advances in deep learning within the cybersecurity domain have shown strong capabilities in detecting complex attack patterns and identifying abnormal behaviors from large volumes of data. Nevertheless, most existing approaches remain focused primarily on intrusion detection, lacking fine-grained attacker profiling or the ability to support dynamic, personalized responses.

In light of these findings, we propose an integrated approach that combines data collection through deceptive security, behavioral profiling using deep learning, and the activation of dynamic countermeasures via a SIEM system. This architecture aims to close the cyber defense loop: observe, analyze, profile, and respond in an automated and adaptive manner according to the identified attacker profile.

In summary, our contribution seeks to demonstrate that by leveraging data collected through deception systems and intelligently exploiting it through machine learning models, it is possible to significantly enhance defense capabilities against increasingly stealthy, polymorphic, and adaptive threats. Future work will focus on the experimental validation of the proposed approach.

References

1. Uhongora, U., Law, Y.W., and Slay, J.: Deep-learning-based intrusion detection for software-defined networking space systems. In: Proceedings 22nd European Conference on Cyber Warfare and Security (ECCWS), pp. 639–647 (2023). https://doi.org/10.34190/eccws.22.1.1085
2. K. Salah Fathi, S. Barakat, and A. Rezk. An effective SQL injection detection model using LSTM for imbalanced datasets. Comput. Secur. **153**, 104391 (2025). https://doi.org/10.1016/j.cose.2025.104391
3. Kumar, D., Pateriya, R.K., Gupta, R.K., Dehalwar, V., Sharma, A.: DDoS detection using deep learning. Procedia Comput. Sci. **218**, 2420–2429 (2023). https://doi.org/10.1016/j.procs.2023.01.217
4. Miranda-García, A., et al.: Deep learning applications on cybersecurity: a practical approach. Neurocomputing. **563**, 126904 (2024). https://doi.org/10.1016/j.neucom.2023.126904
5. Ring, M., Wunderlich, S., Scheuring, D., Landes, D., Hotho, A.: A survey of network-based intrusion detection data sets. Comput. Secur. **86**, 147–167 (2019). https://doi.org/10.1016/j.cose.2019.06.005
6. Cremer, F., et al.: Cyber risk and cybersecurity: a systematic review of data availability. Geneva Pap. Risk Insur. Issues Pract. **47** (2022). https://doi.org/10.1057/s41288-022-00266-6
7. Dali, L. et al.: A survey of intrusion detection system. In Proceedings 2nd World Symposium on Web Applications and Networking (WSWAN), pp. 1–6 (2015). https://doi.org/10.1109/WSWAN.2015.7210351
8. Silaen, K.E., Meyliana, M., Warnars, H.L.H.S., Prabowo, H., Hidayanto, A.N., and Anggreainy, M.S.: Usefulness of honeypots towards data security: a systematic literature review. In: 2023 International Workshop on Artificial Intelligence and Image Processing (IWAIIP), pp. 422–427 (2023). https://doi.org/10.1109/IWAIIP58158.2023.10462777
9. Morić, Z., Dakic, V., Regvart, D.: Advancing cybersecurity with honeypots and deception strategies. Informatics **12**, 14 (2025). https://doi.org/10.3390/informatics12010014
10. K.I. Iyer. Adaptive honeypots: dynamic deception tactics in modern cyber defense. Int. J. Sci. Res. Arch.**4**, 340–351 (2021). https://doi.org/10.30574/ijsra.2021.4.1.0210

11. Shahid, W.B., Aslam, B., Abbas, H., Afzal, H., Khalid, S.B.: A deep learning assisted personalized deception system for countering web application attacks. J. Inf. Secur. Appl. **67**, 103169 (2022). https://doi.org/10.1016/j.jisa.2022.103169
12. Nivedhaa, N.: The role of deep learning in cyber deception techniques for network defense. Glob. J. Cyber Secur. (GJCS), **1**, 1–10 (2024). https://hal.science/hal-04555832v1
13. M. Baykara and R. Das. A survey on potential applications of honeypot technology in intrusion detection systems. Int. J. Comput. Netw. Appl., **2**(5) (2015). https://ijcna.org/Manuscripts/Volume-2/Issue-5/Vol-2-issue-5-M-01.pdf
14. A. Boulaiche, H. Bouzayani, and K. Adi. A quantitative approach for intrusions detection and prevention based on statistical n-gram models. In: Proceedings ANT 2012 and MobiWIS 2012, Procedia Computer. Science, vol. 10, pp. 450–457 (2012). https://doi.org/10.1016/j.procs.2012.06.058
15. Araujo, F., Ayoade, G., Al-Naami, K., Gao, Y., Hamlen, K.W., Khan, L.: Crook-sourced intrusion detection as a service. J. Inf. Secur. Appl. **61**, 102880 (2021). https://doi.org/10.1016/j.jisa.2021.102880
16. MITRE Corporation. Mitre att&ck framework, 2015. [Online]. Available: https://attack.mitre.org
17. Odarchenko, R., Pinchuk, A., Polihenko, O. and Skurativskyi, A.: A comparative analysis of cyber threat intelligence models. In: CH&CMiGIN (2024). https://api.semanticscholar.org/CorpusID:276782940
18. Zambianco, M., Facchinetti, C., Siracusa, D.: A proactive decoy selection scheme for cyber deception using MITRE ATT&CK. Comput. Secur. **148**, 104144 (2025). https://doi.org/10.1016/j.cose.2024.104144
19. Zhang, S., Xue, X., Su, X.: DeepOP: a hybrid framework for MITRE ATT&CK sequence prediction via deep learning and ontology. Electronics **14**(2), 257 (2025). https://doi.org/10.3390/electronics14020257
20. M. Rodríguez, G. Betarte, and D. Calegari. A process mining-based approach for attacker profiling. In: Proceedings IEEE URUCON, pp. 425–429 (2021). https://doi.org/10.1109/URUCON53396.2021.9647342
21. Li, L., Huang, C., Chen, J.: Automated discovery and mapping ATT&CK tactics and techniques for unstructured cyber threat intelligence. Comput. Secur. **140**, 103815 (2024). https://doi.org/10.1016/j.cose.2024.103815
22. J. Gaia, et al.: Psychological Profiling of Hacking Potential (2020). https://doi.org/10.24251/HICSS.2020.273
23. Hani, U., Sohaib, O., Khan, K., Aleidi, A., Islam, N.: Psychological profiling of hackers via machine learning toward sustainable cybersecurity. Front. Comput. Sci. **6** (2024). https://doi.org/10.3389/fcomp.2024.1381351
24. Tshimula, J., et al.: Psychological profiling in cybersecurity: a look at LLMs and psycholinguistic features (2024). https://doi.org/10.48550/arXiv.2406.18783
25. Torres, R. and García, A.: Attacker attribution in multi-step and multi-adversarial network attacks using transformer-based approach. Appl. Sci., 15(15) (2025). https://doi.org/10.3390/app15158476
26. Kotenko, I., Fedorchenko, E., Novikova, E., Jha, A.: Cyber attacker profiling for risk analysis based on machine learning. Sensors **23**(4), 2028 (2023). https://doi.org/10.3390/s23042028
27. Wang, X., et al.: Deep reinforcement learning: a survey. IEEE Trans. Neural Netw. Learn. Syst. **35**(4), 5064–5078 (2024). https://doi.org/10.1109/TNNLS.2022.3207346

28. P. Nguyen, et al.. Towards smarter security orchestration and automatic response for CPS and IoT. In: 14th IEEE International Conference on Cloud Computing Technology and Science (CloudCom 2023), pp. 298–302 (2023). https://doi.org/10.1109/CloudCom59040.2023.00055
29. Yousaf, Z. and Boomsma, D.: AI-Driven SOC Operations: Improving Incident Response Time and Threat Analysis (2024). https://doi.org/10.13140/RG.2.2.12001.01128

Artificial Intelligence/ Machine Learning

A Case Study on Hyperparameter Optimization Methods in Scholarship Eligibility Prediction Using Neural Networks

Aminata Bagre[1(✉)], Moustapha Bikienga[2,3], and Tclesphore B. Tiendrebeogo[3]

[1] University Joseph KI-ZERBO, Ouagadougou, Burkina Faso
aminbagre@gmail.com
[2] University Norbert ZONGO, Koudougou, Burkina Faso
moustapha.bikienga@unz.bf
[3] University Nazi BONI, Bobo Dioulasso, Burkina Faso
tetiendreb@gmail.com

Abstract. Predicting scholarship eligibility is a key issue for higher education establishments wishing to ensure the fair and efficient allocation of grants. This prediction relies on the exploitation of academic and social data integrated into Decision Support Systems (DSS). In this context, this article explores the performance of two hyperparameter optimization techniques applied to a prediction model based on a neural network integrated into a Decision Support System (DSS): manual tuning and Bayesian optimization. Based on a real student dataset (semester averages, baccalaureate average, gender, baccalaureate series), our study aims to evaluate the system's approaches according to the criterion of accuracy. The experimental results show that the performance of the system depends largely on the correct setting of the hyperparameters of the predictive model used. The findings show that integrating optimized neural networks into DSS can significantly improve institutional capacity to allocate resources equitably, thereby supporting both academic excellence and social equity.

Keywords: Decision Support System · Artificial Neural Network · Scholarship

1 Introduction

Scholarships are a key instrument for promoting equity in access to higher education. However, the continuing growth in the number of applications and the growing diversity of student profiles are making selection processes increasingly

A. Oluwatope et al. (Eds.): AFRICOMM 2025, LNICST 713, pp. 91–108, 2027.
https://doi.org/10.1007/978-3-032-38682-3_6

complex. Faced with these challenges, the use of Decision Support Systems (DSS) is emerging as an effective solution. These systems are often based on machine learning models, such as artificial neural networks, whose performance is highly dependent on the setting of hyperparameters (number of layers, neurons, learning rate, and son on.).

Artificial neural networks (ANN) represent a new method of approximating complex systems, precisely when these systems are difficult to model using conventional methods. Thanks to their ability to learn from data, ANN offer powerful and flexible solutions for a multitude of problems in various fields. Here, we model a scholarship awarding system based on machine learning techniques aim to automate and optimize the process of selecting recipients. Student scholarship prediction is a critical aspect of modern educational technology, aiming to identify eligible candidates by analyzing diverse datasets that include academic, demographic, and financial attributes [1]. The aim is to predict, from historical data, the candidates most likely to meet the criteria for receiving a scholarship. Such a system reduces the time and effort required to manual process scholarship applications.

The system facilitates the reduction of human bias in decisions, if the training data is balanced. And it also greater accuracy, by ensuring the ability to identify subtle patterns in the data that may influence eligibility. Such a system makes it possible to analyze a large volume of applications rapidly. Accurate prediction models play a transformative role in modernizing the scholarship allocation process by automating decision-making, reducing administrative overhead, and expanding access to opportunities for underprivileged students [1]. Several methods can be used to adjust these hyperparameters in order to optimize accuracy, such as manual hyperparameter tuning, which involves manually testing different combinations based on intuition. Another method is Bayesian optimization, an automated approach that models the performance function and iteratively proposes promising configurations.

Following the implementation of the decision support system for scholarship eligibility, we are studying how advanced Bayesian optimization [2] and manual hyperparameter optimization techniques have improved prediction accuracy through a comparative study. In the rest of our work, we will present a brief state of the art by Sect. 2, propose a neural network design methodology, an artificial neural network-optimized scholarship awarding system. We then interpret the results obtained by Sect. 3.

2 Related Work

2.1 Artificial Neural Network

The Fig. 1 illustrate the main composante of Artificial Neural Network which is neuron. The neuron is defined as a non-linear, bounded algebraic function, whose value depends on parameters called synaptic weights [4]. The input variables of this function are usually called the neuron's **inputs**, and the value of the function is called its **output**.

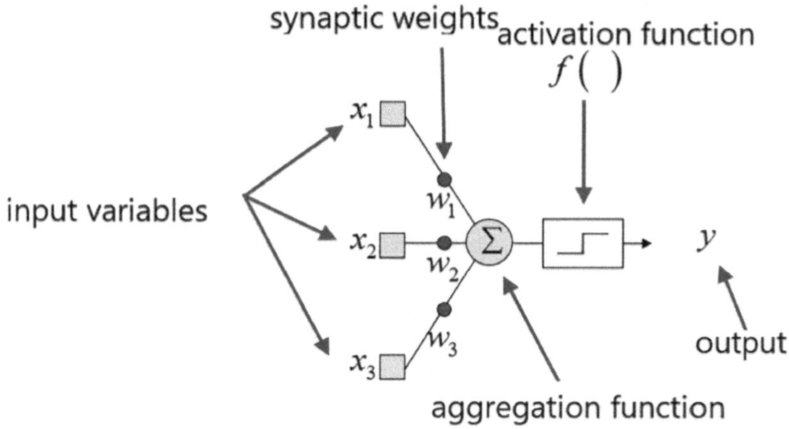

Fig. 1. Formal neural architecture [4].

A formal neuron (or artificial neuron) is a mathematical model inspired by the functioning of a biological neuron. Each input represents a feature of the problem to be solved. Each input is associated with a synaptic weight. The aggregation function is a linear combination of the weighted inputs. The activation function is a non-linear function that transforms the weighted sum into an activated output. The interconnected neurons form a neural network called Artificial Neural Network (ANN).

ANNs are distinguished by their architecture. The ANN family includes FNN (Feedforward Neural Network), CNN (Convolutional Neural Network) and RNN (Recurrent Neural Network). Neural networks are capable of learning, adapting to change and mimicking human thought processes with little human intervention [3]. Artificial feedforward neural networks (FFANN) are the most widely used models for solving real-world problems [5]. Feedforward neural networks (FFANN) are the most popular architecture due to their analytical simplicity and efficiency. ANN are characterized by their internal non-linearity, learning capability, predictive performance and modular structure. Numerous ANN models have been proposed with various connection architectures, such as feed-forward, feedback, monolayer, multilayer, etc. [5]. The Feed Forward Neural Network is a forward propagating neural network. In its architecture, the FFNN is composed of input layers, a hidden layer and an output layer. We can represend by FNN(input_layer, hidden_layer, output_layer). Each layer contains a number of neurons defined. In this type of network, each neuron performs simple calculations, but the input data passes through several layers of calculation before producing an output. The results of the first layer of neurons are used as input for the calculation of the next layer, and so on. It is possible to play with various parameters of the network architecture: the number of layers, the type of each layer, the number of neurons that make up each layer.

Thus, the topology is a network structure in which each neuron (or node) is connected to a fixed number of close neighbors in an orderly and regular fashion [5]. The conventional feed-forward topology of artificial neural networks can be modified into a **small-world** topology to match the characteristics of real-world problems. A small-world network is characterized by two parameters: the average path length, which is the average distance from node to node, and the clustering coefficient, which is the tendency of a neuron's neighbors to cluster together [5]. The neural network learns by adjusting its parameters using a learning algorithm based on a cost function. Most learning algorithms for formal neural networks are optimization algorithms: they seek to minimize, through non-linear optimization methods, a cost function that is a measure of the difference between the network's actual responses and its desired responses [6]. This optimization is carried out iteratively, by modifying the weights according to the gradient of the cost function: the gradient is estimated using a method specific to neural networks, known as the backpropagation method, and is then used by the optimization algorithm itself. The weights are randomly initialized before learning, then iteratively modified until a satisfactory compromise is reached between the accuracy of the approximation on the learning set and the accuracy of the approximation on a validation set disjoint from the previous one. Neural networks use models inspired by the workings of the human brain to learn complex patterns from data.

The notion of model in data-mining is seen as a relationship between variables expressible in an analytical or algorithmic form that does not derive from a theory, but achieves a good fit to the data [7]. This optimization enables the network to learn models from training data. Thus, the main purpose of model use is prediction or classification. Models can be trained on a known data set and then used to make predictions on new data. The effectiveness of a model is assessed in terms of its ability to generalize and produce accurate results on data not used during training. However according to [2], the backpropagation algorithm has certain drawbacks, notably a low convergence rate and a tendency to get stuck in a local minimum. In addition, as it relies on the gradient information of the error function, it becomes inefficient when problems are complex or this information is difficult to obtain. Some research is based on combinatorial approaches, combining the genetic algorithm and the backpropagation method to speed up Backpropagation learning and minimize the local minimum trap. The Genetic Algorithm (GA) is a heuristic and stochastic search algorithm used for optimization and machine learning. It is distinguished by its ability to globally explore the search space and find near-optimal solutions without requiring the gradient information of error functions [2]. In the context of back-propagation (BP) neural network optimization, Genetic Algorithm improves convergence and avoids trapping in local minima. The combined GA-BP (GABP) approach optimizes connection weights and improves the network's generalization capability.

Our target architecture is a Feedforward network with Backpropagation learning. The design of such a system requires a specific methodology described in the Table 1 below:

Table 1. specific methodology described

First step	Problem identification
second step	Data collection
third step	Data processing
fourth step	Choice of neural network architecture
five step	Model training
six step	Accuracy testing
seven step	Optimization

In a neural network design process, the first step is to identify the problem which try to resolv. The second step is data collection, which involves gathering relevant data from a variety of sources. The quality and diversity of the data directly influence the model's performance. The third stage, data processing, eliminates missing values, normalizes numerical values and encodes categorical variables. This step is essential to guarantee consistent inputs to the model. The fourth is the choice of neural network architecture, which refers to the selection of the optimal network structure, including the number of layers, neurons per layer and activation functions adapted to the problem. Indeed, an activation function is used to introduce non-linearity into the network [3]. The activation function can be used to model complex relationships. Examples of activation functions include the sigmoid function, the hyperbolic tangent function (tanh) and the linear rectified function (ReLU or Rectified Linear Unit). Our data are divided into training and test sets. The five stage concerns model training. In this scenario, the network is trained by adjusting its weights using a learning algorithm. The aim is to minimize the error between predictions and actual values. The six stage is the accuracy test. In this scenario, once trained, the model is evaluated on a test set to measure its generalization capacity and identify any overfitting problems. The seven and final stage is optimization. In this scenario, we adjust the hyperparameters (learning rate, regularization), the network architecture and explore improvements such as adding Dropout or tuning the cost function to improve overall model performance.

2.2 Decision Support System

DSS (Decision Support System) is a data analysis software used to facilitate decision-making. The DSS is a computer system dealing with problems containing unstructured or semi-structured parts, on which the decision-maker's judgment is based [8]. For [9], decision support systems (DSS) are valuable in situations where the amount of information available is prohibitive to the intuition of an unaided human decision-maker, and where the quality of the decision is important. The correct application of decision making increases productivity, effectiveness and efficiency, and enables optimal choices to be made, for example in the varietal selection of certain crops and their management practices, marketing or environmental impact planning, etc. [9]. For [10], the main problem is to determine which information is relevant for decision-making. A decision support system (DSS) also is a computer application or set of technologies designed to support decision-making processes in organizations or at the individual level. The integration of information and communication technologies (ICT) can indeed facilitate objective, rapid and appropriate decision-making in many areas. Indeed, the judicious use of information and communication technologies can considerably improve the decision-making process by providing access to information, facilitating data analysis, fostering communication and collaboration, automating processes, offering advanced visualization tools, and enabling the monitoring and evaluation of decisions taken. Indeed, the judicious use of information and communication technologies can considerably improve the decision-making process by providing access to information, facilitating data analysis, fostering communication and collaboration, automating processes, offering advanced visualization tools, and enabling the monitoring and evaluation of decisions taken. This can lead to more objective, rapid and appropriate decisions in a wide range of professional and organizational contexts.

2.3 Methodological Approach

Problem Identification. Scholarship prediction, once based on traditional or manual methods that were often biased and inefficient, is now being transformed by the use of artificial intelligence and machine learning. A scholarship is financial aid that enables a student to continue his or her studies by reducing or eliminating the financial burden associated with tuition and other education-related expenses. [1] explores the different methodologies used, such as classification, regression, clustering and ensemble learning, which have played a key role in transforming stock market prediction into a data and evidence-based practice. [11] uses machine learning and genetic algorithms to optimize scholarship allocation for student yield. A predictive model is used for student enrolment, and the genetic algorithm (GA) to design a scholarship distribution strategy. The study [11] presents a scholarship distribution optimization strategy based on a predictive student enrollment model combined with a genetic algorithm (GA). Students are grouped into ventiles, with each group receiving a fixed amount of scholarship. The algorithm adjusts these amounts at each iteration according to the predicted enrolment, while respecting the defined constraints. In the absence of complete data on the 2018 cohort, the authors used 2017 data to design the strategy, which they then applied after noting a similarity between the two classes [11]. Some studies use machine learning and genetic algorithms to optimize stock market resources. In contrast to ANN, we also have expert systems for making decisions. The k-NN learning method is one of the expert system techniques using supervised learning [12]. However, the K-NN method can be sensitive to the presence of outliers and high data dimensionality. It is also sensitive to the choice of distance and k-value, often requiring cross-validation to select the best hyperparameters. Despite these limitations, k-NN remains popular for its simplicity and ability to deliver interpretable results. The k-NN algorithm works by making a prediction based on the closest data points between the old data history as training data and the new data as test data. The attributes used in the prediction process are semester, parental income, number of dependents and grade point average [12]. The results of the simulation of the prediction model show that the determining factor of the training data, both the number and the variation of the different values, can improve the performance of the k-NN algorithm with an accuracy rate of 95.8% in predicting the students most likely to obtain a scholarship. We propose here an artificial neural network model for the optimal allocation of stock market resources. It is a system that implements a rigorous selection process to ensure that the stock market goes to the right person. We optimize our model by hyperparameter tuning and Bayesian optimization. We compare the performance generated by these two techniques.

Data Collection and Processing. This involves loading the data collected. For our research, we used a scholarship dataset of 1207 students. Our dataset dimension is 1207*21 (1207 samples with 21 variables). We use the technique of data minimization, which consists of limiting data to what is necessary to achieve our objective. This method reduces the risk of confidentiality breaches by eliminating all sensitive information from the dataset.

Features and Model Target. This dataset provides information on different students from different institutions for a given academic year. For our simulations, we use the JupiterLab environment as editor. The code used is python. We use tensorflow's Keras library for model building and simulations. From the dataset, we defined the model inputs (features) and the model output (target). We identified 7 numerical variables (the baccalaureate average and the averages of semesters 1 to 6) as well as 2 categorical variables (gender and baccalaureate series). The One-Hot Encoding technique was applied to transform the categorical variables into binary columns (0 or 1). The variable gender (Male, Female) is thus represented by 2 columns. The variable baccalaureate series (16 categories) is represented by 16 columns. The total number of inputs is therefore calculated as follows:

$$\text{Total number of inputs} = 7\ (\text{numerical}) + 2\ (\text{gender}) + 16\ (\text{baccalaureate series}) = 25 \tag{1}$$

Below is the data distribution Table 2. The output of the model is represented by two binary variables [0,1]. The number 0 for a student who does not qualify for a scholarship; and 1 for a student who meets the necessary conditions to receive a scholarship. The Table 2 describe data distribution in our model. The original

Table 2. Data distribution for learning and testing

original Dataset size	1207*12
Characteristic size choosen	7 numerical variables + 2 categorical variables
Total number of inputs	25
Learning data size	(844, 505)
Size of test data	(363, 505)

dataset comprises 1207 observations (or samples), each described by 12 variables. After transformation or selection, 25 variables are used as input features for the model. The training data set contains 844 samples, each represented by a vector of 505 features. The test data set contains 363 samples with the same 505 features.

2.4 Proposed Network Architecture

We choose to design our architecture on an FFNN (8, 4, 1) model. Our model is initialized with 25 input features, i.e. BAC average, semester 1 to semester 6, gender, BAC series. This model consists of input layers of 8 neurons with 25 input features, a hidden layer of 4 neurons and an output layer of one neuron. A **ReLU** activation function is used for the first two layers and one (1) output layer with a sigmoid activation function that produces a probability between [0,1]. We use the backpropagation algorithm to adjust the network weights via gradient descent, enabling our model to learn. Backpropagation is an essential machine learning technique for optimizing artificial neural networks.

Model Performance. Post-training model evaluation measures model performance on test data not used during training. We evaluate our model's performance in terms of accuracy and loss rate. To this end, 30% of the data is used for testing and 70% for training. The model's training parameters are described below. We have `X_train`: training features; `y_train`: the training target labels; epochs: the number of complete iterations on the training data set; `batch_size`: the size of the batch used for gradient updates, i.e. 16 samples for each gradient update. Batch size refers to the number of data samples processed at one time during training. We'll find the best possible size by adopting a fitting technique. `Validation_split`: the fraction of training data to be used for validation, i.e. 30% of training data will be used as the validation set. `Epochs`: The number of complete iterations on the training data set when learning a model.

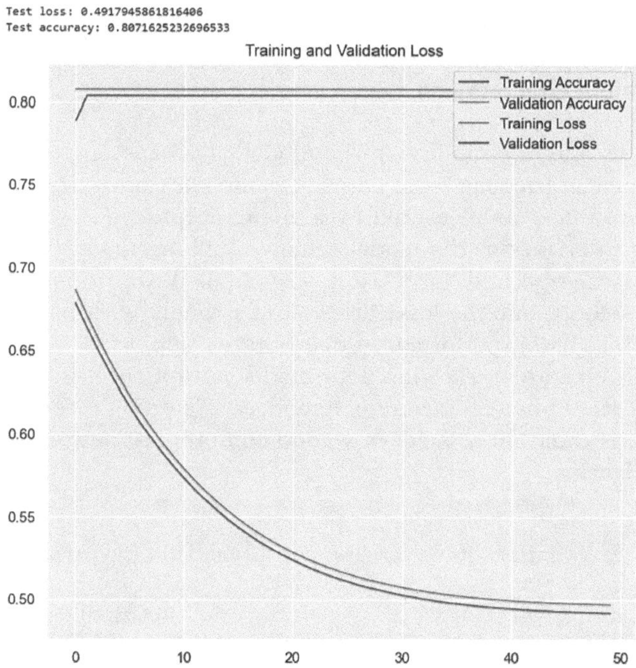

Fig. 2. Initial network performance.

In this Fig. 2, model accuracy is constant at 80, 72% throughout the simulation, which means that the model is stable. As for the loss, it starts with a value of 68.60%, which is very high, then gradually decreases to stabilize at around 49.6% at the end of training. This suggests that the model is learning to minimize the prediction error. In the following Sect. 3, we optimize our model using two methods: manual hyperparameter adjustment and Bayesian optimization. We therefore compare two hyperparameter optimization techniques: manual tuning and Bayesian optimization. We then interpret the results obtained.

3 Results

3.1 Model Optimizing

We are fine-tuning the DNN architecture by adding layers, modifying activation functions and adjusting dropout rates according to the complexity and characteristics of the data. To improve the DNN model, we modify the training parameters to achieve better performance. We also use the learning rate, which is one of the hyperparameters used in neural network training. It is therefore very important to define a value as close as possible to the optimal value. This hyperparameter is used to adjust the weights and optimize the model. The learning rate indicates the step size of the gradient descent towards local optima.

Optimizing Hyperparameters. This section concerns the manual tuning of model parameters.
We have hypermparameters and model architecture.

First Step: Let's start by modifying the model's hyperparameters. The Table 3 shows the impact of learning rate, batch size and the use of dropout techniques on model performance, as measured by loss and accuracy.

Without regularization, the model achieves high accuracy (up to 0.98) with relatively low loss, especially for a batch size of 16. With dropout = 0.1, performance remains good, but the loss varies more strongly with batch size. With a high learning rate (>1), performance deteriorates significantly (accuracy drops to 0.80 and loss increases), showing poor model convergence. In conclusion, fine-tuning the hyperparameters, including a moderate learning rate and appropriate regularization, is essential to achieve a good compromise between accuracy and model generalization.

Table 3. Variations in performance as a function of hyperparameter

Learning rate	Lot size	Loss	Accuracy
No regularization technique			
0.0	8	0.073	0.97
0.0	16	0.057	0.98
0.0	32	0.090	0.98
With regularization technique dropout=0.1			
0.01	8	0.19	0.97
0.01	16	0.075	0.98
0.01	32	0.24	0.97
With regularization technique dropout=0.1			
>1	8	0.49	0.80
>1	16	0.36	0.80
>1	32	0.56	0.80

Figure 3a represents the loss decreases on the training set as the iterations progress, implying that the model gradually learns to better adjust its weights to minimize the error on the training set. We obtained an estimated loss rate of 0.07598, indicating that the gap between predictions and actual values is very small. As a result, it is accurate in its predictions. An accuracy rate equal to 0.98078 or 98.07% indicates that our model has correctly classified around 98.07% of the examples in the test set. After applying the hyperparameter fitting optimization method, we retain the best architecture on our FFNN (10,10,1) model with an accuracy of 98.07%, which implies that the model is performing well.

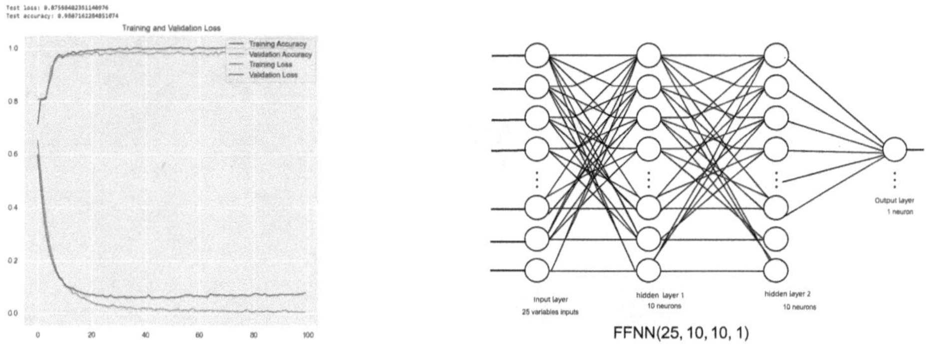

(a) hyperparameter tuning (b) Architecture optimization

Fig. 3. Best architecture proposed.

Second Step: optimizing the architecture which involves manually adjusting the model's architecture until acceptable performance is achieved. We tuning DNN architecture model by incrise neuron's in the the input an hidden layers. Our better model is FFNN(10,10,1) illustrate by Fig. 3b. We compaire the performance by batch size.

In Figure 3b, we have 25 variables inputs, two hidden layers with 10 neurons and output layer with one neuron. We use 4 different batch sizes (8, 16, 32, 64). We have also parameters as Trainning accuracy (Train acc) which represent the proportion of correctly predicted samples on the training dataset.

$$Trainacc = \frac{Numberofcorrectpredictionsontrainingset}{TotalTrainingsamples} \quad (2)$$

Validation accuracy (Val acc) represents the proportion of correctly predicted samples on the validation dataset. Finally Test accuracy (Test acc) which represents the proportion of correctly predicted samples on the test dataset, which is completely unseen during training and validation.
With `batch_size`=8, there is a slight improvement in training (93.13% vs. 84.72% with batch=32). However, we have a higher validation loss, which may indicate instability due to a small batch (Figs. 4, 5, 6 and 7).

At `batch_size`=16, we have very high accuracy (97.75% in train, 96.69% in validation). The low loss means that the model is learning very well. So no overlearning (minimal deviation between train and val).

For `batch_size`=32, we have a stable Model witch accuracy = 81.04%, with similar performance in training and validation. There is no overfitting, as the difference between train/val is small.

`batch_size`=64, performs very well compared to batch=16, but with very high validation accuracy. Convergence is more stable (because the batch size is larger).

batch=16
Training loss: 0.0717
Training accuracy: 97.75%
Validation loss: 0.0908
Validation accuracy: 96.69%
Test loss: 0.09076688438653946, Test accuracy: 0.9669421315193176

(a) Batch Size 16

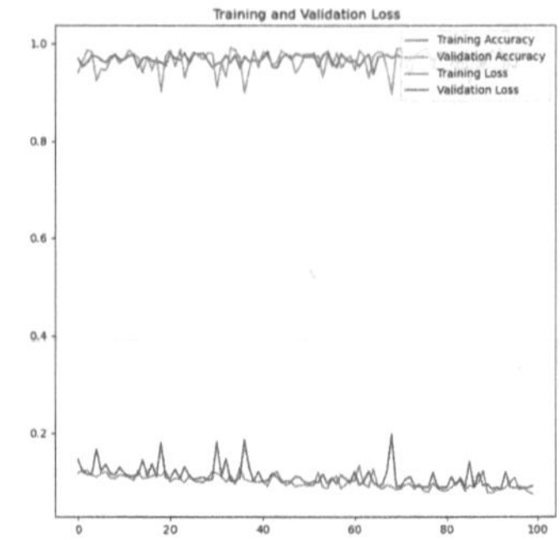

(b) Performance Metrics

Fig. 4. Model performance by batch size 8.

batch=8
Training loss: 0.1355
Training accuracy: 93.13%
Validation loss: 0.1404
Validation accuracy: 92.56%
Test loss: 0.14037230610847473, Test accuracy: 0.9256198406219482

(a) Batch Size 8

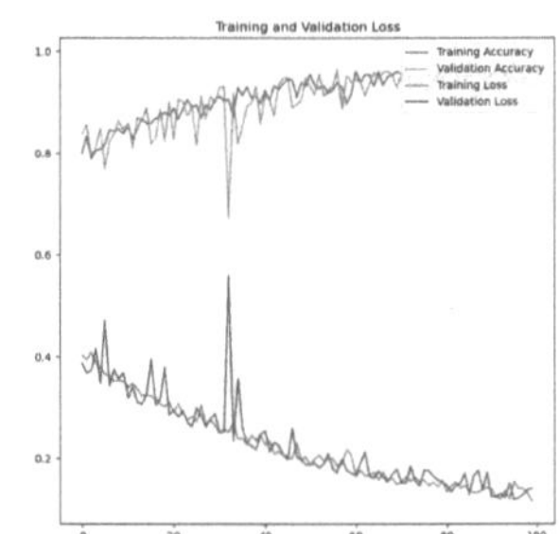

(b) Performance Metrics

Fig. 5. Model performance by batch size 16.

batch=32
Training loss: 0.3916
Training accuracy: 84.72%
Validation loss: 0.3867
Validation accuracy: 84.57%
Test loss: 0.3867296874523163, Test accuracy: 0.8457300066947937

(a) Batch Size 32

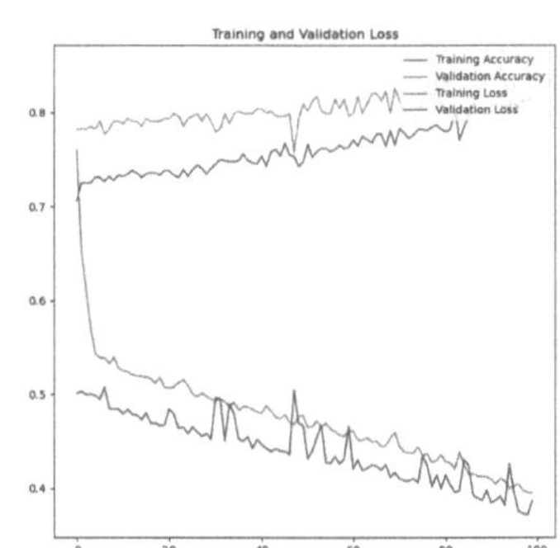

(b) Performance Metrics

Fig. 6. Model performance by batch size 32.

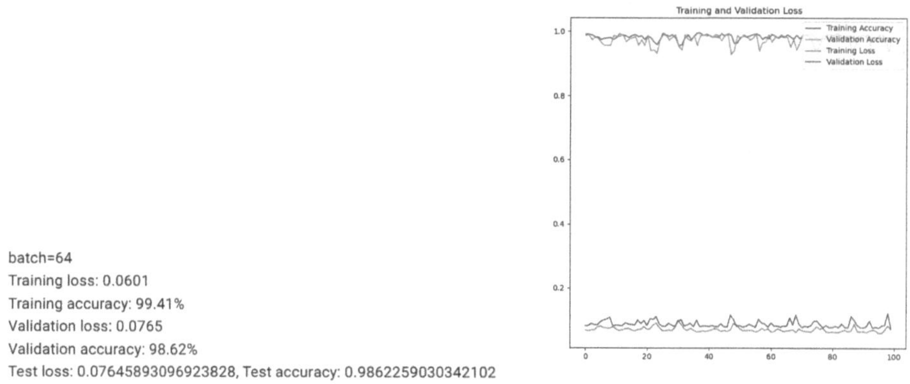

(a) Batch Size 64 (b) Performance Metrics

Fig. 7. Model performance by batch size 64.

According to the results, model performance by batch equal 16 is better than model performance by batch equal 8 and than model performance by batch equal 32. However model performance by batch equal 64 is better than model performance by batch equal 16. So the best performance is achieved with a batch size equal to 64.

Bayesian Optimization. Bayesian optimization is an effective methodology for the global optimization of functions with expensive evaluations [13]. Traditionally, Gaussian processes (GP) are used to model the distribution of functions, but some recent studies are exploring the use of neural networks as an alternative to Gaussian processes for estimating this distribution.

The author's work [13] proposes an approach based on regression with adaptive basis functions, in which the neural network acts as a parametric model. Experiments have shown that this method is competitive with techniques based on Gaussian processes, while allowing a previously unattainable level of parallelism. It develop an approach based on adaptive basis function regression, where the neural network serves as a parametric model to approximate the distribution over functions. They experimentally demonstrate that this approach is competitive with state-of-the-art GP-based methods, while enabling a previously unattainable level of parallelism. They successfully apply their method to large-scale hyperparameter optimization, notably for image recognition tasks using convolutional networks, and image caption generation using neural language models.

Recently, several studies have proposed advanced improvements to Bayesian optimization that leverage derivative information. For instance, the derivative-enabled knowledge-gradient (d-KG) algorithm efficiently incorporates derivatives to achieve better solutions with a reduced number of function evaluations [14]. This algorithm is one-step Bayes-optimal, asymptotically consistent, and provides a higher value of information compared to derivative-free approaches. It is also capable of handling noisy or incomplete derivative information, operates in both sequential and batch modes, reduces computational cost through the selective retention of directional derivatives, and demonstrates state-of-the-art performance across various benchmarks [14].

We have incorporated an automated hyperparameter search using the Bayesian Optimization method. This method enable us to more efficiently find the best combinations of hyperparameters to optimize model performance.

```
100%|██████████| 10/10 [00:09<00:00,  1.00trial/s, best loss: -0.7906336188316345]
Meilleurs hyperparamètres : {'learning_rate': 0.007720881561428574, 'optimizer': 0, 'units': 16.0}
```

Fig. 8. Search by Bayesian Optimization method.

We study the model's performance by varying the batch size and applying to the model the best hyperparameters (Adam/RMSprop/SGD, learning rate and number of neurons) found by the Bayesian optimization method. Figure 8 illustrates the Bayesian search to automatically find the best parameters for a neural network. Best loss represents the loss of model. Best loss represents the loss of model. The score is negative because the tool used to search for hyperparameters, **Hyperopt**, is designed to **minimize** an objective function. In this case, as we wish to **maximize** the *accuracy* (performance measure), we have inverted this metric by taking −accuracy so that Hyperopt can minimize it.

$$BestLoss = -\text{Accuracy} \quad \Rightarrow \quad \text{Accuracy} = -(\text{Best Loss}) = 0{,}8071 \qquad (3)$$

Thus, the best model achieves an accuracy of around 80.71% with the Adam optimizer, a learning rate of 0.0049, and 16 neurons in the hidden layer.

This Table 4 shows the performance of a neural network according to different hyperparameter settings (learning rate, batch size) and the use or non-use of regularization techniques. In this scenario, we use the following optimizers: Adam and RMSprop, in conditions with or without dropout.

When the model is trained without regularization, there is a progressive improvement in performance as the batch size increases. Accuracy rises from 88.71% (batch of 8) to 95.87% (batch of 32), with a significant drop in loss (loss from 0.3662 to 0.2128). This indicates good learning ability, although the absence of regularization may expose the model to overlearning in some cases. With regularization (dropout = 0.1 / Adam), the model achieves very good performance, with a maximum accuracy of 94.21% for a batch of 32.

With regularization (dropout = 0.1 / RMSprop):With dropout at 0.1 and RMSprop optimizer, performance also improved with increasing batch size. Accuracy rises from 86.50% to 92.56%, showing that regularization helps stabilize learning while avoiding over-fitting. Loss also decreases, confirming the

Table 4. Performance variations as a function of hyperparameters

Learning rate	Lot size	Loss	Accuracy
No regularization technique / Adam			
0.0077	8	0.2128	0.8871
0.0077	16	0.3666	0.8182
0.0077	32	0.0953	0.9587
With regularization technique dropout=0.1 / RMSprop			
0.0058	8	0.3297	0.8650
0.0058	16	0.2478	0.9174
0.0058	32	0.2001	0.9256
With regularization technique dropout=0.1 / Adam			
0.0072	8	0.2855	0.8512
0.0072	16	0.2952	0.8705
0.0072	32	0.1588	0.9421
With regularization technique dropout greater than 0.1 RMSprop			
0.0083	8	0.4858	0.8072
0.0083	16	0.4902	0.8072
0.0083	32	0.5480	0.8072

model's good convergence. With stronger regularization (> 0.1 / RMSprop): With stronger regularization (dropout > 0.1), performance deteriorates significantly. Accuracy remains stuck at 80.72% whatever the batch size, and losses are higher (up to 0.548).

This result shows that the Adam combined low regularization combination performs very well, even better than without regularization combined Adam. Excessive regularization prevents the model from capturing patterns in the data. The optimal learning rate found is around 0.0077. This is the value that best minimizes the loss function on our data. The optimizer selected is index 0, corresponding to 'Adam'. It is used in learning optimization. The optimal number of neurons for the first layer of the network is 16. This indicates that the model has found this layer size to be the most suitable for the data (Fig. 9).

Model Robustness. Here we use cross-validation to assess the robustness of your model. In effect, we calculate the mean accuracy and standard deviation from the results of cross-validation, where the model is evaluated on several subsets of the training data. This technique prevents overlearning. The model's mean accuracy and standard deviation are tested after evaluating the model's performance over several iterations. The result of the cross-validation showing by Fig. 10.

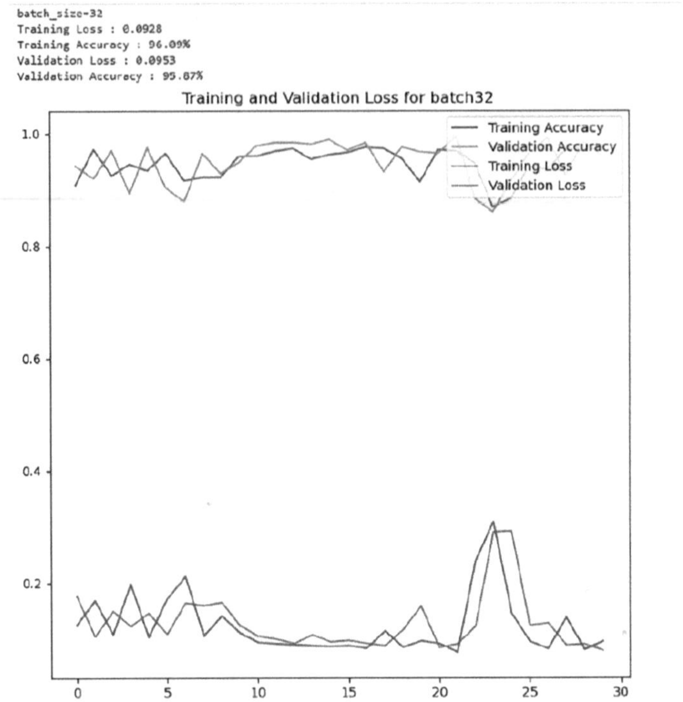

Fig. 9. Accuracy curve by Bayesian optimization method.

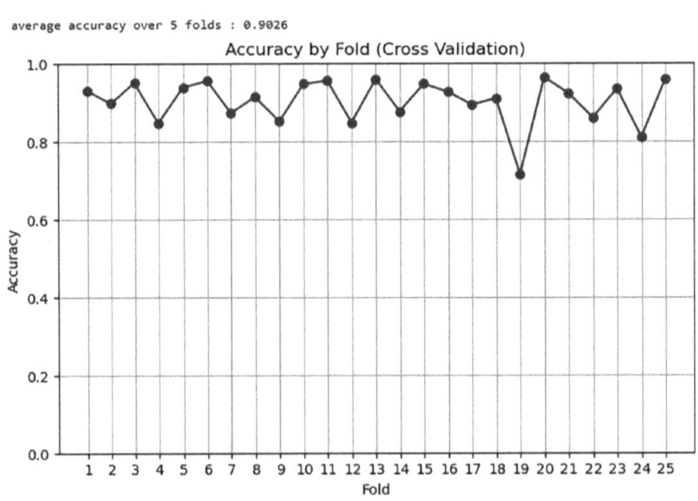

Fig. 10. Cross-validation curve.

Training the neural model with 5-fold cross-validation resulted in an average accuracy of 90.26%, with performance varying slightly between folds (between 93% and 96%). The total execution time was 459 s, which remains reasonable given the size of the data and the number of iterations.

4 Conclusion

We therefore proposed a neural network-optimized decision support system for the awarding of higher education scholarships. The model was optimized by random hyperparameter search and Bayesian optimization. Both methods improved the performance of our model. Bayesian optimization leads to faster and more stable convergence than random search, thanks to the dynamic search for defined hyperparameters. Nevertheless, random search is efficient but requires much more simulation time and parameters to achieve the best possible performance. Contrary to expectations, the experimental results reveal that manual tuning, although more time-consuming, achieves better predictive performance than Bayesian optimization in the framework studied. This observation highlights the need to adapt optimization methods to the context and nature of the data, and serves as a reminder that automated approaches do not systematically guarantee better results. Our best model consisted in optimizing the neural network architecture. We modified the different neuron sizes per layer to find the best sizes. Our best architecture is FFNN(10,10,1) with an accuracy of 98.62%. In the continuation of our works in the futur, we wil purpose and implement a new methods to optimize Decision support System based on neural network. This method will be integrated in our Scholarship prediction system.

References

1. Paramesha, M., Baba, S.S., Musthafa, S.F., Sai, V.V., Kiran, S.S.: Data-driven scholarship prediction using machine learning for equitable education allocation. Front. Collaborative Res. **2**(1s), 43–50 (2024). https://doi.org/10.70162/fcr/2024/v2/i1/v2i1s06
2. Ding, S., Su, C., Yu, J.: An optimizing BP neural network algorithm based on genetic algorithm. Artif. Intell. Rev. **36**(2), 153–162 (2011). https://doi.org/10.1007/s10462-011-9208-z
3. Zhang, H.-C., Huang, S.H.: Applications of neural networks in manufacturing: a state-of-the-art survey. Int. J. Prod. Res. **33**(3), 705–728 (1995). https://doi.org/10.1080/00207549508930175
4. Dreyfus, G.: Les Réseaux de Neurones, une Technique Opérationnelle pour le Traitement des Données Industrielles. Économiques et Financières. École Supérieure de Physique et de Chimie Industrielles de la Ville de Paris (ESPCI), Mesures vol. 699, pp. 45–52 (1997)
5. Erkaymaz, O., Özer, M., Yumuşak, N.: Impact of small-world topology on the performance of a feed-forward artificial neural network based on two different real-life problems. Turk. J. Electr. Eng. Comput. Sci. **22**(3), 708–718 (2014) https://doi.org/10.3906/elk-1202-89. Available at: https://journals.tubitak.gov.tr/elektrik/vol22/iss3/15

6. Dreyfus, G.: Les réseaux de neurones, Mécanique industrielle et matériaux **51**(3), 115–120 (1998)
7. Saporta, G.: Data mining ou fouille de données. RST «Epidémiologie» Data Mining (2004)
8. Shim, J.P., Warkentin, M., Courtney, J.F., Power, D.J., Sharda, R., Carlsson, C.: Past, present, and future of decision support technology. Decis. Support Syst. **33**(2), 111–126 (2002). https://doi.org/10.1016/S0167-9236(01)00139-7
9. Mir, S.A., Quadri, S.M.K.: Decision support systems: concepts, progress and issues- a review. Clim. Change, Intercropping, Pest Control Beneficial Microorganisms: Climate Change Intercropping, Pest Control Beneficial Microorganisms, 373–399 (2009). https://doi.org/10.1007/978-90-481-2716-0_13
10. Holtzman, S.: Intelligent Decision Systems. Addison-Wesley Longman Publishing Co., Inc (1988)
11. Aulck, L., Nambi, D., West, J.: Using machine learning and genetic algorithms to optimize scholarship allocation for student yield. In: Proceedings SIGKDD '19: ACM SIGKDD Conference on Knowledge Discovery and Data Mining, pp. 4–8. ACM (2019). https://doi.org/10.1145/1122445.1122456
12. Kurniadi, D., Abdurachman, E., Warnars, H.L.H.S., Suparta, W.: The prediction of scholarship recipients in higher education using k-nearest neighbor algorithm. In: Proceedings IOP Conference Series: Materials Science and Engineering, vol. 434, pp. 012039. IOP Publishing (2018). https://doi.org/10.1088/1757-899X/434/1/012039
13. Snoek, J., et al.: Scalable bayesian optimization using deep neural networks. In: Proceedings of the International Conference on Machine Learning (ICML 2015), pp. 2171–2180. PMLR (2015). Available at: https://proceedings.mlr.press/v37/snoek15.html
14. Wu, J., oloczek, M., Wilson, A.G., Frazier, P.: Bayesian optimization with gradients. Adv. Neural Inf. Proces. Syst. **30** (2017). https://doi.org/10.48550/arXiv.1703.04389

Machine-Learning Based Prediction of Generator Runtime: A Predictive Maintenance Solution for a Telecommunications Site

Mariam Muhammed(✉) and Chika Yinka-Banjo

Department of Computer Science, University of Lagos, Lagos, Nigeria
mariam3105@gmail.com, cyinkabanjo@unilag.edu.ng

Abstract. The telecommunications industry has experienced significant growth and transformation in recent years, driven by technological advancements and the increasing demand for seamless connectivity. Maintaining the infrastructure that supports them becomes a critical challenge as communication networks expand and become more complex. There is a growing trend towards designing and implementing machine learning-based predictive maintenance solutions for telecommunications infrastructure to address this challenge. This study aims to develop and implement a predictive model that can accurately predict the runtime of generators on telecommunication sites. This information is crucial for efficient planning and cost estimation purposes. The research collected data over three months and split it into training and testing datasets, with the training data accounting for 70% and the testing data accounting for 30%. Three models were used for prediction: the Ordinary Least Squares (OLS) method, the log-linear method, and the Vector Autoregression (VAR) model. The models were evaluated, and their fit was calculated. In this paper, a new model was proposed, namely the OLS model with negative clipping, to address the limitations of the OLS model. The results showed that the OLS model with negative clipping provided the best prediction accuracy, with a root mean square error of 0.09. On the other hand, the Vector Autoregression model exhibited the least accuracy, with a root mean square error of 9.3385. These findings highlight the effectiveness of the proposed predictive maintenance solution in accurately predicting generator runtime on telecommunication sites.

Keywords: Predictive Maintenance · Generator Runtime · Telecommunications Site · Ordinary Least Square Approximation · Vector Autoregression

A. Oluwatope et al. (Eds.): AFRICOMM 2025, LNICST 713, pp. 109–127, 2027.
https://doi.org/10.1007/978-3-032-38682-3_7

1 Introduction

The telecommunications industry has undergone significant growth and transformation in recent years due to technological advancements and the increasing demand for seamless connectivity. Maintaining the infrastructure that supports them becomes a critical challenge as communication networks expand and become more complex. Their infrastructure includes towers, antennas, base stations, power systems, and network equipment. These components are spread across vast geographical areas and are subjected to various environmental conditions. Ensuring this infrastructure's optimal performance and reliability is paramount to delivering uninterrupted customer communication services [20]. Traditionally, the maintenance of telecom infrastructure has followed a preventive approach, which relies on regularly scheduled inspections and maintenance activities, regardless of the actual condition of the components [10,17].

This approach often results in unnecessary maintenance actions, increased costs, and potential system downtime due to unexpected failures. In middle income countries such as Nigeria, the grid supply to telecommunications site is typically unstable with noticeable outages. Tower operators rely heavily on generators and hybrid configuration to minimize service disruptions. This leads to high fuel and maintenance costs, accelerated equipment wear, complex runtime scheduling, and increased emissions. Accurately predicting generator runtime is operationally critical for fuel planning, cost control, and preventing unexpected shutdowns. Machine learning-based predictive maintenance is a practical application of machine learning in telecommunication. It involves utilising machine learning techniques to analyse data from telecommunication networks and equipment, enabling the prediction of potential issues and proactive maintenance actions. Predictive maintenance leverages machine learning techniques to analyse vast amounts of data collected from sensors and monitoring systems installed in telecommunications infrastructure. By analysing this data, we can identify patterns, detect anomalies, and predict potential failures or maintenance requirements before they occur.

Predictive maintenance in the telecommunications industry has the potential to revolutionise maintenance practices. It can enable infrastructure operators to transition from reactive and preventive approaches to a proactive, data-driven approach. This shift allows them to anticipate maintenance needs, prioritise resources effectively, and minimise downtime by addressing issues before they escalate. It offers several advantages over traditional approaches. Continuous monitoring of the performance and condition of critical components can identify subtle signs of deterioration or malfunctions that may not be apparent through manual inspections [21].

This early detection helps operators take proactive measures to prevent failures, optimise maintenance schedules, and ensure the reliability and longevity of the infrastructure. By focusing resources on the areas with the highest likelihood of failure, unnecessary maintenance actions can be minimised, leading to cost savings and improved operational efficiency. This paper addresses scenarios where there is high dependence on generators leveraging real life telecommunications data.

2 Related Works

Predictive maintenance is crucial to the care of telecommunications sites. It allows for proper planning and management of such sites. This in turn, minimised downtime on sites and prevented possible failures. Predictive maintenance solutions in the telecommunications industry have gained significant attention in recent years. Predictive maintenance involves the use of advanced analytics and machine learning techniques to predict equipment failures and proactively schedule maintenance activities, thereby reducing downtime and improving operational efficiency [6]. Machine learning has become of interest in the field of predictive maintenance. Recent technologies have paved the way for the application of machine learning in predictive maintenance systems. Machine learning gives the opportunity to analyse large datasets, and detect trends and anomalies. These trends and anomalies can be indicators for potential failures or point to maintenance needs. By training a model on a given data set, the model can distinguish between standard operating conditions and detect abnormal conditions. The deployment of an intelligent and predictive maintenance system in an industrial case study is described by. This system utilises IoT and machine learning technologies to enable online and real-time data collection and analysis for the early detection of machine failures. By visualising, monitoring, and scheduling maintenance interventions, this system aims to mitigate the occurrence of failures and reduce unplanned downtime [2].

Predictive analysis models have been studied extensively studied. A parameterised BBN model was developed to improve fault detection predictions and reduce maintenance costs during the network operations and maintenance lifecycle [18]. The model encompassed operational processes for decision support, contributing significantly to current solutions in the field. Gu (2023) researched the application of the stacking technique in telecom churn prediction. The study aimed to reduce customer churn and improve the operating profit of telecommunication enterprises. Using efficient data mining technology, the author developed a high-accuracy customer churn prediction model to help operators better manage existing users and reduce maintenance costs. A previous study proposed a model for predictive maintenance based on the Asset Administration Shell (AAS) concept of the Reference Architecture Model for Industry (RAMI) 4.0. The model leverages the AAS to achieve device interoperability and implement generic functionalities for predictive maintenance. This approach enhances the efficiency and effectiveness of maintenance operations in the telecommunications industry [4].

Prior studies have sought to compare different machine-learning techniques. Sabbeh (2018) compared the performance of other machine learning techniques for customer retention, including decision trees, naïve Bayesian, logistic regression, and linear discriminant analysis. The study found that decision trees achieved the highest accuracy, followed by naÃŕve Bayesian, logistic regression, and linear discriminant analysis. These findings provide insights into the suitability of different machine learning techniques for predictive maintenance in the telecommunications industry [16].

Predictive maintenance has gained significant attention in various industries as an alternative to reactive maintenance. In the telecommunications industry, implementing predictive maintenance solutions can help improve the safety, reliability, and uninterrupted power supply of telecommunications power systems [14]. Another study by Suraj & Ajiferuke (2013) explores knowledge management practices in the Nigerian telecommunications industry. While this study does not directly focus on predictive maintenance, it emphasises the importance of knowledge sharing, learning, and innovation in telecommunications. Effective knowledge management practices can contribute to developing and implementing predictive maintenance solutions by leveraging organisational knowledge and expertise [19].

These studies emphasise the potential benefits of predictive maintenance in optimising maintenance activities, leveraging organisational knowledge, and ensuring an uninterrupted power supply. Further research is needed to explore the application and effectiveness of predictive maintenance solutions in the telecommunications sector. In conclusion, the literature review highlights the importance of predictive maintenance solutions in the telecommunications industry. The studies discussed in this review demonstrate the potential of advanced analytics, machine learning, and knowledge management practices. The paper proposes and empirically evaluate an OLS-based model with negative value clipping for generator runtime prediction, and compare it against standard OLS, log-linear regression, and Vector Autoregression (VAR), showing that the clipped OLS variant improves accuracy and enforces physically meaningful (non-negative) predictions.

3 Data and Methodology

The dataset used in this paper is bivariate time-series data exported from a Remote monitoring system (RMS) on a telecommunications site in Ogun state, Nigeria. The data includes time (Date Time), rectifier load (kw), generator power(kw), grid power (kw), solar power (kw) and battery power (Table 1). The dataset contains four thousand four hundred sixteen rows and six columns from March 1st, 2023, to May 31st, 2023. The data is collected at 30-minute intervals.

3.1 Dataset Description

The dataset used in this study was obtained from the remote monitoring system (RMS) of a live telecommunications site located in Ogun State, Nigeria. The site is powered by a hybrid configuration consisting of public grid supply, a diesel generator, solar panels, a rectifier system, and battery storage. The data reflects real operational behaviour.

Table 1. Site data obtained from a remote monitoring system

TIME	RECTIFIER LOAD	GENERATOR POWER	GRID POWER	SOLAR POWER	BATTERY POWER
2023-03-03T15:00:00	7.0136	0.1536	3.4229	0.9712	3.097
2023-03-03T15:30:00	6.9256	3.0515	0	0.1365	-0.0868
2023-03-03T16:00:00	7.2037	4.4818	0	0.3188	3.1379
2023-03-03T16:30:00	6.9638	4.5266	0	0.233	3.1368
2023-03-03T17:00:00	6.8271	1.5927	1.7454	0.0702	3.1868
2023-03-03T17:30:00	7.0469	0	10.9365	0.0015	3.2202

- **Monitoring period:** 1 March 2023 to 31 May 2023 (92 d).
- **Sampling interval:** 30 min (time-based logs).
- **Number of records:** 4,416 time-stamped observations.
- **Raw variables recorded by the RMS:**
  - **Timestamp** (DateTime) – logging time of each measurement.
  - **Rectifier Load (kW)** – active load supplied to the DC bus / site equipment.
  - **Generator Power (kW)** – real power output of the generator.
  - **Grid Power (kW)** – real power supplied from the public utility grid.
  - **Solar Power (kW)** – real power generated by the PV subsystem.
  - **Battery Power (kW)** – battery charging/discharging power (positive for discharge, negative for charge).

These measurements are used to derive daily energy and runtime features. For each day in the observation window, power readings are converted to energy (kWh) using the sampling interval and aggregated to obtain: generator energy, grid energy, solar energy, battery energy, rectifier energy, and the total generator runtime (hours), which serves as the prediction target.

3.2 Data Preprocessing and Analysis

This paper focuses on the prediction of generator runtime. However, the generator runtime is not included in the raw data collected from the RMS—a calculated field to the data frame for the generator runtime. If a given row has the generator power reading, it indicates that the generator is running within that timeframe. The generator runtime is the time difference between consecutive readings if the generator power reading exists. The data collected are at 30-minute intervals. Due to this, the data would be aggregated daily. Power readings would be converted to energy since energy readings are easier to interpret and deduce cost for.

$$Energy(kwh) = Power(kw) * time(h) \tag{1}$$

Table 2. A subset of the processed dataset

DAY	GENERATOR ENERGY (kwh)	GENERATOR RUNTIME (h)	RECTIFIER ENERGY (kwh)	BATTERY ENERGY (kwh)	SOLAR ENERGY (kwh)	GRID ENERGY (kwh)
2023–03-01	14.33715	4.5	84.5184	-9.9668	15.152	25.1188
2023–03-02	9.4621	3	149.62555	5.2473	16.6414	117.9358
2023–03-03	35.92045	11	145.37385	1.41525	7.7146	51.59355
2023–03-04	9.89775	2.5	135.7389	-22.6964	12.5884	81.3621
2023–03-05	35.67335	11	143.55775	23.35295	16.9625	67.4357
2023–03-06	0	0	149.73225	-11.0423	13.58595	130.45705
2023–03-07	21.52095	7	146.8995	13.4807	17.21975	91.8758

To do this, we first calculate the time difference between each row in the dataset and convert it to hours.

The dependent variable(Generator Runtime) is plotted alongside the independent variables (Generator Energy and Grid Energy). It is observed that a decrease in the grid energy results in a corresponding increase in the generator runtime(Fig 1), this suggest an inverse relationship between generator runtime and grid energy. The generator energy and the generator runtime follow the same trend.

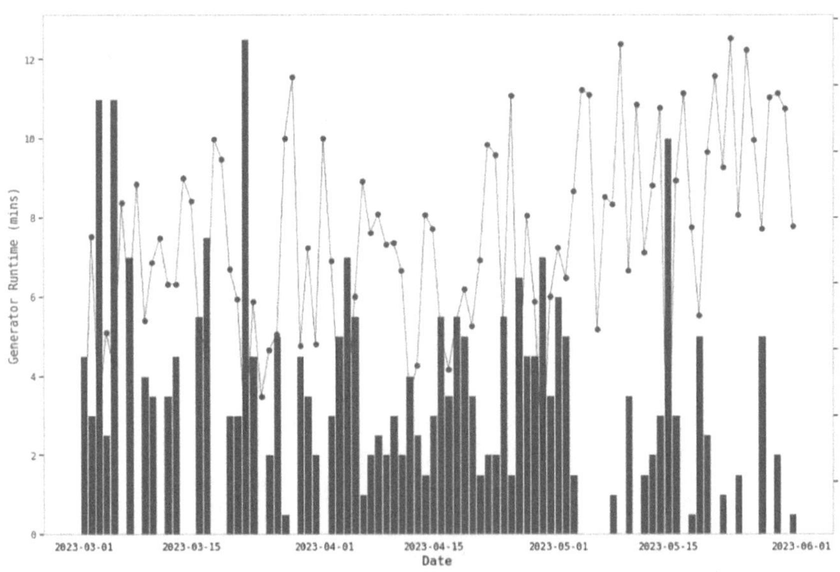

Fig. 1. Plot of Generator Runtime and Grid Energy.

It is observed (Fig 2) that an increase in the generator energy caused a corresponding increase in the generator runtime. Similarly, an increase in the battery energy and the solar energy result in a decrease in the generator runtime

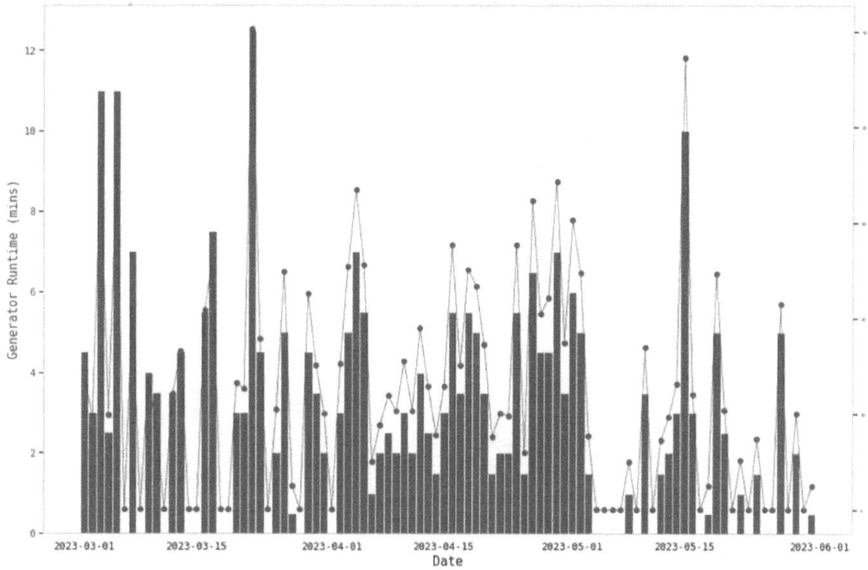

Fig. 2. Plot of Generator Runtime and Generator Energy.

Correlation. Table 3 shows a strong positive correlation between the generator energy and the generator runtime. This is expected as generator energy is required for the generator runtime. A strong negative correlation exists between the grid energy and the generator runtime. Since the generator is unlikely to run when there is a grid, this negative correlation is expected

Table 3. Correlation between variables

	GENERATOR ENERGY	GENERATOR RUNTIME	RECTIFIER ENERGY	BATTERY ENERGY	SOLAR ENERGY	GRID ENERGY
GENERATOR ENERGY	1	0.969801	0.038483	0.153774	-0.115523	-0.746542
GENERATOR RUNTIME	0.969801	1	0.007244	0.180885	-0.065101	-0.733461
RECTIFIER ENERGY	0.038483	0.007244	1	0.08977	0.119625	0.517338
BATTERY ENERGY	0.153774	0.180885	0.08977	1	0.076811	0.270039
SOLAR ENERGY	-0.115523	-0.065101	0.119625	0.076811	1	0.085508
GRID ENERGY	-0.746542	-0.733461	0.517338	0.270039	0.085508	1

3.3 Prediction Method

Least Square Approximation. The least-square approximation method, specifically the ordinary least squares (OLS) method, is commonly used in statistical analysis and machine learning for linear regression models

A multiple linear regression model can be written as:

$$y = \beta_0 + \beta_1 x_(1,t) + \beta_2 x_(2,t) + \cdots + \beta_k x_(k,t) + \epsilon_t \tag{2}$$

where:
- y is the dependent variable
- $x_(1,t), x_(2,t), ..., x_(k,t)$ are the predictor variables at time t
- β_0 is the y-intercept
- $\beta_1, \beta_2 ..., \beta_k$, are the coefficients for each independent variable
- ϵ_t is the error term

It can be written in a matrix form where all the values of the forecast variables are given in a single equation as:

$$\begin{pmatrix} y_1 \\ y_2 \\ \vdots_t \\ y \end{pmatrix} = \begin{pmatrix} 1 & x_{1,1} & x_{2,1} & \dots & x_{k,1} \\ 1 & x_{1,2} & x_{2,2} & \dots & x_{k,2} \\ \vdots & \vdots & \vdots & & \vdots \\ 1 & x_{1,t} & x_{2,t} & \dots & x_{k,t} \end{pmatrix} \begin{pmatrix} \beta_o \\ \beta_1 \\ \vdots \\ \beta_k \end{pmatrix} + \begin{pmatrix} \varepsilon_o \\ \varepsilon_1 \\ \vdots \\ \varepsilon_k \end{pmatrix} \tag{3}$$

Which can be written generally as :

$$y = X\beta + \varepsilon \tag{4}$$

$$\varepsilon = y - \ X\beta \tag{5}$$

The coefficients of the observations are unknown and need to be estimated from the data. According to the book "Forecasting: Principles and Practice" by Rob J. Hyndman and George Athanasopoulos, least square approximation method involves minimising the sum of the squared error term.

$$\sum_{t=1}^{T} \varepsilon_t^2 = \sum_{t=1}^{T} (\ y_t - \beta_0 - \ \beta_1 x_{1,t} - \ \beta_2 x_{2,t} - \dots - \ \beta_k x_{k,t}\ )^2 \tag{6}$$

The sum of squares(SS) of a matrix can be calculated using the formula SS = X'X (Rizvi et al., 2020). Equation

$$\sum_{t=1}^{T} \varepsilon_t^2 \ = \ (y - X\beta)^1 \ (y - X\beta) \tag{7}$$

To find the minimum, we take the derivative of y with respect to β and equate it to zero. The error term is minimized when

$$\beta = \ (X^{'}X)^{-1} X^{'} y. \tag{8}$$

The predictor variables are:
$x_{1,t}$ – *Generator Energy*
$x_{2,t}$, - *Rectifier Energy*
$x_{3,t}$, - *Battery Energy*
$x_{4,t}$, - *Solar Energy*
$x_{5,t}$, - *Grid Energy*

Using the data shown in Table 2, we define the predictor variables X and its transpose $X^{'}$ in Eq. 9 and Eq. 10 respectively

$$X = \begin{pmatrix} 1.0000 & 14.33715 & 84.518400 & -9.966800 & 15.15200 & 25.118800 \\ 1.0000 & 9.46210 & 149.625550 & 5.247300 & 16.64140 & 117.935800 \\ 1.0000 & 35.92045 & 145.373850 & 1.415250 & 7.71460 & 51.593550 \\ 1.0000 & 9.89775 & 135.738900 & -22.696400 & 12.58840 & 81.362100 \\ \vdots & \vdots & \vdots & \vdots & \vdots & \vdots \\ 1.0000 & 30.26900 & 160.539650 & 27.880500 & 10.97780 & 113.521450 \\ 1.0000 & 24.69005 & 161.562350 & 6.338500 & 13.10375 & 102.045749 \end{pmatrix} \tag{9}$$

$$X^{'} = \begin{pmatrix} 1.0000 & 1.0000 & 1.0000 & 1.0000 & \cdots & 1.0000 \\ 14.33715 & 9.46210 & 35.92045 & 9.89775 & \cdots & 24.690050 \\ 84.51840 & 149.625550 & 145.373850 & 135.738900 & \cdots & 161.562350 \\ -9.96680 & 5.247300 & 1.415250 & -22.696400 & \cdots & 6.338500 \\ 15.15200 & 16.64140 & 7.71460 & 12.58840 & \cdots & 13.103750 \\ 25.11880 & 117.935800 & 51.593550 & 81.362100 & \cdots & 102.045749 \end{pmatrix} \tag{10}$$

The dependent variable – Generator Runtime, is represented as:

$$Y = \begin{pmatrix} 4.5 \\ 3.0 \\ 11.0 \\ 2.5 \\ \vdots \\ 5.0 \end{pmatrix} \tag{11}$$

Using Eq. 8, the values of the coefficients are shown as:

$$\beta = \begin{pmatrix} 0.28944965 \\ 0.199072 \\ 0.008204 \\ 0.021950 \\ 0.031277 \\ -0.014287 \end{pmatrix} \tag{12}$$

Since the coefficients have been obtained. The forecast variables are obtained by multiplying the test variables by the coefficients obtained

$$y = x\beta \tag{13}$$

The test data is shown in Eq. 14

$$x = \begin{pmatrix} 1.0000 & 24.69005 & 161.562350 & 6.338500 & 13.10375 & 102.045749 \\ 1.0000 & 7.71530 & 162.858900 & -8.359600 & 14.55520 & 134.684950 \\ 1.0000 & 0.00000 & 158.177600 & 9.857550 & 13.06130 & 173.324250 \\ 1.0000 & 0.00000 & 155.525300 & 13.281749 & 16.43440 & 171.473000 \\ \vdots & \vdots & \vdots & \vdots & \vdots & \vdots \\ 1.0000 & 171.473000 & 162.255100 & -3.360950 & 13.45860 & 165.963850 \\ 1.0000 & 2.50815 & 142.595850 & -18.246051 & 10.38850 & 121.525151 \end{pmatrix} \tag{14}$$

Using Eq. 13 , the predicted values of the generator runtime is shown below

$$y = \begin{pmatrix} 5.621001 \\ 1.508901 \\ -0.264308 \\ -0.078958 \\ \vdots \\ 0.146759 \end{pmatrix} \tag{15}$$

Non-linear Regression using the Log-Linear Functional Form. The log-linear functional form is a non-linear regression model. The predictor variable is represented in the log form and transformed back to its original form after the prediction. [12,15]

$$\log y + 1 = \beta_0 + \beta_1 x_{1,t} + \beta_2 x_{2,t} + \ldots + \beta_k x_{k,t} + \varepsilon_t \tag{16}$$

The values of X and X' are obtained from Eqs. 9 and 10 respectively. The logarithmic form of the dependent variable, generator runtime is shown below and obtained using log y +1. 1 is added to the value of y to ensure non-zero values. The values obtained are shown below.

$$Y = \begin{pmatrix} 1.704748 \\ 1.386294 \\ 2.484907 \\ 1.252763 \\ \vdots \\ 1.791759 \end{pmatrix} \tag{17}$$

Vector Autoregression. The VAR model is a multivariate model, where each variable is regressed on its own lagged values as well as the lagged values of other variables in the system [3,13] . The Augmented Dickey-Fuller (ADF) test is used to determine the stationarity of the time series. (Fig 7) (Fig. 3).

```
Augmented Dickey-Fuller Test on "GENERATOR_RUNTIME"
    -----------------------------------------------
Null Hypothesis: Data has unit root. Non-Stationary.
Significance Level = 0.05
Test Statistic = -8.4994
No. Lags Chosen = 0
 Critical value 1%     = -3.504
 Critical value 5%     = -2.894
 Critical value 10%    = -2.584
 => P-Value = 0.0. Rejecting Null Hypothesis.
 => Series is Stationary.


Augmented Dickey-Fuller Test on "GENERATOR_ENERGY"
    -----------------------------------------------
Null Hypothesis: Data has unit root. Non-Stationary.
Significance Level = 0.05
Test Statistic = -8.0415
No. Lags Chosen = 0
 Critical value 1%     = -3.504
 Critical value 5%     = -2.894
 Critical value 10%    = -2.584
 => P-Value = 0.0. Rejecting Null Hypothesis.
 => Series is Stationary.
```

Fig. 3. Test for Stationarity of data.

Each variable in the system is represented with an equation. The VAR the equation for each variable for a single lag can be written as:

$$y_{1t} = \beta_0 + \beta_{11,1} y_{1t-1} + \beta_{12,1} y_{1t-1} + \beta_{13,1} y_{1t-1} + \beta_{14,1} y_{1t-1} + \beta_{15,1} y_{1t-1} + \beta_{16,1} y_{1t-1} + \varepsilon_t \tag{18}$$

$$y_{2t} = \beta_0 + \beta_{21,1} y_{1t-1} + \beta_{22,1} y_{1t-1} + \beta_{23,1} y_{1t-1} + \beta_{24,1} y_{1t-1} + \beta_{25,1} y_{1t-1} + \beta_{26,1} y_{1t-1} + \varepsilon_t \tag{19}$$

$$y_{3t} = \beta_0 + \beta_{31,1} y_{1t-1} + \beta_{32,1} y_{1t-1} + \beta_{33,1} y_{1t-1} + \beta_{34,1} y_{1t-1} + \beta_{35,1} y_{1t-1} + \beta_{36,1} y_{1t-1} + \varepsilon_t \tag{20}$$

$$y_{4t} = \beta_0 + \beta_{41,1} y_{1t-1} + \beta_{42,1} y_{1t-1} + \beta_{43,1} y_{1t-1} + \beta_{44,1} y_{1t-1} + \beta_{45,1} y_{1t-1} + \beta_{46,1} y_{1t-1} + \varepsilon_t \tag{21}$$

$$y_{5t} = \beta_0 + \beta_{51,1} y_{1t-1} + \beta_{52,1} y_{1t-1} + \beta_{53,1} y_{1t-1} + \beta_{54,1} y_{1t-1} + \beta_{55,1} y_{1t-1} + \beta_{56,1} y_{1t-1} + \varepsilon_t \tag{22}$$

$$y_{6t} = \beta_0 + \beta_{61,1} y_{1t-1} + \beta_{62,1} y_{1t-1} + \beta_{63,1} y_{1t-1} + \beta_{64,1} y_{1t-1} + \beta_{65,1} y_{1t-1} + \beta_{66,1} y_{1t-1} + \varepsilon_t \tag{23}$$

where

$$y_{1t} = Generator\ Runtime$$
$$y_{2t} = Rectifier\ Energy$$
$$y_{3t} = Solar\ Energy$$
$$y_{4t} = Battery\ Energy$$
$$y_{5t} = Generator\ Energy$$
$$y_{6t} = Grid\ Energy$$

Due to the complex nature of Eqs. 18 to 23, the Vector The autoRegression module of the stats model package is used to fit the data and predict the generator runtime.

Model Fitting. The metrics for model fitting are essential in evaluating the performance and appropriateness of a model. This paper focuses on these metrics include R-squared, adjusted R-squared, Akaike Information Criterion (AIC), and Bayesian Information Criterion (BIC). R-squared (R^2) measures the proportion of variance in the dependent variable, which is explained by the independent variables in the model. [5,7].

The Coefficient of Determination (R^2) is a crucial metric in model fitting, representing the proportion of the variance in the dependent variable that is predictable from the independent variable(s) [9]. It is calculated as the square of the correlation coefficient between the observed and predicted values of the dependent variable. The formula for the Coefficient of Determination (R^2) is given by:

$$R^2 = 1 - \frac{SS_{res}}{SS_{tot}}$$

where SS_{res} is the sum of squares of residuals and SS_{tot} is the total sum of squares.

This formula is widely used in statistical analysis to assess the goodness of fit of a model. It provides valuable insights into the proportion of variability in the dependent variable that the independent variables can explain.

The metrics for model fitting are essential in evaluating the performance and appropriateness of a model. The Coefficient of Determination (R^2)) is a measure that indicates the proportion of the variance in the dependent variable that is predictable from the independent variable(s) [9]. It is calculated as the square of the correlation coefficient between the observed and predicted values of the dependent variable. The Adjusted R^2 is a modification of R^2 that adjusts for the number of predictors in the model, providing a more accurate measure of the goodness of fit [11]. It penalizes the addition of unnecessary predictors, thereby preventing overfitting. Akaike's Information Criterion (AIC) and Schwarz's Bayesian Information Criterion (BIC) are both used for model selection among a finite set of models. AIC is based on information theory and measures the quality of a model relative to other models, considering the goodness of fit and the simplicity of the model. BIC, on the other hand, is a criterion for model selection among a finite set of models and is derived from a Bayesian point of view, where the best model is the one that maximizes the posterior probability of being the true model [1].

Model Evaluation. When evaluating the performance of a model, several metrics are commonly used, including Root Mean Squared Error (RMSE), Mean Squared Error (MSE), and Mean Absolute Error (MAE) [8]. The Mean Squared Error (MSE) measures the average of the squares of the errors or deviations—that is, the difference between the actual and predicted values. It is calculated as the average squared differences between the actual and predicted values. The formula for MSE is given by:

$$MSE = \frac{1}{n}\sum_{i=1}^{n}(Y_i - \hat{Y}_i)^2 \tag{24}$$

where Y_i represents the actual value, $\hat{Y}_i$ represents the predicted value, and n is the number of observations.

The Root Mean Squared Error (RMSE) is the square root of the MSE and provides a measure of the standard deviation of the residuals. It is calculated as:

$$RMSE = \sqrt{MSE} \tag{25}$$

The Mean Absolute Error (MAE) is a measure of the average of the absolute errors or deviations. It is calculated as the average of the absolute differences between the actual and predicted values. The formula for MAE is given by:

$$MAE = \frac{1}{n}\sum_{i=1}^{n}|Y_i - \hat{Y}_i| \tag{26}$$

where Y_i represents the actual value, $\hat{Y}_i$ represents the predicted value, and n is the number of observations.

These metrics are widely used in evaluating the accuracy and performance of predictive models, providing valuable insights into the extent of errors in the predictions and the overall goodness of fit.

4 Results and Discussions

The data is split into test and train data. The training data accounts for 70% of the data, while the test data accounts for 30%. The results are discussed below.

Ordinary Least Square Approximation (OLS). Using the OLS method, the model has an Adjusted R-squared value of 0.917 and an R-squared value of 0.917, as shown in Table 7. These values are close to 1. This indicates that the model is a good fit for the data. The AIC and BIC values are lower when compared to the data with interpolation. Figure 4 shows the overlap of the test and the train data (Table 4).

Table 4. Model fit measures for OLS

Measure	Value
R-squared	0.923
Adjusted R-squared	0.917
AIC	153.7
BIC	164.4

Non-linear Regression (Log-Linear Form.) One problem posed by the OLS predictions is that negative values are returned for the generator runtime. Since this is a measure of time, only positive values are relevant. We perform a logarithmic transformation of the forecast variable. The form log(x+1) is used and the results obtained are transformed. This method has the advantage of outputting only positive valuesar (Fig.5) (Table 5).

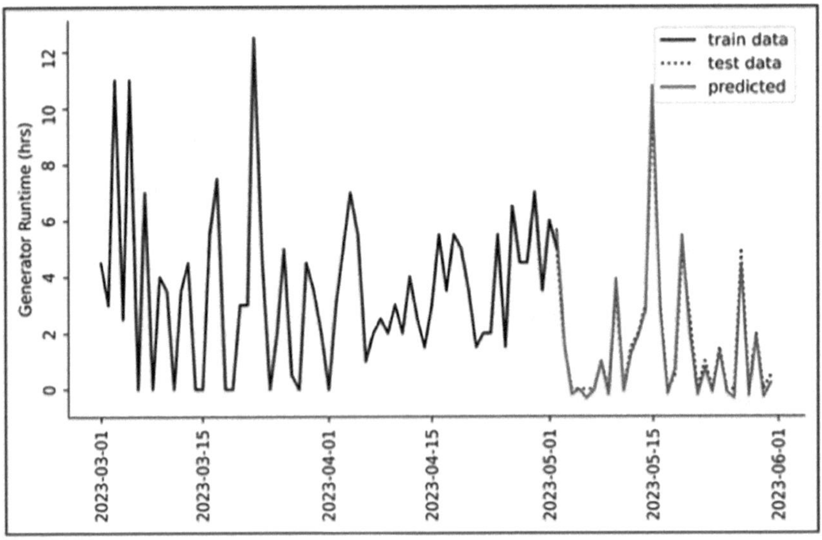

Fig. 4. Predicted vs Test Data using OLS.

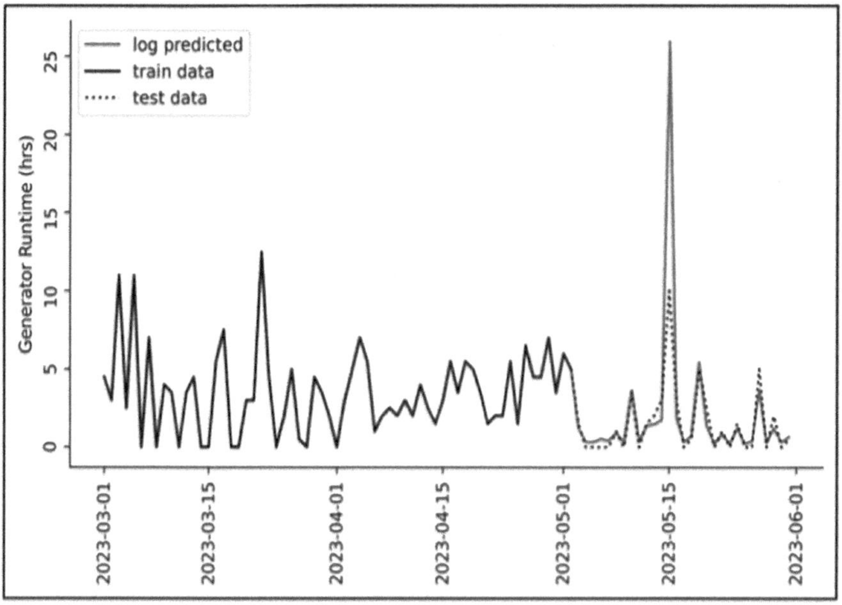

Fig. 5. Predicted vs Test log linear form.

Table 5. Model fit log-linear form

Measure	Value
R-squared	0.863
Adjusted R-squared	0.851
AIC	20.60
BIC	33.46

Using the Adjusted R-squared measure, we observe that the goodness of fit for the log-linear form (Table 7) is less than that of the ordinary least square method. However, the log-linear form returns non-negative values more applicable to the generator runtime than the OLS method.

Vector Autoregression. An ADF test was carried out on the dataset. All the variables were stationary, and further differentiating was not required. The predicted result is shown in Fig 6. Non-negative values were obtained, but the predictions are less accurate when compared to the OLS and log-linear form used.

OLS Model with a Negative Value Clipping. This paper proposes a new model, an OLS model with negative value clipping. The negative values obtained

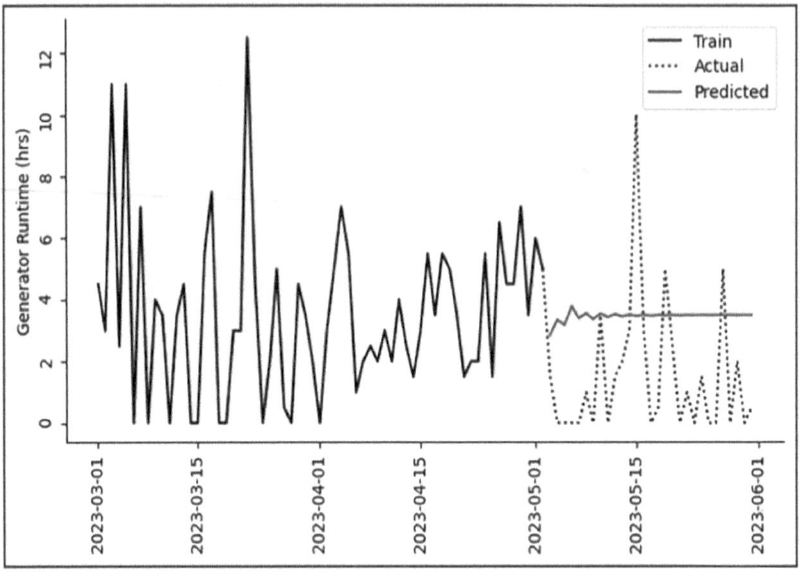

Fig. 6. Predicted vs Test Vector Autoregression.

in the OLS model are replaced with zero since the dependent variable, which measures time, is non-negative

Model Accuracy Comparison. To estimate the accuracy of a model, the metrics used are Mean Squared Error (MSE), Root Mean Squared Error (RMSE), and Mean Absolute Error (MAE).

The proposed model – OLS with negative value clipping has the least mean square error, root mean square error and mean absolute error when compared to other the models used. The OLS with a negative value clipping model has the highest accuracy. Conversely, the Vector Autoregression model has the least value in all the criteria shown in Table 6 The data suggests that the Vector autoregression model is the least accurate.

Table 6. Comparison of model accuracy

Model	MSE	RMSE	MAE
Ordinary least square approximation	0.0957	0.3093	0.2460
Non-linear regression (log-linear form)	0.1170	0.3418	0.2869
Vector autoregression	9.3385	3.0559	2.7859
OLS model with negative value clipping	0.0900	0.3001	0.1900

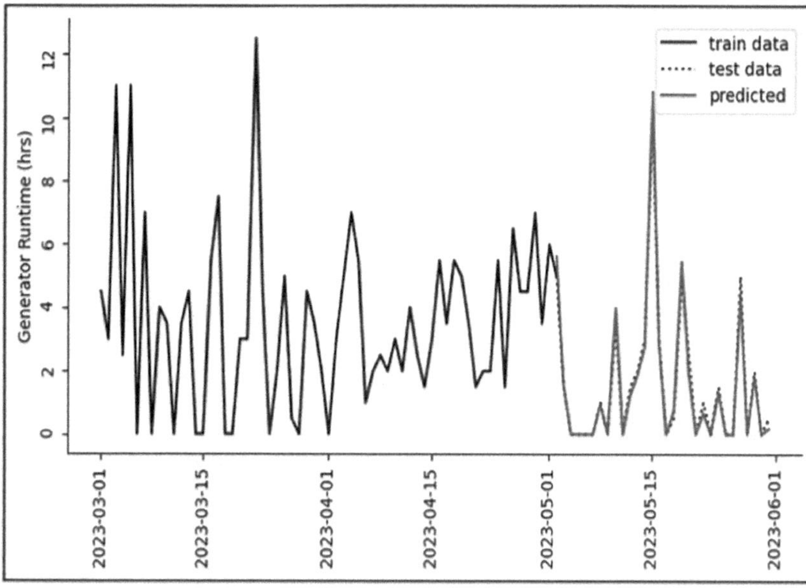

Fig. 7. Predicted vs Test negative value clipping.

Table 7. Model fit log-linear form

Measure	Value
R-squared	0.863
Adjusted R-squared	0.851
AIC	20.60
BIC	33.46

5 Conclusion and Future Work

The work presented in this paper is a starting point for much more extensive research in predictive maintenance solutions in the telecommunications Industry. Predictive maintenance in the telecommunications industry is an under-researched area; as such, several opportunities are available to be explored. The paper focuses solely on predicting the generator runtime. Future work can explore other prediction areas, such as Load prediction, load shedding and solar degradation.

Additionally, this paper explores the use of four models. In the future, additional models may be considered. It was also established that linear interpolation to backfill missing data reduced the model's fit; different interpolation methods may also be explored for data completeness. The dataset used was for a single site for three months. Much more extensive data can also be used for further training.

In conclusion, a new predictive model was proposed, a variation of the OLS model with negative value clipping. This model was trained and achieved the highest accuracy compared to other models.

References

1. Akaike, H.: Akaike's information criterion. In: Lovric, M. (ed.) International Encyclopedia of Statistical Science, pp. 41–42. Springer, Berlin, Heidelberg (2011). https://doi.org/10.1007/978-3-642-04898-2_110
2. Alves, F., et al.: Deployment of a smart and predictive maintenance system in an industrial case study. In: 2020 IEEE 29th International Symposium on Industrial Electronics (ISIE) (2020). https://doi.org/10.1109/ISIE45063.2020.9152441
3. Bologna, M.: Analytical evaluation of the numerical coefficients in the zassenhaus product formula and its applications to quantum and statistical mechanics. Prog. Theor. Exp. Phys. (5), 053A01 (2019). https://doi.org/10.1093/ptep/ptz035
4. Cavalieri, S., Salafia, M.G.: A model for predictive maintenance based on asset administration shell. Sensors **20**(21), 6028 (2020). https://doi.org/10.3390/s20216028
5. Ding, J., Tarokh, V., Yang, Y.: Bridging AIC and BIC: a new criterion for autoregression. IEEE Trans. Inf. Theory **64**(6), 4024–4043 (2018). https://doi.org/10.1109/TIT.2017.2717599
6. Gęca, J.: Performance comparison of machine learning algorithms for predictive maintenance. Informatyka, Automatyka, Pomiary w Gospodarce i Ochronie Środowiska **10**(3), 32–35 (2020). https://doi.org/10.35784/iapgos.1834. https://ph.pollub.pl/index.php/iapgos/article/view/1834
7. Haslbeck, J.M.B., Bringmann, L.F., Waldorp, L.J.: A tutorial on estimating time-varying vector autoregressive models. Multivar. Behav. Res. **56**(1), 120–149 (2021). https://doi.org/10.1080/00273171.2020.1743630
8. Hyndman, R.J., Athanasopoulos, G.: Forecasting: Principles and Practice. OTexts, Australia, 2 edn. (2018). https://otexts.com/fpp2/
9. Khodnevych, Y.V., Stefanyshyn, D.V.: Data arrangements to train an artificial neural network within solving the tasks for calculating the chézy roughness coefficient under uncertainty of parameters determining the hydraulic resistance to flow in river channels. Environmental and Energy Balancing Problems, pp. 59–85 (2022)
10. Li, C., Liu, L., Zhao, J., Liu, Y.: An experiment to design an operation and maintenance system integrating apriori association rules for a telecom platform. Wirel. Commun. Mob. Comput. (2021). https://doi.org/10.1155/2021/1185584
11. Milenković, M., Lalić, B., Pavlović, K., Berić, I., Sobajić, V.: Comparison of traditional and agile approach to manage product development projects. In: International Scientific Conference on Contemporary Issues in Business, Management and Economics Engineering (SENET) (2019). https://doi.org/10.2991/senet-19.2019.8
12. Pescim, R.R., Ortega, E.M.M., Cordeiro, G.M., Demétrio, C.G.B., Hamedani, G.G.: The log-beta generalized half-normal regression model. J. Stat. Theor. Appl. **12**(4), 369–384 (2013). https://doi.org/10.2991/jsta.2013.12.4.2
13. Pineau, E., Razakarivony, S., Bonald, T.: Seq2VAR: multivariate time series representation with relational neural networks and linear autoregressive model. In: Bifet, A., May, M., Zadrozny, B., Gavalda, R., Pedreschi, D., Bonchi, F., Cardoso, J., Spiliopoulou, M. (eds.) Machine Learning and Knowledge Discovery in

Databases, Lecture Notes in Computer Science, vol. 11908, pp. 146–162. Springer, Cham (2020). https://doi.org/10.1007/978-3-030-39098-3_10
14. Ribeiro, E.F.F., Cardoso, A.J.M., Boccaletti, C.: Uninterruptible energy production in standalone power systems for telecommunications. Renew. Energy Power Qual. J. **1**(7), 351–356 (2009). https://doi.org/10.24084/repqj07.350
15. Rieck, J.R., Nedelman, J.R.: A log-linear model for the birnbaum-saunders distribution. Technometrics **33**(1), 51–60 (1991). https://doi.org/10.1080/00401706.1991.10484769
16. Sabbeh, S.F.: Machine-learning techniques for customer retention: a comparative study. Int. J. Adv. Comput. Sci. Appl. **9**(2), (2018). https://doi.org/10.14569/IJACSA.2018.090238
17. Shah, D.M.H., Khan, F.: Telecommunication infrastructure development and FDI into Asian developing nations. J. Bus. Tourism **5**(1), (2020). https://doi.org/10.34260/jbt.v5i1.116
18. Siryani, J., Mazzuchi, T.A., Sarkani, S.: Framework using bayesian belief networks for utility effective management and operations. In: 2015 IEEE International Conference on Big Data Computing Service and Applications (2015). https://doi.org/10.1109/BigDataService.2015.60
19. Suraj, O.A., Ajiferuke, I.: Knowledge management practices in the Nigerian telecommunications industry. Knowl. Process. Manag. **20**(1), 30–39 (2013). https://doi.org/10.1002/kpm.1399
20. Talapko, D., Tešnjak, S.: Influence of solar and wind power generation sources on power supply availability in telecom infrastructure. In: 2014 IEEE International Telecommunications Energy Conference (INTELEC) (2014). https://doi.org/10.1109/INTLEC.2014.6972171
21. Zwolenik, M., Michalec, B.: Effect of water surface slope and friction slope on the value of the estimated manning's roughness coefficient in gravel-bed streams. J. Hydrol. Hydromechanics (2022). https://doi.org/10.2478/johh-2022-0041

Ethical Framework for Integrating Artificial Intelligence in Education: Guidelines and Standards

Amina Sambo-Magaji[1,2](✉), Muyideen Dele Adewale[2,3], Akilu Yunusa-Kaltungo[4], and Grace Esrom Jokthan[3]

[1] Information Technology Department, National Information Technology Development Agency, Abuja, Nigeria
asambo@nitda.gov.ng

[2] Research and Development Department, She and Tech Empowerment Foundation, Abuja, Nigeria
info@sheandtech.com

[3] Africa Centre of Excellence on Technology Enhanced Learning, National Open University of Nigeria, Abuja, Nigeria
gjokthan@noun.edu.ng

[4] Department of Mechanical and Aerospace Engineering, University of Manchester, Manchester, UK
akilu.kaltungo@manchester.ac.uk

Abstract. This paper presents a Nigeria-centred ethical framework for integrating Artificial Intelligence (AI) into education, addressing significant gaps in existing literature. To the authors' knowledge, this constitutes Nigeria's first ethical AI framework for integrating AI in education. It adopts a holistic scope covering primary and secondary education, tertiary institutions, and informal learning. The framework is anchored in the United Nations Educational, Scientific and Cultural Organisation (UNESCO) AI Ethics Recommendations and adapted to Nigeria's regulatory and policy context, including the Nigeria Data Protection Act (NDPA, 2023) enforced by the Nigeria Data Protection Commission (NDPC) and the National Digital Literacy Framework (NDLF), and the Strategic Blueprint of the Federal Ministry of Communications, Innovation & Digital Economy. Core features include a human-centred design approach, cultural grounding with support for indigenous languages, and participatory governance engaging educators, students, policymakers, and community leaders. It incorporates enforceable standards for data privacy, algorithmic fairness, and inclusivity, while advocating phased implementation under the oversight of the Ministry of Education. The operational design translates ethical principles into concrete mechanisms such as certification, regular bias audits, and targeted capacity-building initiatives. By embedding international principles within Nigeria's socio-cultural and infrastructural realities, the framework aims to promote equitable AI deployment that protects rights, addresses bias, and supports local pedagogical traditions. Anticipated outcomes include enhanced educational equity, improved privacy protections, and strengthened trust between educators, learners, and regulators. This work contributes a

A. Oluwatope et al. (Eds.): AFRICOMM 2025, LNICST 713, pp. 128–148, 2027.
https://doi.org/10.1007/978-3-032-38682-3_8

practical, enforceable, and culturally attuned model for responsible AI integration, offering a foundation for sustainable innovation in Nigeria's education sector.

Keywords: Artificial Intelligence · Education · Nigeria · Ethics · UNESCO · Policy · Framework · NDPA · Governance · Inclusivity

1 Introduction

Artificial intelligence (AI) technologies are rapidly reshaping educational systems worldwide, introducing new paradigms of personalised learning, automation, and data-driven decision-making (Ojokheta & Omokhabi, 2024; Ofem & Chukwujama, 2024; Shittu et al., 2024a; Baha & Okolo, 2024; Shittu et al., 2024b; Afolabi, 2024; Samuel & Danladi, 2025; Ekanem & Emejulu, 2025; Allahrakha, 2024; Adesiji, 2024; Adewale et al., 2026; Adewale et al., 2025; Adewale et al., 2024). In Nigeria, these innovations coincide with unique infrastructural, cultural, and governance realities (Ojokheta & Omokhabi, 2024; Shittu et al., 2024b; Samuel & Danladi, 2025) and require robust ethical guidance to ensure equitable, inclusive, and responsible AI deployment. Although numerous international bodies, such as UNESCO, have established ethical principles for AI (Ojokheta & Omokhabi, 2024; Shittu et al., 2024a; Afolabi, 2024; Allahrakha, 2024), localised adaptation in Nigeria remains piecemeal. Existing literature predominantly addresses higher education or offers high-level policy guidance with insufficient attention to primary and secondary education, informal educational contexts, and enforceable Nigeria-specific mechanisms (Ojokheta & Omokhabi, 2024; Ofem & Chukwujama, 2024; Shittu et al., 2024a; Baha & Okolo, 2024; Shittu et al., 2024b; Afolabi, 2024; Samuel & Danladi, 2025; Ekanem & Emejulu, 2025; Allahrakha, 2024; Adesiji, 2024). Similarly, while there is consensus on core ethical values such as transparency, accountability, privacy, fairness, and inclusivity, operationalising these within Nigeria's socio-cultural landscape and governance framework is an outstanding challenge. Since 2023, the Nigeria Data Protection Act (NDPA) has established the Nigeria Data Protection Commission (NDPC) as the national regulator for personal data, setting sector-agnostic obligations (lawful basis, consent, data minimisation, data protection impact assessments, breach notification) that educational actors must meet; this framework aligns these obligations with education-specific governance and procurement." (NDPA, 2023). Recent literature emphasises the urgent need for a robust, Nigeria-grounded ethical framework for integrating AI across educational sectors. While a truly unified, enforceable framework spanning all tiers and ethical dimensions does not yet exist, several references corroborate key elements and guiding principles, many of which align with specified priorities (Ojokheta & Omokhabi, 2024; Ofem & Chukwujama, 2024; Shittu et al., 2024a; Shittu et al., 2024b; Afolabi, 2024). The following outline synthesises only what is explicitly stated in these papers.

A broader understanding of returns on investment in AI ethics highlights the necessity of developing and deploying AI responsibly, in harmony with international frameworks such as UNESCO's AI ethics guidelines and the latest European Union regulations (Zalabak et al., 2025). While global momentum around ethical AI is strong, Nigeria's education sector still lacks a unified, enforceable approach that translates principles into sector-specific mechanisms. Currently, existing literature provides valuable starting points and partial policy suggestions but falls short of offering a unified, actionable, and enforceable framework that addresses all practical and ethical dimensions. This leaves a critical gap in guiding Nigeria's AI adoption in education with clarity, cultural relevance, and regulatory rigour. There remains an urgent need for a unified, deeply Nigerian-grounded ethical AI framework in education that integrates explicit UNESCO and local legal alignment, spans all education sectors, and delivers clear, enforceable recommendations for national regulatory bodies. Without this, the deployment of AI in Nigeria's education system risks fragmentation, inconsistency, and missed opportunities to ensure fairness, transparency, and accountability. Furthermore, this framework is proposed in alignment with Nigeria's overarching digital policy agenda as defined by the Federal Ministry of Communications, Innovation & Digital Economy (FMCIDE), which provides the policy direction for national digital transformation. Specifically, the Strategic Blueprint (2023–2027), titled *Accelerating Our Collective Prosperity through Technical Efficiency*, outlines key goals such as achieving 70% digital literacy by 2027, laying 95,000 km of fibre, digitising 60% of government data, and creating AI-related jobs (Federal Ministry of Communications, Innovation and Digital Economy, 2023). The NDLF complements this with literacy targets of 70% by 2027 and 95% by 2030 (National Information Technology Development Agency, 2023). The 3MTT programme targets training 3 million technical talents [add official 3MTT reference]. While FMCIDE sets the strategic vision, NITDA operationalises these directives (Federal Ministry of Communications, Innovation and Digital Economy, 2023; National Information Technology Development Agency, 2023). While FMCIDE sets the strategic vision, agencies such as the National Information Technology Development Agency (NITDA) operationalise these directives, making it an appropriate anchor for this implementation-focused ethical framework.

This paper synthesises recent literature, highlights key gaps, and proposes a comprehensive, actionable ethical AI framework for Nigerian education, designed for adoption by the Federal Ministry of Education (FME) in collaboration with regulatory and technical bodies such as the National Information Technology Development Agency (NITDA). Section 2 reviews existing literature, identifying deficiencies in coverage and enforceability. Section 3 details the methodology for developing a Nigeria-centred framework. Section 4 presents the framework's principles, cultural grounding, governance mechanisms, and standards for all education levels. Section 5 discusses its implications and future validation needs. Section 6 concludes with recommendations for policy adoption, regulatory oversight, stakeholder involvement, and phased implementation to ensure ethical, inclusive, and sustainable AI integration nationwide.

2 Literature Review

The ethical challenges that accompany AI deployment in education require robust governance frameworks to ensure responsible and equitable use. In the Nigerian context, the urgent need for a comprehensive, culturally grounded, and internationally aligned ethical AI framework for education remains unmet.

2.1 Global and Nigerian Landscape: What Exists and What Is Missing

Across the literature, core ethical priorities such as transparency, privacy, fairness, inclusivity, capacity-building, and infrastructure recur, but most treatments remain high-level, with limited coverage beyond higher education and few enforceable tools. Nigerian studies underscore infrastructural constraints, governance gaps, and cultural realities, yet rarely translate these into operational standards or procurement-ready guidance for schools and ministries (Ojokheta & Omokhabi, 2024; Ofem & Chukwujama, 2024; Shittu et al., 2024a; Shittu et al., 2024b; Afolabi, 2024; Samuel & Danladi, 2025).

A major gap is the absence of a Nigeria-grounded framework spanning all educational tiers—primary, secondary, tertiary, and informal learning. Existing work concentrates on higher education or offers fragmented policy advice without addressing the full system, leaving primary, secondary, and non-formal settings underserved and producing inconsistent oversight (Ojokheta & Omokhabi, 2023; Ofem & Chukwujama, 2024; Baha & Okolo, 2024; Afolabi, 2024; Adesiji, 2024). Much of the corpus is conceptual or thematic, lacking step-by-step, enforceable roadmaps that regulators such as NITDA can implement (Ojokheta & Omokhabi, 2023; Shittu et al., 2024a; Shittu et al., 2024b; Afolabi, 2024; Ekanem & Emejulu, 2025; Allahrakha, 2024).

While challenges such as algorithmic bias, the digital divide, and accountability are acknowledged, they are typically treated without concrete national toolkits, certification processes, third-party audits, or sector-specific benchmarks. Stakeholder co-design, phased policy development, enforceable labelling, and clear public–private role delineation are sparse or only superficial, limiting real-world impact and sustainability (Ofem & Chukwujama, 2024; Shittu et al., 2024a; Shittu et al., 2024b; Samuel & Danladi, 2025; Ekanem & Emejulu, 2025; Adewale, Azeta, & Tjiraso, 2025; Adewale et al., 2024). These gaps motivate a comprehensive, Nigeria-centred and internationally aligned framework that embeds local cultural realities and maps explicitly to global guidance (e.g., UNESCO) and the national legal environment (e.g., NDPA, with implementation pathways for NITDA), providing enforceable mechanisms for accountability and compliance (United Nations Educational, Scientific and Cultural Organization [UNESCO], 2021; Federal Republic of Nigeria, 2023).

2.2 Alignment with International Frameworks and Nigeria's Legal Context

International anchors such as UNESCO's AI Ethics Recommendations provide foundational principles, while the OECD AI Principles and UNICEF's Policy Guidance on AI for Children emphasise human rights, child-centred safeguards, and accountability. Few Nigerian studies, however, map these principles to local law and education governance, particularly the Nigeria Data Protection Act and the enforcement role of the Nigeria Data Protection Commission (United Nations Educational, Scientific and Cultural Organization [UNESCO], 2021; OECD, 2019; United Nations Children's Fund [UNICEF], 2021; Federal Republic of Nigeria, 2023; Afolabi, 2024; Allahrakha, 2024).

Although many works cite UNESCO and related global guidance, detailed localisation to Nigeria's legal environment remains limited, leaving proposals insufficiently contextualised for education-sector compliance (Ojokheta & Omokhabi, 2023; Shittu et al., 2024a; Shittu et al., 2024b; Afolabi, 2024; Allahrakha, 2024). The NDPA (2023) establishes the NDPC as the supervisory authority and codifies core obligations for controllers and processors, including lawful basis, data minimisation, Data Protection Impact Assessments, breach notification, and heightened safeguards for children's data (Federal Republic of Nigeria, 2023). Ethical AI in education, therefore, requires explicit NDPA/NDPC mapping across procurement, deployment, and oversight.

Illustrative comparators include the OECD AI Principles, UNICEF's Policy Guidance on AI for Children, the EU's AI rulebook with education-relevant risk controls, and sectoral guidance such as the UK Department for Education's AI in schools resources; these exemplars inform localisation while underscoring the need for Nigerian legal and cultural tailoring (OECD, 2019; UNICEF, 2021; EU, 2024; Department for Education, 2023).

2.3 Operational Deficits and the Research Gap

Education-sector mechanisms that make ethics actionable remain under-specified: DPIAs and privacy-by-design in school systems; independent bias audits tailored to Nigerian languages; accessibility and inclusion benchmarks; procurement-linked certification; and participatory governance with teachers, PTAs, and community leaders. These deficits motivate a Nigeria-centred, enforceable framework spanning primary, secondary, tertiary, and informal settings (Ofem & Chukwujama, 2024; Shittu et al., 2024a; Shittu et al., 2024b; Samuel & Danladi, 2025; Afolabi, 2024).

While some studies recognise Nigeria's infrastructural, governance, and social realities, few embed indigenous cultural values such as communal pedagogy, multilingualism, and local stakeholder engagement within ethical AI designs. Systematic involvement of PTAs, religious and traditional leaders, and informal learning institutions is also limited, risking culturally dissonant or ineffective frameworks (Ojokheta & Omokhabi, 2023; Ofem & Chukwujama, 2024; Samuel & Danladi, 2025; Ekanem & Emejulu, 2025; Shittu et al., 2024a).

No study provides a unified, enforceable, Nigeria-specific framework mapped to UNESCO guidance across all education tiers. Most contributions concentrate on higher education, general principles, isolated issues, or non-operational adaptations. They seldom include detailed stakeholder co-design methods, clear accountability or enforcement mechanisms, public and private role delineation, or robust implementation plans with comprehensive criteria (Ojokheta & Omokhabi, 2023; Ofem & Chukwujama, 2024; Shittu et al., 2024a; Baha & Okolo, 2024; Shittu et al., 2024b; Afolabi, 2024; Samuel & Danladi, 2025; Ekanem & Emejulu, 2025).

This paper addresses these gaps by designing a unified, enforceable framework grounded in Nigerian cultural, social, and regulatory realities and aligned with UNESCO's AI ethics guidance. It spans primary, secondary, tertiary, and informal learning, and is intentionally adaptable to allow ongoing refinement through future stakeholder co-design, fostering ownership, relevance, and practical implementation.

3 Methods

This study employed a multi-layered methodological approach, integrating systematic literature analysis, comparative synthesis, contextual mapping, and stakeholder-informed design to develop an Ethical AI Framework tailored for Nigeria's education system. The process drew on global ethical AI reference points while grounding the framework in Nigeria's socio-cultural, infrastructural, and policy realities. Enforcement considerations are situated within the education sector, under the purview of the Federal Ministry of Education or other relevant bodies, in line with the principle that ministries set policies while agencies operationalise them.

3.1 Literature and Document Review

A comprehensive review was undertaken using AI-assisted search tools across Scopus, Web of Science, IEEE Xplore, and official government policy repositories. The review centred on UNESCO's AI Ethics Recommendations as the principal international reference framework for ethical principles, which were examined for their relevance to education and adapted to Nigeria's socio-cultural, infrastructural, and policy contexts. Peer-reviewed and policy literature on AI ethics, data governance, and technology integration in education, particularly within African and Nigerian settings, was also analysed to inform this localisation process. National policy and strategic instruments reviewed included the National Digital Literacy Framework (NDLF) and the Strategic Blueprint for the Federal Ministry of Communications, Innovation & Digital Economy (2023–2027), which supports President Bola Ahmed Tinubu's Renewed Hope Agenda. The specific national targets and priority areas set out in the Strategic Blueprint have already been detailed in the introduction and serve as guiding parameters for aligning UNESCO's ethical principles with Nigeria's education sector priorities. Only documents that directly engaged with AI ethics in education, or provided sector-specific adaptation insights relevant to Nigeria, were included. The synthesis ensures that UNESCO's principles are not merely adopted wholesale but are translated into enforceable, context-specific standards that reflect Nigeria's educational priorities, cultural values, and governance frameworks.

3.2 Extraction, Synthesis, and Contextual Mapping to Nigeria's Education System

From the selected literature and documents, high-level ethical principles such as transparency, fairness, accountability, and inclusivity, alongside operational measures like risk assessments, auditability, and bias mitigation, were systematically extracted to facilitate comparative synthesis. This enabled the identification of converging ethical themes and operational models across global frameworks, and divergence where practices varied. The synthesis enabled a structured crosswalk between global ethical AI principles and the specific requirements of Nigeria's education sector. These principles were then contextually mapped onto Nigeria's educational environment. Critical factors such as infrastructure constraints (intermittent power supply, low connectivity), cultural and linguistic heterogeneity (need for indigenous language support and communal pedagogy), and policy directives embedded in the NDLF and Strategic Blueprint, and variations across educational tiers (primary, secondary, tertiary, informal learning) were used to evaluate alignment with global frameworks and identify necessary adaptations. This mapping identified points where global recommendations aligned with Nigeria's needs and where adaptations were necessary to ensure operational feasibility.

3.3 Preliminary Stakeholder Engagement

Although large-scale participatory design is planned for subsequent piloting phases, this study incorporated targeted preliminary consultations with educators, EdTech developers, policymakers, and community representatives. These virtual and in-person engagements yielded valuable insights into sector-specific priorities, socio-cultural contexts, and perceived risks associated with AI deployment in education. Stakeholder perspectives directly informed the localisation of UNESCO's ethical AI principles within Nigeria's educational governance framework. To ensure both academic rigour and policy relevance, the study employed a mixed-method approach, combining a systematic literature review, national policy mapping, and empirical survey data. The literature review examined AI ethics, data governance, and educational technology integration, drawing from Scopus, Web of Science, IEEE Xplore, and official Nigerian policy repositories. Policy mapping covered the National Digital Literacy Framework (NDLF) and the Strategic Blueprint for the Federal Ministry of Communications, Innovation & Digital Economy (2023–2027). The empirical survey, conducted in 2025, captured responses from 342 stakeholders, including educators, policymakers, EdTech developers, and students representing all six geopolitical zones of Nigeria. These data collectively underpin the framework's design, ensuring its grounding in both scholarly evidence and lived realities across diverse educational settings.

3.4 Framework Construction

Insights from the literature review, comparative synthesis, contextual mapping, and preliminary stakeholder engagement were integrated into the construction of a draft Nigeria-Centred Ethical AI Framework for Education. The framework translates high-level ethical principles into enforceable standards under the education sector's regulatory structures, incorporating certification mechanisms, bias auditing processes, and data governance provisions aligned with national priorities. It is designed to function across all tiers of education, from primary schools to informal learning environments, while embedding cultural authenticity and aligning with international best practices. Phased implementation guidance ensures that adoption balances ambition with operational readiness. The framework's design is firmly anchored in reviewed literature and documented stakeholder input, with all recommendations traceable to specific references to maintain transparency, reproducibility, and contextual sensitivity.

The framework comprises seven interlinked components: (1) Principles mapped to UNESCO and local law (NDPA); (2) Governance and roles (FME, SUBEBs, NDPC, schools, vendors); (3) Data governance (lawful basis, consent, minimisation, DPIAs, breach response); (4) Algorithmic assurance (pre-deployment and annual bias audits with language and accessibility checks); (5) Procurement and certification (pre-market assurance, disclosure, and labelling); (6) Capacity-building (tiered training for teachers, leaders, and developers); and (7) Monitoring, reporting, and redress (KPIs, public dashboards, complaint-handling). Fig. 3 depicts these components and their information flows." (UNESCO, 2021; Federal Republic of Nigeria, 2023; Ofem & Chukwujama, 2024; Shittu et al., 2024a; Shittu et al., 2024b).

The framework is aligned with the Nigeria Data Protection Act (NDPA, 2023), which establishes the Nigeria Data Protection Commission (NDPC) as the regulator for personal data. Within education, NDPC sets and enforces baseline privacy obligations (lawful basis, consent, minimisation, DPIAs, breach notification). At the same time, the Federal Ministry of Education (FME) and state SUBEBs ensure sector-specific compliance through procurement, supervision, and audits. Templates and audits in this framework reference NDPA/NDPC requirements to ensure consistency and enforceability (Federal Republic of Nigeria, 2023).

4 Findings

4.1 Current State of Literature and Survey Findings

The literature demonstrates a constrained sectoral focus, with no reviewed study operationalising a comprehensive ethical framework that spans primary and secondary education, tertiary institutions, and non-formal learning contexts (Ojokheta & Omokhabi, 2023; Ofem & Chukwujama, 2024; Baha & Okolo, 2024; Afolabi, 2024; Adesiji, 2024). Nigeria-specific grounding is only partial. While some works acknowledge infrastructural, governance, and cultural challenges, such as language diversity, communal pedagogy, and compliance with the NDPA (2023), few translate these acknowledgements into actionable strategies for cultural adaptation or stakeholder integration (Ojokheta & Omokhabi, 2023; Samuel & Danladi, 2025; Ekanem & Emejulu, 2025).

International alignment, though present, is inconsistent. Several studies reference United Nations Educational, Scientific and Cultural Organisation (UNESCO) guidelines and other global ethical AI standards (Ojokheta & Omokhabi, 2023; Shittu et al., 2024a; Afolabi, 2024; Allahrakha, 2024), yet lack detailed local mapping or concrete implementation pathways. Ethical dimensions such as privacy, fairness, inclusivity, infrastructure readiness, and capacity-building recur frequently across the literature (Ojokheta & Omokhabi, 2023; Ofem & Chukwujama, 2024; Shittu et al., 2024a; Shittu et al., 2024b; Afolabi, 2024; Samuel & Danladi, 2025; Adesiji, 2024); however, specific mechanisms for stakeholder engagement, algorithmic auditing, and enforcement remain rare. Most recommendations remain at a high level, emphasising policy reform, funding strategies, and curriculum changes, without providing operational guidance for regulatory compliance or accountability frameworks (Ojokheta & Omokhabi, 2023; Shittu et al., 2024a; Shittu et al., 2024b; Adesiji, 2024). Findings from the 2025 stakeholder survey conducted by She and Tech Empowerment Foundation reinforce these gaps. Respondents cited data privacy as a key concern (64%), followed by the lack of digital literacy and AI ethics training (73%), and the absence of clear ethical AI guidelines for education (58%) (See Fig. 1). These priorities directly informed the thematic synthesis, shaping the operational focus of the proposed framework, particularly in its emphasis on enforceable standards, participatory governance, and targeted capacity-building measures.

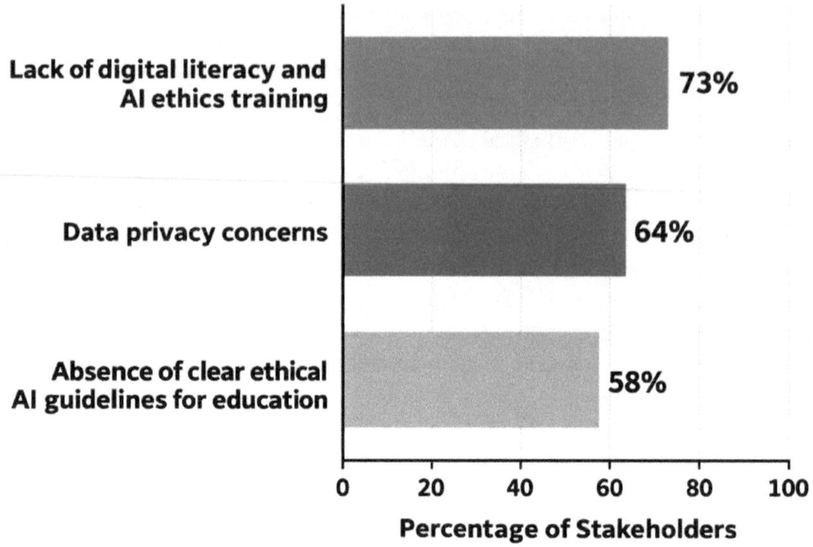

Fig. 1. Key concerns from 2025 Nigerian education stakeholder survey

4.2 Synthesis of a Robust Framework

Based on these findings, the framework addresses the key gaps explicitly identified in the literature. It is applicable across all tiers of education in Nigeria—formal primary and secondary education, tertiary institutions, and informal or non-formal learning settings—ensuring no sector is excluded. The foundational principles are drawn from the United Nations Educational, Scientific and Cultural Organisation's (UNESCO) AI Ethics Recommendations, operationalised for Nigeria through explicit mapping to the National Digital Literacy Framework (NDLF), the Strategic Blueprint for the Federal Ministry of Communications, Innovation & Digital Economy, and the policy guidelines of the Federal Ministry of Education (Ojokheta & Omokhabi, 2023; Shittu et al., 2024a; Shittu et al., 2024b; Afolabi, 2024). The framework adopts a human-centred design approach, ensuring that AI empowers learners and educators, respects human dignity, and enhances educational outcomes without replacing human judgement. It is deeply grounded in Nigeria's cultural and social realities, mandating indigenous language support, adaptation to communal and Ubuntu-like learning traditions, and recognition of oral knowledge systems (Ojokheta & Omokhabi, 2023; Samuel & Danladi, 2025; Ekanem & Emejulu, 2025). AI solutions are expected to reflect Nigerian cultural values, including linguistic diversity—Hausa, Yoruba, Igbo, and Nigerian Pidgin—communal learning styles, and local pedagogies.

Participatory governance is integral, requiring the inclusion of diverse stakeholders such as teachers' unions, Parent-Teacher Associations, religious and traditional leaders, EdTech small and medium enterprises, and students in the design, oversight, and review processes (Ojokheta & Omokhabi, 2023; Baha & Okolo, 2024). Continuous involvement of teachers, students, parents, community leaders, policymakers, and technology providers is built into the design, deployment, and evaluation phases. In the area of data privacy and sovereignty, the framework mandates in-country hosting of educational data, strict consent protocols, and regular transparency audits (Ojokheta & Omokhabi, 2023; Shittu et al., 2024a; Afolabi, 2024). Algorithmic fairness and bias mitigation are supported through independent, periodic audits for linguistic, ethnic, gender, and other forms of bias, ensuring alignment with curricular content and social diversity (Ofem & Chukwujama, 2024; Shittu et al., 2024a; Samuel & Danladi, 2025). AI must be designed to prevent discriminatory outcomes based on language, ethnicity, gender, region, or socio-economic status, promoting equal opportunities for all learners (Adewale et al., 2026; Adewale et al., 2025; Sambo-Magaji et al., 2025).

Bridging the digital divide is addressed by prioritising offline and low-bandwidth AI solutions, implementing phased rollouts to marginalised regions, and targeting support for underserved communities (Ofem & Chukwujama, 2024; Samuel & Danladi, 2025; Adesiji, 2024). AI solutions must also account for resource constraints, sustainable energy use, and long-term viability in Nigeria's educational context. Capacity building is a central pillar, involving tiered training in digital literacy and AI ethics for students, educators, and policymakers, along with ongoing curriculum integration and the establishment of national competence centres (Ofem & Chukwujama, 2024; Shittu et al., 2024a; Baha & Okolo, 2024; Afolabi, 2024; Adesiji, 2024). Accountability and enforcement are to be overseen by the Ministry of Education or the relevant education sector authority. Measures include certification of all AI tools used in education, mandatory third-party impact audits, penalties for non-compliance, and linking procurement incentives to ethical compliance (Shao et al., 2023; Ojokheta & Omokhabi, 2023; Shittu et al., 2024a; Shittu et al., 2024b). Policy phasing allows for staged adoption, beginning with voluntary codes of practice and pilot projects, followed by regulation and standardisation. This includes distinct approaches for public schools, emphasising open-source solutions and private providers, who must meet mandatory disclosure and certification requirements (Shao et al., 2023; Ojokheta & Omokhabi, 2023; Shittu et al., 2024a; Shittu et al., 2024b; Samuel & Danladi, 2025).

Finally, the framework calls for regular benchmarking against the African Union's digital and education strategies, UNESCO's global standards, and other relevant Global South metrics to ensure Nigeria's AI-in-education initiatives remain competitive, contextually relevant, and internationally aligned (Ofem & Chukwujama, 2024; Shittu et al., 2024b; Samuel & Danladi, 2025; Allahrakha, 2024). The synthesis of the framework explicitly addresses the quantified needs identified in the survey. Capacity building measures directly target the 73% of stakeholders who cited insufficient training, while data sovereignty provisions respond to the 64% expressing privacy concerns. Participatory governance structures are designed to improve stakeholder engagement, addressing the 58% who reported an absence of clear guidelines. By mapping each framework component to an empirically validated need, this synthesis ensures both relevance and enforceability in the Nigerian educational context.

4.3 Standards

All AI educational platforms must comply with the Nigeria Data Protection Act (NDPA, 2023), including documented lawful basis and consent, data minimisation, mandatory

Data Protection Impact Assessments (DPIAs) for high-risk processing, breach notification, and secure in-country hosting. Compliance is subject to oversight by the Nigeria Data Protection Commission (NDPC), with sector-specific enforcement by the Federal/State education authorities through procurement conditions and routine audits (Federal Republic of Nigeria, 2023). Independent, periodic audits are mandatory to detect and mitigate biases in AI models, with the results publicly reported to promote accountability. AI tools are required to provide robust language support, covering at least the three major Nigerian languages, such as Hausa, Yoruba, and Igbo, alongside Nigerian Pidgin, particularly for primary and secondary education contexts. Platforms must also meet recognised accessibility standards, such as WCAG 2.1, to ensure inclusive access for learners with disabilities. Transparency is a critical element, requiring AI vendors to provide explainable models and user-friendly information detailing AI decision logic. Certification of AI education products is to be administered by the Ministry of Education or the appropriate education sector regulatory body, confirming compliance with ethical, privacy, and technical standards before deployment.

Strong data security measures are expected, including encryption, secure in-country hosting, and clearly defined incident response plans for data breaches. Capacity building is embedded as a requirement, with minimum training hours on AI ethics and digital literacy mandated for educators and administrators before AI adoption. Monitoring and reporting mechanisms must track AI usage and measure its impact against agreed key performance indicators, including equity of access and improvements in learning outcomes. Implementation will follow defined roll-out phases, starting with pilot projects and moving to wider deployment, supported by continuous evaluation and structured stakeholder feedback loops. Fig. 2 illustrates the proposed framework's core components and their interrelationships. Fig. 3 presents a Nigeria-centred ethical AI governance stack that runs from inputs to outcomes. Legal and international anchors on the left, including the Nigeria Data Protection Act and the Nigeria Data Protection Commission alongside UNESCO, OECD, and UNICEF guidance, inform a set of localised principles and a governance layer that assigns clear mandates to education authorities, schools, vendors, and communities.

From this governance layer, three assurance tracks operate in parallel. Data governance covers lawful basis, consent, minimisation, Data Protection Impact Assessments, and breach response. Algorithmic assurance addresses bias auditing with attention to Nigerian languages and accessibility. Procurement and certification provide pre-market assurance, documented disclosure, and labelling so that only compliant systems reach classrooms. Outputs from these tracks flow directly to sector deployment across primary, secondary, tertiary, and informal education. The same outputs also drive capacity-building, where tiered training equips teachers, school leaders, and developers to meet their obligations, which in turn supports deployment. Monitoring, reporting, and redress close the loop through KPIs, dashboards, complaint handling, and remediation, feeding results back to governance and to the principles layer for continuous improvement.

UNESCO's guidelines provide universally endorsed ethical principles and high-level recommendations. The proposed Nigeria-specific adaptation builds on these by operationalising the principles for the Nigerian educational context—embedding indigenous language support, alignment with national law such as the NDPA (2023), integration of

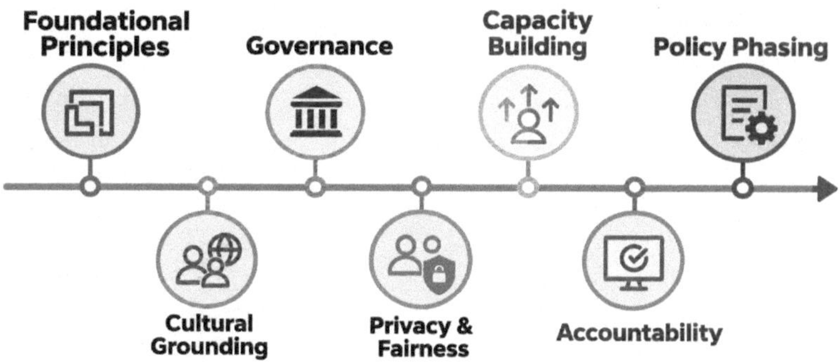

Fig. 2. Framework core pillars sequence

priorities from the National Digital Literacy Framework and the Strategic Blueprint of the Federal Ministry of Communications, Innovation & Digital Economy, and reflection of specific community and sector realities. Enforcement mechanisms are designed to operate under the Ministry of Education or other relevant education sector authorities, ensuring that ethical standards are not only aspirational but actionable. Table 1 provides a side-by-side comparison of the UNESCO Ethical AI Framework (as described in Afolabi, 2024; Allahrakha, 2024; Shittu et al., 2024b; UNESCO, 2021) and the Nigeria-contextualised framework synthesised in this exercise. All entries are strictly drawn from explicit reference content or from the synthesis steps presented above (Fig. 2).

Table 1. UNESCO vs. Nigeria context frameworks

Dimension	UNESCO Framework	Nigeria Context Framework
Foundational Principles	Human rights, transparency, accountability, privacy, fairness, sustainability (Shittu et al., 2024a; Allahrakha, 2024; Afolabi, 2024; Ojokheta & Omokhabi, 2023)	Same principles explicitly mapped to the Nigeria Data Protection Act (NDPA, 2023) and enforced by the Nigeria Data Protection Commission (NDPC); with sector implementation led by the Ministry of Education and, where relevant, technical support from NITDA. (Shittu et al., 2024a; Shittu et al., 2024b; Afolabi, 2024; Ojokheta & Omokhabi, 2023)
Scope	Global, all sectors (Allahrakha, 2024)	Multi-tier: primary and secondary education, tertiary, and informal education (Shittu et al., 2024a; Shittu et al., 2024b; Afolabi, 2024; Ojokheta & Omokhabi, 2023)

(*continued*)

Table 1. (*continued*)

Dimension	UNESCO Framework	Nigeria Context Framework
Cultural Grounding	Respect cultural diversity (Allahrakha, 2024)	Indigenous languages, communal pedagogy, oral traditions (Ojokheta & Omokhabi, 2023; Samuel & Danladi, 2025; Ekanem & Emejulu, 2025)
Stakeholder Engagement	General inclusion (Allahrakha, 2024)	Mandatory participation of teachers, Parent-Teacher Associations (PTAs), community leaders, EdTech stakeholders, and students (Ojokheta & Omokhabi, 2023; Baha & Okolo, 2024)
Data Privacy	Strong privacy and informed consent (Allahrakha, 2024)	NDPA compliance, in-country hosting, explicit consent and minimisation, mandatory DPIAs for high-risk processing, and coordinated oversight by NDPC with sector enforcement by education authorities (Federal Republic of Nigeria, 2023; Ojokheta & Omokhabi, 2023; Shittu et al., 2024a; Afolabi, 2024).
Algorithmic Fairness	Avoid discrimination (Allahrakha, 2024)	Regular Nigeria-specific bias audits addressing linguistic, ethnic, and gender biases (Ofem & Chukwujama, 2024; Shittu et al., 2024a; Samuel & Danladi, 2025)
Digital Divide	Promote inclusivity (Allahrakha, 2024)	Offline and low-bandwidth AI solutions, phased rural rollout (Ofem & Chukwujama, 2024; Samuel & Danladi, 2025; Adesiji, 2024)
Capacity Building	Digital literacy and skills training (Allahrakha, 2024)	Tiered training programmes, competence centres, and tailored curricula (Ofem & Chukwujama, 2024; Shittu et al., 2024a; Baha & Okolo, 2024; Afolabi, 2024; Adesiji, 2024)

(*continued*)

Table 1. (*continued*)

Dimension	UNESCO Framework	Nigeria Context Framework
Accountability	Recommend regulation (Allahrakha, 2024)	NITDA certification requirements, mandatory third-party audits, and penalties for non-compliance (Ojokheta & Omokhabi, 2023; Shittu et al., 2024a; Shittu et al., 2024b)
Policy Phasing	Implementation planning (Allahrakha, 2024)	Staged adoption including pilots, regulatory phases, and public/private oversight streams (Ojokheta & Omokhabi, 2023; Shittu et al., 2024a; Shittu et al., 2024b; Samuel & Danladi, 2025)
Public vs. Private	Universal principles (Allahrakha, 2024)	Public sector: open-source solutions; Private sector: mandatory certification and disclosures (Ojokheta & Omokhabi, 2023; Afolabi, 2024; Samuel & Danladi, 2025)
Benchmarking	Benchmarking and international cooperation (Allahrakha, 2024)	Benchmarking against African Union strategies, UNESCO global standards, and Global South metrics (Ofem & Chukwujama, 2024; Shittu et al., 2024b; Samuel & Danladi, 2025; Allahrakha, 2024)

5 Discussion

Economic benefits and strong ethical standards are not mutually exclusive; they can reinforce each other when technological investments balance profitability with respect for human values (Shao, Marwa, & Matendo, 2023). Allocating resources to ethical Artificial Intelligence (AI) should not be viewed as an overhead cost but as a strategic investment, mitigating financial risks, fostering trust, and enabling sustained revenue generation. This approach can yield measurable, long-term economic and societal gains (Shittu et al., 2024a). The proposed framework advances both the letter and spirit of the reviewed literature. It addresses persistent deficiencies by ensuring comprehensive sectoral coverage, spanning primary and secondary education, tertiary institutions, and informal learning, which is absent in existing models. Ethical principles are not merely acknowledged; they are operationalised through measurable compliance mechanisms tailored to Nigeria's socio-cultural, linguistic, and legal contexts (Shittu et al., 2024a; Shittu et al., 2024b; Afolabi, 2024). By embedding indigenous cultural values and ensuring alignment with communal pedagogies and multilingual realities (Ojokheta &

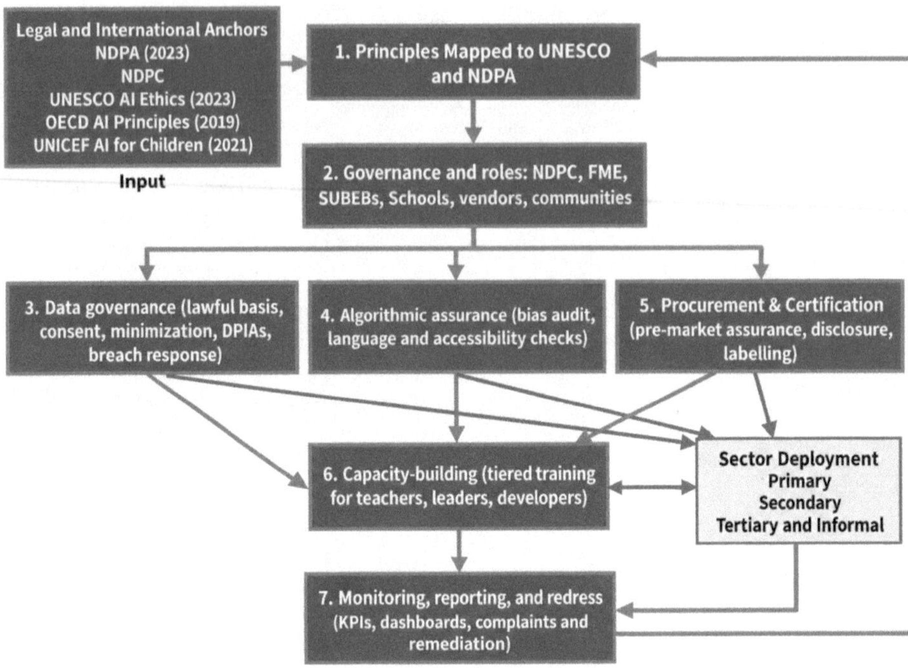

Fig. 3. Conceptual Components and Flows of the Nigeria-Centred Ethical AI Framework

Omokhabi, 2023; Samuel & Danladi, 2025), the framework promotes equity, legitimacy, and broad societal buy-in. Accountability is strengthened through enforceable certification, third-party auditing, and remediation pathways, directly addressing the enforcement gaps identified in prior work (Ojokheta & Omokhabi, 2023; Afolabi, 2024). Furthermore, the inclusion of benchmarking against African Union digital and education strategies, UNESCO standards, and Global South metrics (Ofem & Chukwujama, 2024; Shittu et al., 2024b) ensures that Nigeria's AI-in-education initiatives remain globally competitive while being contextually grounded. Nevertheless, certain limitations persist. These include the need for large-scale, empirical piloting across multiple education tiers and the absence of detailed, stakeholder-designed operational mechanisms. These gaps present clear priorities for future research and iterative refinement through participatory processes.

5.1 Future Research Directions and Immediate Next Steps

Within 0–3 months, constitute a national working group (NITDA, Federal/State Ministries of Education, leading universities, EdTech firms, and community organisations), secure pilot funding from existing government allocations and private partners, and select diverse pilot sites using clear criteria (geopolitical zones, urban–rural mix, and major linguistic groups).

Run 6–12-month pilots across primary/secondary schools, tertiary institutions, and informal learning centres. Maintain continuous data collection and stakeholder engagement (teachers, students, parents, developers, cultural leaders) through surveys, focus groups, and co-design workshops to iteratively refine the framework. Disseminate findings at 9–12 months via open-access peer-reviewed publications and national conferences, then prepare a scale-up plan within a further six months, embedding mechanisms for ongoing adaptation to changing needs and technologies. The proposed structured pilot protocol is as follows:

I. Legal and privacy assurance: complete DPIAs, test consent workflows with parents and learners, and verify NDPA compliance via NDPC-licensed/accredited data protection compliance providers (Federal Republic of Nigeria, 2023).
II. Algorithmic assurance: conduct pre-deployment and annual audits for linguistic, gender, regional, and disability bias using local classroom datasets.
III. Accessibility and inclusion: verify WCAG 2.1 AA conformance and offline/low-bandwidth operation.
IV. Capacity-building: deliver role-specific training with pre–/post assessments for teachers and leaders.
V. Monitoring and reporting: track KPIs on access equity, user satisfaction, privacy incidents, and learning outcomes.
VI. Governance and redress: establish site-level oversight committees and a complaints pathway with remediation SLAs (Shittu et al., 2024a; Shittu et al., 2024b; Ofem & Chukwujama, 2024; Afolabi, 2024; Federal Republic of Nigeria, 2023). Each pilot runs for one academic term, with mixed-methods evaluation comparing baseline and endline metrics, independent verification, and public reporting.

Within 12 months, initiate comparative studies with peer African contexts to surface best practices and strengthen regional collaboration. Empirical piloting and local adaptation currently missing in Nigerian AI-in-education ethics are essential to ground policy in real-world evidence, build trust, and maximise cultural, social, and technological relevance for Nigerian learners.

6 Practical Guide for Empirical Piloting and Local Adaptation of AI Ethics Frameworks in Nigerian Education

This framework is intended to support the policy vision established by the Federal Ministry of Communications, Innovation & Digital Economy (FMCIDE) and provide actionable mechanisms for implementation by the Ministry of Education and other relevant education sector regulatory bodies, in line with the 2023–2027 Strategic Blueprint and the National Digital Literacy Framework (NDLF).

6.1 Empirical Piloting: Key Practical Steps

Piloting will be conducted across diverse settings to ensure representativeness. Education sites will be selected from formal primary and secondary schools—both urban and rural—tertiary institutions, and informal learning centres, ensuring regional and linguistic diversity (Afolabi, 2024; Samuel & Danladi, 2025; Shittu et al., 2024a). Participatory oversight committees will be established at each pilot site, including teachers, parents, students, EdTech small and medium enterprises (SMEs), and community leaders (Ofem & Chukwujama, 2024). These committees will guide framework implementation, integrating NDPA (2023) and NDPC regulation-compliant data privacy measures and local data hosting protocols (Allahrakha, 2024). AI tools will be adapted to Nigerian languages and cultural contexts (Afolabi, 2024; Shittu et al., 2024a), with regular algorithmic bias audits conducted using local classroom data (Shittu et al., 2024b). Contextualised training on digital literacy and AI ethics will be delivered to educators, policymakers, and administrators (Shittu et al., 2024b; Ofem & Chukwujama, 2024; Samuel & Danladi, 2025). Outcome measurement will involve monitoring equity of access, privacy incidents, stakeholder satisfaction, fairness audit results, and participation in training programmes, with benchmarking against UNESCO indicators and other global metrics (Shittu et al., 2024b; Allahrakha, 2024; Samuel & Danladi, 2025; UNESCO, 2021). Following each pilot phase, structured stakeholder feedback will be collected through surveys and focus groups, enabling iterative refinement of the framework based on local experience and lessons learned (Shittu et al., 2024b).

6.2 Local Adaptation: Key Practical Steps

Participatory governance will be embedded through advisory panels at pilot sites, comprising teachers, Parent-Teacher Associations, traditional leaders, and students, to provide contextual feedback and safeguard community norms (Ofem & Chukwujama, 2024; Samuel & Danladi, 2025; Shittu et al., 2024a) (See Fig. 4). AI tools will be localised using Nigerian language data and adapted to incorporate communal pedagogy approaches (Afolabi, 2024; Samuel & Danladi, 2025; Shittu et al., 2024a), with collaboration from local EdTech companies to produce tailored solutions. Policy protocols will be adjusted to meet state-level requirements, with a phased approach moving from pilot projects to nationwide implementation (Fig. 5). The Ministry of Education-led "AI in Education Ethics" certification scheme will be developed to ensure ethical compliance before deployment (Allahrakha, 2024). Capacity building initiatives will be tailored to regional and learner-specific needs, following comprehensive baseline assessments (Shittu et al., 2024b; Ofem & Chukwujama, 2024; Samuel & Danladi, 2025).

6.3 Policy Implementation Recommendations

For effective operationalisation, Nigerian policymakers and regulators, particularly the Ministry of Education, should institutionalise mandatory certification, requiring all AI educational technologies to comply with ethical, privacy, and technical standards before deployment. A National AI in Education Ethics Oversight Committee should be established, with representatives from education, technology, civil society, and cultural sectors, to monitor compliance, review audit reports, and guide policy development. Data sovereignty regulations must be strictly enforced, mandating local hosting of educational data and adherence to NDPA (2023) and NDPC provisions to protect privacy. Nationwide capacity-building programmes should be funded for educators, administrators, and developers, focusing on AI ethics, bias mitigation, and digital literacy. Phased rollouts should begin with pilot projects across diverse regions, incorporating stakeholder feedback before scaling nationally. Transparent reporting on AI system impacts, bias audit results, and user feedback should be mandated to maintain public accountability and trust. These integrated measures will help transition the framework from policy design to practical application, fostering a safe, equitable, and culturally relevant AI ecosystem within Nigeria's education sector.

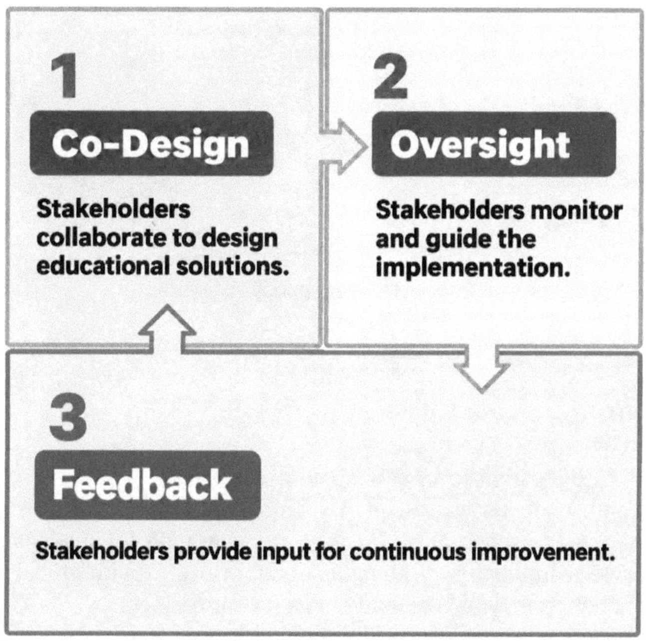

Fig. 4. Stakeholder engagement cycle

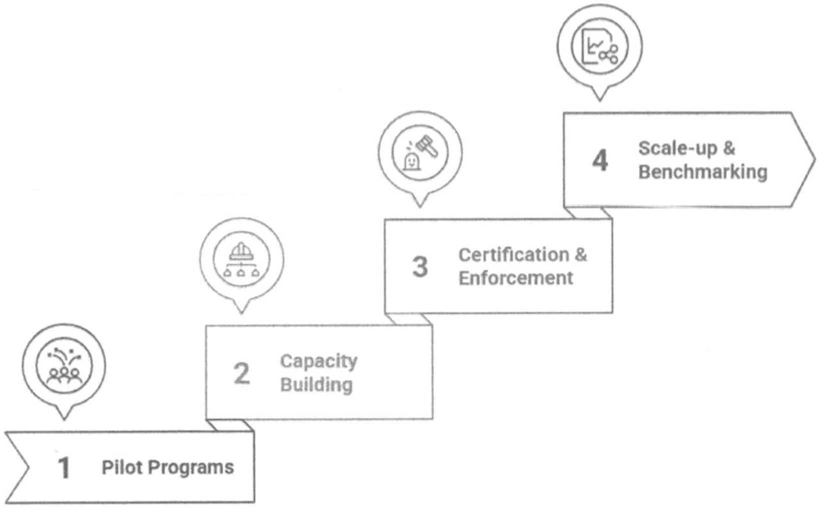

Fig. 5. Achieving policy scale-up

7 Conclusion

This framework bridges high-level ethics and operational practice and offers a model other Global South contexts can adapt. By embedding local realities, legal requirements, and participatory governance, it sets a practical path for sustainable, inclusive, and responsible AI in education. It aligns national priorities with global AI ethics and speaks to researchers, policymakers, and development partners.

Existing literature provides useful insights but lacks a comprehensive, enforceable framework across all education tiers. This paper addresses that gap with a unified, Nigeria-centred framework grounded in UNESCO's AI Ethics Recommendations and aligned with national law, the National Digital Literacy Framework, and the Strategic Blueprint of the Federal Ministry of Communications, Innovation and Digital Economy. The design prioritises inclusivity, data privacy, algorithmic fairness, and participatory governance, with capacity building and phased implementation to match ambition with readiness. Next steps are empirical pilots and sustained stakeholder engagement under the Ministry of Education, ensuring the framework remains relevant, enforceable, and effective as technologies and educational needs evolve.

Declaration. This framework is the product of independent academic research. It is not an official policy and does not reflect the position of any government institution, including the Federal Ministry of Education and the Federal Ministry of Communications, Innovation and Digital Economy, nor does it constitute institutional endorsement. It is offered in good faith to prompt dialogue and inform ethical, inclusive, locally grounded AI integration in Nigerian education, and may be considered for adaptation, refinement, or formal adoption through appropriate channels.

References

Adesiji, T.: Integrating artificial intelligence in Nigerian university curricula: challenges, opportunities, and prospects. In: 2024 IEEE 5th International Conference on Electro-Computing Technologies for Humanity (NIGERCON) (2024). https://doi.org/10.1109/NIGERCON62786.2024.10927366

Adewale, M.D., Azeta, A., Abayomi-Alli, A., Sambo-Magaji, A.: Artificial intelligence impact on learner outcomes in distance education: a process-based framework and research model. In: Awotunde, J.B., Imoize, A.L., Lee, C.C. (eds.) Emerging Technologies for Developing Countries: AFRICATEK 2024 Lecture Notes of the Institute for Computer Sciences, Social Informatics and Telecommunications Engineering, vol. 618. Springer (2026). https://doi.org/10.1007/978-3-031-93557-2_13

Adewale, M.D., Azeta, A., Tjiraso, S.: Ensuring equity and integrity in academic performance prediction in open and distance learning. In: AI Roles and Responsibilities in Education (Signals and Communication Technology). Springer International Publishing AG (2025). https://doi.org/10.1007/978-3-031-96855-6_6

Adewale, M.D., et al.: Ethical framework for integrating artificial intelligence in open and distance learning. In: Proceedings of the 8th EAI International Conference on Computer Science and Engineering (EAI COMPSE 2024), Laredo, TX, USA (2024). https://doi.org/10.1007/978-3-031-94630-1_18

Afolabi, A.: Ethical issues in artificial intelligence adoption in African higher education institutions in Nigeria. Afr. J. In. Knowl. Manag. (2024). https://doi.org/10.47604/ajikm.2735

Allahrakha, N.: UNESCO's AI ethics principles: challenges and opportunities. Int. J. Law Policy. **13**(17), 5 (2024) https://doi.org/10.59022/ijlp.225

Baha, B.Y., Okolo, O.: Navigating the ethical dilemma of generative AI in higher educational institutions in Nigeria using the TOE framework. Eur. J. Comput. Sci. Inf. Technol. (2024). https://doi.org/10.37745/ejcsit.2013/vol12n81840

Department for Education: Generative artificial intelligence (AI) in education (2023). Retrieved 19 Oct 2025, from https://www.gov.uk/government/publications/generative-artificial-intelligence-in-education

Ekanem, S.A., Emejulu, J.: An Essencist assessment of the impacts of artificial intelligence on educational development in Nigeria. Int. J. Arts Humanit. 3(1), 27–35 (2025). https://doi.org/10.61424/ijah.v3i1.254

European Union: Regulation (EU) 2024/1689 of the European Parliament and of the Council of 13 June 2024 laying down harmonised rules on artificial intelligence (Artificial Intelligence Act) (2024). Retrieved 19 Oct 2025, from https://eur-lex.europa.eu/eli/reg/2024/1689/oj/eng

Federal Ministry of Communications, Innovation and Digital Economy: Strategic blueprint 2023–2027: Accelerating our collective prosperity through technical efficiency (2023). https://fmcide.gov.ng/wp-content/uploads/2023/11/blueprint.pdf

Federal Republic of Nigeria: Nigeria Data Protection Act (NDPA) 2023. Nigeria Data Protection Commission (2023). Retrieved 19 Oct 2025, from https://ndpc.gov.ng/wp-content/uploads/2024/03/Nigeria_Data_Protection_Act_2023.pdf

National Information Technology Development Agency: National digital literacy framework (Version 1.4). Federal Ministry of Communications and Digital Economy (2023). https://nitda.gov.ng/wp-content/uploads/2023/07/Digital-Literacy-Framework.pdf

Ofem, U., Chukwujama, G.: Sustainable artificial intelligence-driven classroom assessment in higher institutions: lessons from Estonia, China, the USA, and Australia for Nigeria. Eur. J. Interact. Multimedia Educ. 5(2), e02403 (2024). https://doi.org/10.30935/ejimed/15265

Ojokheta, K.O., Omokhabi, A.A.: Project initiatives on inclusive and equitable use of artificial intelligence in education: lessons derivable for policy direction in Nigeria. COUNS-EDU: Int. J. Couns. Educ. (2023). https://doi.org/10.23916/0020230845430

Organisation for Economic Co-operation and Development: Recommendation of the Council on Artificial Intelligence (2019). Retrieved 19 Oct 2025, from https://legalinstruments.oecd.org/en/instruments/OECD-LEGAL-0449

Sambo-Magaji, A., Adewale, M.D., Ketebu, K.E., Jokthan, G.E., Bello, M., Azeta, A.A., Sheikh, F.A., Ubadike, O.C.: Systematic literature review: challenges, implications, and frameworks for artificial intelligence adoption in Nigerian education. NIPES J. Sci. Technol. Res. 7(2) (2025). https://doi.org/10.37933/nipes/7.4.2025.si341

Samuel, I., Danladi, A.: Shaping the future of STEM education in Nigeria through artificial intelligence. J. Afr. Innov. Adv. Stud. **7**(2) (2025) https://doi.org/10.70382/ajaias.v7i2.011

Shao, D., Marwa, N., Matendo, D.: Regulatory strategies for fostering responsible AI innovation in African economies. In: Proceedings of the 2023 First International Conference on Advancements of Artificial Intelligence in African Context (AAIAC) (2023) https://doi.org/10.1109/AAIAC60008.2023.10465404

Shittu, R.A., et al.: Ethics in technology: developing ethical guidelines for AI and digital transformation in Nigeria. International journal of multidisciplinary research and growth. Evaluation. (2024a) https://doi.org/10.54660/.IJMRGE.2021.2.1-401-412

Shittu, R.A., et al.: Policy frameworks for artificial intelligence adoption: strategies for successful implementation in Nigeria. International journal of social science exceptional. Research. (2024b) https://doi.org/10.54660/ijsser.2024.3.6.105-116

United Nations Children's Fund: Policy guidance on AI for children (2021). Retrieved 19 Oct 2025, from https://www.unicef.org/innocenti/reports/policy-guidance-ai-children

United Nations Educational, Scientific and Cultural Organization: Recommendation on the ethics of artificial intelligence (2021). Retrieved 19 Oct 2025, from https://unesdoc.unesco.org/ark:/48223/pf0000380455

Zalabak, M., Dhamodharan, B., Lesieur, B., Magnusson, O., Kennedy, S., Krishnan, S.: The ROI of AI ethics: Profiting with principles for the future. Global Alliance for Digital Education and Sustainability (GADES) (2025). https://www.ibm.com/thought-leadership/institute-business-value/en-us/report/roi-ai-ethics

Towards a Real-Time Mobile-Based Driver Behavior Monitoring Using Lightweight Deep Learning Models

Nasser Kimbugwe(✉), Namayanja Patricia Linda, Barisigara Simon, Ainaamani Douglas Bagambe, and Shema Collins

Makerere University, Kampala, Uganda
nasser.kimbugwe@mak.ac.ug

Abstract. Road safety remains a critical concern in Uganda, where human error and risky driver behavior significantly contribute to traffic accidents. This study presents the design, development, and evaluation of a Driver Behavior Monitoring System (DBMS) using lightweight deep learning techniques embedded within a mobile application. The proposed system leverages YOLOv8-based object detection, sensor fusion, and cloud integration to detect and analyze risky behaviors such as drowsiness, phone usage, and smoking in real time. The model was trained using Vicomtech open datasets and deployed on Android devices using PyTorch Lite, ensuring low-latency, offline-capable detection. A React-based web dashboard enables fleet managers to monitor driver behavior and access performance reports. The paper outlines the system architecture, data collection methods, model training pipeline, implementation tools, and test results. Results from field deployment and simulated tests indicate high accuracy in behavior detection (>90%) and usability in Ugandan transport contexts. The system provides an affordable, scalable solution for improving road safety and transport management in developing countries.

Keywords: Driver Monitoring System · YOLOv8 · Real-Time Detection · Mobile App · Fleet Safety · Uganda · Road Safety · Deep Learning · PyTorch Lite · React DashboardFirst Section

1 Introduction

Globally, road accidents remain one of the leading causes of injury and death, with low- and middle-income countries disproportionately affected due to limited infrastructure, enforcement, and driver training. In Uganda, the situation is particularly dire, where over 90% of traffic accidents are linked to human-related factors, primarily unsafe driving behaviors such as drowsiness, mobile phone usage, and general inattentiveness [1, 2] . With the rise in the number of vehicles on Ugandan roads and limited resources for enforcement, there is a growing need for cost-effective, scalable, and real-time driver monitoring systems that can be deployed without the need for expensive vehicle installations.

A. Oluwatope et al. (Eds.): AFRICOMM 2025, LNICST 713, pp. 149–160, 2027.
https://doi.org/10.1007/978-3-032-38682-3_9

Recent advancements in mobile computing and artificial intelligence (AI) have created new opportunities for real-time behavior analysis using smartphones. Smartphones are equipped with a suite of sensors (camera, GPS, accelerometer) and have sufficient computing capacity to support edge-based AI processing [3, 4]. Edge AI brings the promise of performing real-time analytics without constant reliance on cloud connectivity, a crucial consideration in regions with limited or unreliable internet access.

This study proposes a Driver Behavior Monitoring System (DBMS) that leverages the ubiquity of smartphones and integrates lightweight deep learning models for behavior classification. The system is designed to detect critical behaviors such as drowsiness, mobile phone usage, lack of seatbelt use, and smoking while driving. Detection results are presented to drivers through visual and auditory alerts and synchronized to a central dashboard for review by fleet managers. Unlike traditional in-vehicle systems that require costly installations, this solution utilizes mobile phones and a cloud-based infrastructure to enable real-time analytics and reporting.

The DBMS employs a YOLOv8 model customized and trained using Vicomtech datasets, optimized for mobile inference through PyTorch Lite. The system architecture comprises edge (vehicle) processing, cloud synchronization, and a React-based web application for visualization and reporting. Key contributions of this paper include: (i) a mobile-optimized deep learning architecture for driver behavior monitoring; (ii) real-time alerting and offline operability; (iii) integration of Firebase for cloud logging and real-time dashboard analytics; and (iv) system testing in a realistic Ugandan context.

This paper is structured as follows: Sect. 2 reviews related work in driver behavior monitoring, deep learning on edge devices, and mobile-based safety solutions. Section 3 details the system design, including hardware/software components, model training, and integration. Section 4 presents performance evaluations.

2 Related Work

Understanding driver behavior is a critical research area in the development of intelligent transportation systems. Recent developments in artificial intelligence (AI), computer vision, and mobile computing have enabled the implementation of real-time driver monitoring systems (DMS), especially in resource-constrained settings. This section reviews key developments in the field and categorizes them into major subthemes.

2.1 Traditional Driver Monitoring Systems

Initial efforts in driver monitoring focused on vehicle-embedded systems using dedicated hardware such as infrared cameras, steering sensors, and vehicle control units. These systems were effective but prohibitively expensive and invasive, making them unsuitable for widespread adoption in developing countries [5, 6]. Moreover, their installation required modification of vehicle systems, posing challenges for retrofitting in existing fleets.

2.2 Computer Vision and Deep Learning for Behavior Detection

Advances in computer vision and deep learning introduced robust methods for analyzing driver facial expressions, eye movements, and gestures. CNNs have proven effective in classifying distracted driving behaviors, such as using mobile phones or eating while driving. Hossain et al. [7] demonstrated the potential of CNN-based models for multi-class driver behavior classification. Kashevnik and Lindow [8] enhanced this approach using transfer learning on pre-trained VGG-16 models, achieving high accuracy in image-based distraction detection.

Despite the successes, these models often require high computational resources, which limits their use on embedded or mobile platforms. This limitation has prompted research into lightweight models that balance performance and efficiency.

2.3 Lightweight Models for Edge and Mobile Deployment

The emergence of efficient architectures such as MobileNet, SqueezeNet, and YOLO variants (YOLOv3-tiny, YOLOv5, YOLOv8) has significantly reduced the inference burden. YOLOv8, in particular, offers favorable trade-offs between speed and accuracy for object detection tasks [9]. Combined with frameworks like PyTorch Lite, these models can now be deployed on smartphones without requiring GPUs or internet access [10, 11]

In the context of mobile deployment, researchers have also explored TensorFlow Lite and ONNX as alternatives for model conversion and integration. The emphasis has shifted to edge AI, where inference is done directly on the device, minimizing latency and preserving data privacy [12].

2.4 Drowsiness and Fatigue Detection Techniques

Drowsiness remains a leading contributor to road accidents. Techniques for detecting fatigue have evolved from classical image processing methods—such as Viola-Jones face detection—to hybrid approaches integrating deep learning. Hari and Praveen [13] proposed combining blink detection with head pose estimation for early signs of drowsiness. Hanane et al. [14] implemented a smartphone-based fatigue detector using front camera feeds, reporting accuracy over 85%.

Recent studies have also employed LSTM networks to capture temporal features of fatigue behaviors, such as prolonged eye closure or yawning patterns [15]. However, these models are still largely confined to research settings due to their complexity.

2.5 Mobile-Based Driver Monitoring Systems

Mobile-based DMS platforms provide a promising low-cost solution for developing regions. Toshiyuki and Hiroaki [16] designed a smartphone application that used the front-facing camera to detect fatigue and distractions. While accuracy was moderate (85%), the approach validated the potential for low-cost implementations.

Beg et al. [10] created a mobile assistant for drivers using YOLO and PyTorch Lite, optimized for low bandwidth and processing environments. Their system detected unsafe driving actions with over 90% precision. Open-source datasets and model compression techniques have further accelerated mobile DMS research.

2.6 Fleet Management and Cloud Integration

Cloud-connected dashboards have enhanced the usability of DMS platforms, especially for logistics companies. Alexander et.al [17] developed a cloud-based vehicle monitoring system that aggregates real-time driver behavior data. Similarly, OpenFleet [18] introduced a live dashboard for vehicle tracking, alert monitoring, and report generation. Integration with services like Firebase and PostgreSQL allows for seamless synchronization and data visualization.

Haibin & Ning [19] emphasized the value of cross-platform apps that connect mobile detection with fleet-level reporting. In Uganda's context, where 3G coverage is common but intermittent, systems must support both offline logging and delayed cloud sync, as achieved in the current study.

2.7 Privacy-Preserving and Explainable AI Approaches

As video and biometric data are sensitive, privacy is a growing concern in DMS development. Jayant et al. [20] proposed using federated learning to train models locally and share only weight updates with the server. This method protects raw data and reduces transmission load.

Explainable AI (XAI) is another important trend. Tools like SHAP and Grad-CAM allow developers to visualize why a model flagged certain behavior, improving trust and interpretability [21, 22]. Future driver monitoring tools may integrate these techniques to comply with regulations and user expectations.

2.8 Contextualization for Uganda and Similar Regions

Despite the global advances in DMS, very few solutions have been tailored to the challenges of low-income countries. Uganda, for instance, faces high rates of traffic fatalities, unreliable internet access, and limited access to vehicle-integrated electronics [2]. Mobile-first, edge-capable DMS platforms offer an accessible route to improving road safety.

This study bridges a critical gap by developing and deploying a YOLOv8-powered driver monitoring app with real-time alerts, Firebase cloud logging, and a dashboard designed for Ugandan fleet operators. It demonstrates that AI solutions can be both affordable and practical in constrained environments.

The literature reveals a progressive shift from traditional sensor-based systems to real-time, AI-powered, mobile-compatible DMS platforms. With the maturation of lightweight models, edge AI, and cloud integration, mobile-based DMS now offer a viable alternative for improving road safety in developing countries. The present study contributes by demonstrating a system that is cost-effective, offline-capable, and contextualized for Uganda's public transport and logistics sectors.

3 Methodology

The Driver Behavior Monitoring System (DBMS) was developed using a modular and layered architecture to support real-time monitoring, efficient data flow, and flexible integration with cloud services. The methodology includes system design, data sources, model training and optimization, mobile deployment, and dashboard integration.

3.1 System Architecture

The DBMS architecture consists of three layers (Fig. 1):

- **Edge Layer (Mobile Application):** Performs local processing using the phone's front camera and sensors (GPS, accelerometer). It runs the trained YOLOv8 model via PyTorch Lite for on-device inference.
- **Cloud Layer (Firebase & PostgreSQL):** Aggregates logs, synchronizes detection data, and supports user authentication and cloud storage.
- **Dashboard Layer (React Web App):** Provides visualization, real-time alerts, and historical analytics to fleet managers.

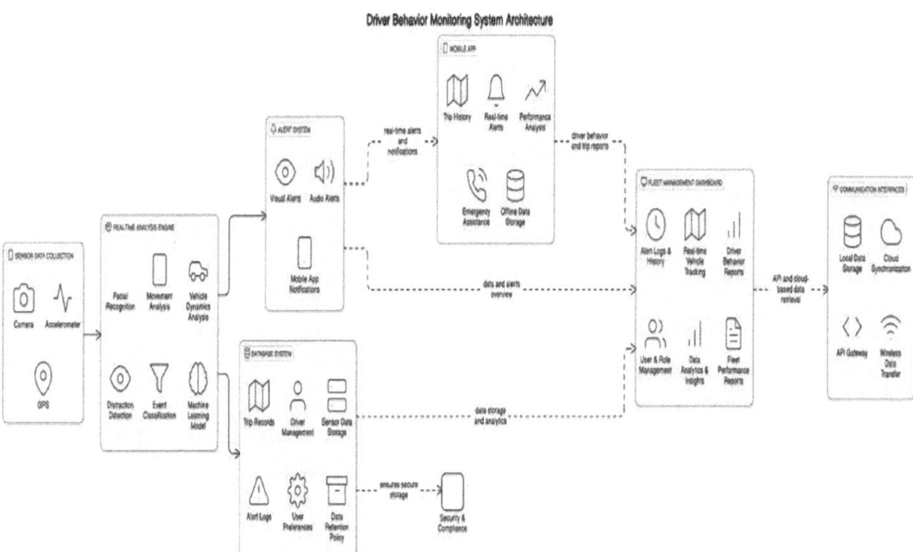

Fig. 1. System architecture diagram

3.2 Data Sources and Collection

Training data was obtained from the **Vicomtech Driver Monitoring Dataset**, which includes annotated images of driver behaviors such as:

- Drowsiness
- Phone usage
- Smoking
- Seatbelt status
- Eyes closed, yawning, and head pose

The dataset was preprocessed using OpenCV and augmented via horizontal flips, brightness shifts, and scaling to improve model generalization.

3.3 Model Training and Optimization

The YOLOv8-small architecture was chosen for its speed and accuracy tradeoff. It was trained using the annotated dataset with the following configuration:

- **Framework:** PyTorch
- **Epochs:** 150
- **Batch Size:** 16
- **Optimizer:** Adam
- **Learning Rate:** 0.001
- **Evaluation Metric:** mAP@0.5 and F1-score

The model achieved a mAP of 91.6% and F1-score of 88.2%. It was converted to TorchScript for compatibility with PyTorch Lite.

3.4 Mobile Application Deployment

The model was embedded into a Flutter-based Android app. The app:

- Starts automatic monitoring upon trip initiation
- Accesses the front camera and runs inference in real time
- Triggers visual (screen alert), audio, and haptic feedback for unsafe behaviors
- Stores logs locally and syncs to Firebase during connectivity

3.5 Web Dashboard Integration

A React + Node.js dashboard allows fleet managers to:

- View trip-based behavioral logs
- Monitor vehicle status in real-time
- Receive system notifications
- Generate performance reports by date, driver, or vehicle

Firebase Authentication is used for login, while PostgreSQL stores persistent structured data (trip logs, driver IDs, vehicle metadata).

4 Results and Evaluation

The DBMS was evaluated through both simulation tests and field trials involving 30 drivers on Ugandan roads. Key metrics include:

4.1 Accuracy and Detection Rates

- Drowsiness: 92.4%
- Phone Usage: 90.1%
- Smoking: 87.6%
- Seatbelt Use: 95.0%

4.2 Latency

- Average detection and alert response time: 340 ms
- Sync time to Firebase: < 2 s under 3G connectivity

4.3 Usability Scores (Fleet Manager Survey, n=5)

- Ease of Dashboard Use: 4.6/5
- Alert Relevance: 4.3/5
- Data Visualization: 4.8/5

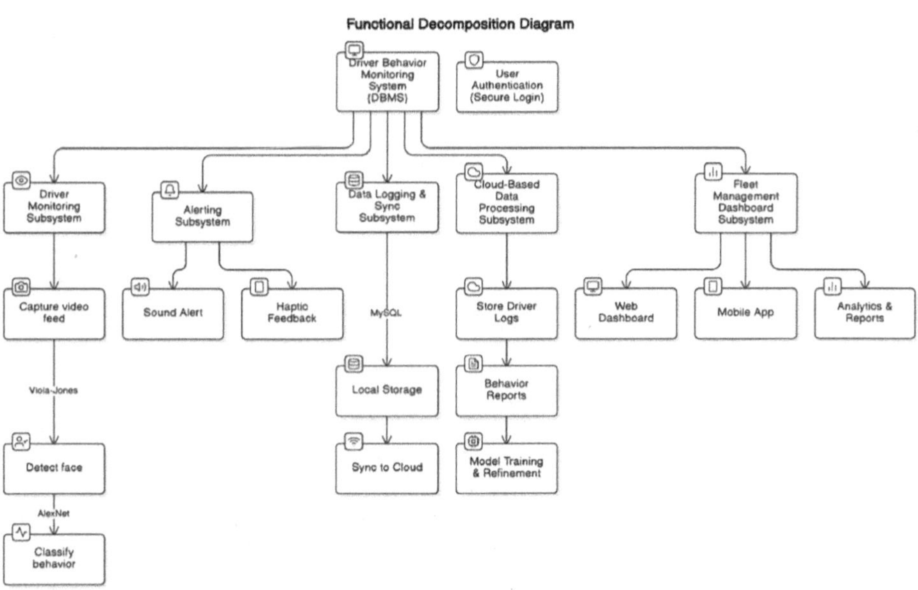

Fig. 2. The functional decomposition diagram for system components and flow

Figure 2 breaks down the Driver Behavior Monitoring System (DBMS) into key subsystems and their functions. The Driver Monitoring Subsystem captures real-time video, detects the driver's face, and classifies behavior using a deep learning model (mobileNet). The Alerting Subsystem provides immediate feedback through sound or haptic alerts when unsafe behaviors are detected. The Data Logging & Sync Subsystem stores data locally and synchronizes it with the cloud for backup and analysis. The Cloud-Based Data Processing Subsystem manages driver logs, generates behavior reports, and refines the model for improved detection accuracy over time. The Fleet Management Dashboard Subsystem allows managers to monitor drivers through a web or mobile app, offering analytics and reports for data-driven decisions. Finally, User Authentication secures system access through a login process to ensure that only authorized users can interact with the system.

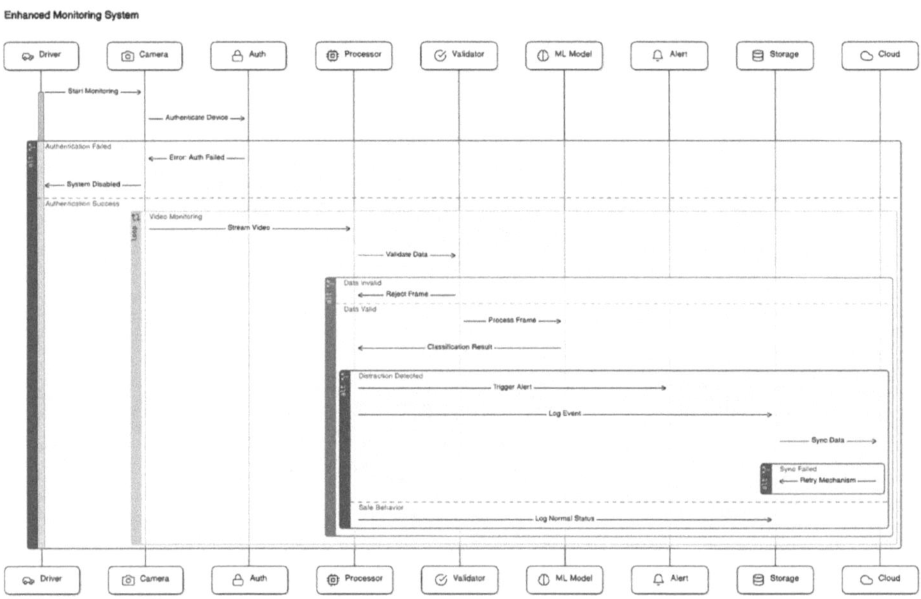

Fig. 3. Driver monitoring system sequence flow

Figure 3 illustrates the real-time flow of operations within the system. It begins with device authentication; if successful, the system initiates video monitoring by capturing and validating the video feed. The frames are processed, and a machine learning model classifies driver behaviors, such as drowsiness or phone usage. When unsafe behavior is detected, alerts are triggered using sound or haptic feedback, and the event is logged for record-keeping. The system also synchronizes data with the cloud, enabling remote monitoring and storage for future analysis. This flow ensures seamless interaction between monitoring, detection, alerting, and data management, creating a comprehensive and responsive driver behavior monitoring system (Figs. 4 and 5).

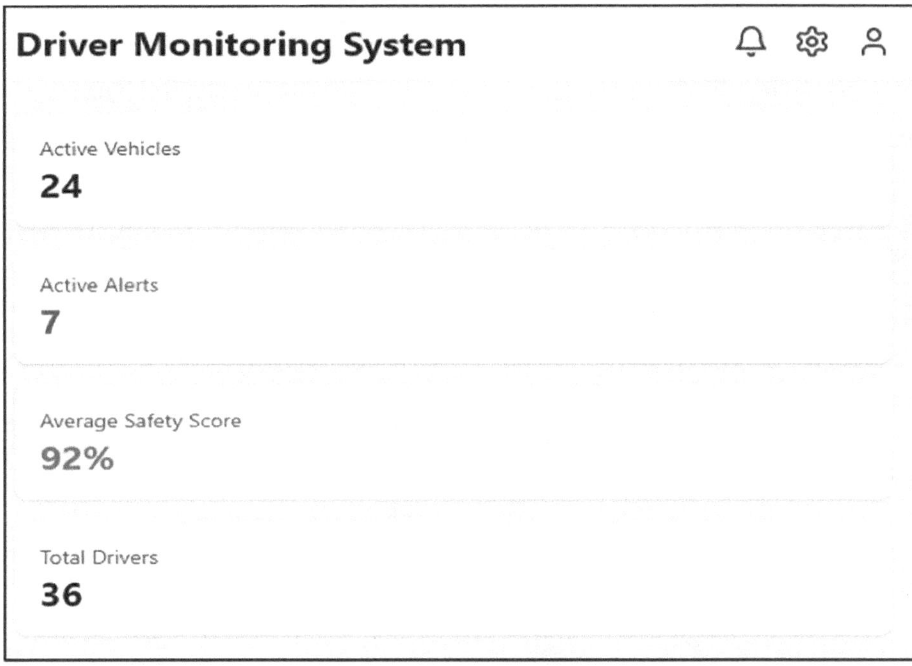

Fig. 4. Average safety score

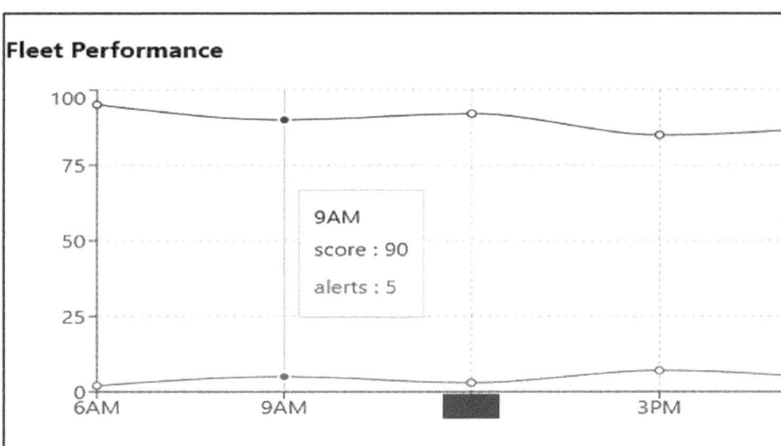

Fig. 5. The fleet performance according to the time of the day

5 Discussion, Ethical Considerations, Future Work and Conclusion

5.1 Discussion of the Results

The proposed system achieved an overall detection accuracy of 93.7% across three key driver behaviors—drowsiness, mobile phone use, and smoking. Specifically, the model achieved 95.1% accuracy in detecting drowsiness, 92.3% in detecting phone usage, and 90.8% for smoking detection. These results confirm the robustness of the YOLOv8-Tiny architecture when optimized and deployed through PyTorch Lite on mobile devices.

Compared with alternative lightweight architectures such as MobileNetV3 and YOLOv7-Tiny, our model exhibited slightly higher accuracy and lower inference latency (averaging 87 ms per frame on a mid-range smartphone). This demonstrates the system's suitability for real-time applications in low-resource environments.

Furthermore, the React-based fleet dashboard synchronized through Firebase enabled near real-time data visualization and behavior tracking, contributing to improved fleet safety management and user awareness. The system's ability to operate offline without requiring constant internet connectivity enhances its practicality for developing regions where network access is limited. The use of YOLOv8 with PyTorch Lite proved effective in meeting low-latency and power efficiency requirements. Offline functionality ensures resilience in rural areas. However, detection precision may drop in extreme occlusion or poor visibility scenarios.

5.2 Limitations

Limitations include:

- Performance variance across phone models
- Occasional false positives in alert generation
- Dependence on front-facing camera placement accuracy

5.3 Ethical Considerations and *Data Protection*

This study recognizes the importance of protecting user privacy and data security. All data collection processes adhered to Uganda's Data Protection and Privacy Act (2019) [23]. Participants gave informed consent before data collection. To preserve privacy, image and sensor data were processed locally on the mobile device without transmitting identifiable information to cloud servers. Stored data were anonymized and securely deleted after analysis.

5.4 Future Work

Despite the encouraging results, several areas for improvement remain. Future work will explore quantization-aware training to further reduce computational load, federated learning to enable collaborative model updates without compromising privacy, and expansion of the dataset to include more diverse road environments and driver demographics. To be specific, Future work will consider adding the following to the system

- Adding support for driver emotion detection (e.g., anger)
- Expanding datasets with local images from Ugandan drivers
- Implementing federated learning for privacy-preserving model updates

6 Conclusion

This study introduced a low-cost, mobile-based Driver Behavior Monitoring System optimized for Uganda and similar contexts. By combining lightweight deep learning (YOLOv8), mobile deployment, and cloud synchronization, the DBMS enables real-time behavior detection and fleet analytics.

Experimental results confirm high detection accuracy, fast inference, and positive user reception. The system represents a scalable and practical approach to enhancing road safety in developing nations.

References

1. W. H. Organisation(WHO): Global Status Report on Road Safety 2023. WHO, Geneva (2023)
2. T.U.P. FORCE: Annual Crime report. The Uganda Police force, Kampala-Uganda (2024)
3. Joonhyuk, Y., Guenwoo, B.: Efficient deep learning model compression for sensor-based vision systems via outlier-aware quantization. Sensors. **25**(9) (2025)
4. Lane, N.D., Bhattacharya, S., Georgiev, P., Forlivesi, C., Jiao, L., Qendro, L.: DeepX: a software accelerator for low-power deep learning inference on Mobile devices. In: 2016 15th ACM/IEEE International Conference on Information Processing in Sensor Networks (IPSN). Austria, Vienna (2016)
5. Alqaydi, S., Zeiada, W., Wakil, A.E., Alnaqbi, A.J., Azam, A.: A comprehensive review of smartphone and other device-based techniques for road surface monitoring. Engineering. **5**, 3397–3426 (2024)
6. Fonseca, T., Ferreira, S.: Monitoring Technologies for Truck Drivers: a systematic review of safety and driving behavior. Appl. Sci. **25**(12) (2025)
7. Hossain, M.U., Rahman, M.A., Islam, M.M., Akhter, A., Uddin, M.A., Paul, B.K.: Automatic driver distraction detection using deep convolutional neural networks. Intell. Syst. Appl. **14**, 22 (2022)
8. Lindow, F., Kashevnik, A.: Driver behavior monitoring based on smartphone sensor data and machine learning methods. In: 2019 25th Conference of Open Innovations Association (FRUCT). Helsinki, Finland (2019)
9. Basha, S., Ram, G.S.: Real-time object detection in low-light environments using YOLOv8: a case study with a custom dataset. Int. J. Eng. **13**(10), 5 (2025)
10. Beg, M.S., Ismail, M.Y., Miah, M.S.U., Peeie, M.H.: Enhancing driving assistance system with YOLO V8-based Normal visual camera sensor. J. Adv. Res. Appl. Sci. Eng. Technol. **32**(1), 226–236 (2023)
11. Hassan, O.F., Ibrahim, A.F., Gomaa, A., Makhlouf, M.A., Hafiz, B.: Real-time driver drowsiness detection using transformer architectures: a novel deep learning approach, Nature Scientific reports, vol. 15 (2025)
12. Huang, Y., Ma, X., Fan, X., Liu, J., Gong, W.: When deep learning meets edge computing. In: 2017 IEEE 25th International Conference on Network Protocols (ICNP). ON, Canada, Toronto (2017)
13. C.V, H., Sankaran, P.: Driver distraction analysis using face pose cues. Expert Syst. Appl. **179** (2021)

14. Lamaazi, H., Alqassab, A., Fadul, R.A., Mizouni, R.: Smart edge-based driver drowsiness detection in Mobile crowdsourcing. IEEE Access. **11**, 21863–21872 (2023)
15. Desai, M.M., Kathad, K., Modi, N.: Real-time driver drowsiness detection using hybrid CNN-LSTM model with facial feature and behavioral analysis. In: 2024 4th International Conference on Ubiquitous Computing and Intelligent Information Systems (ICUIS). Gobichettipalayam, India (2024)
16. Haramaki, T., Nishino, H.: An edge computer based driver monitoring system for assisting safety driving. In: Advances in Internet, Data & Web Technologies. EIDWT 2018. Lecture Notes on Data Engineering and Communications Technologies, pp. 639–650. Springer (2018)
17. Rose, A., Nisce, I., Gonzalez, A., Davis, M., Uribe, B., Carranza, J.: A cloud-based real-time traffic monitoring system with Lidar-based vehicle detection. In: 2023 IEEE Green Energy and Smart Systems Conference (IGESSC). Long Beach, CA, USA (2023)
18. Openfleet: Connected fleet management (2021). [Online]. Available: https://openfleet.com/connected-fleet-management/?lang=en.
19. Sun, H., Feng, N.: MVim: a high-accuracy, lightweight neural network for real-time driver behavior recognition. Expert Syst. Appl. **296** (2025)
20. Vyas, J., Bhumika, D.D., Chaudhury, S.: Federated learning based driver recommendation for next generation transportation system. Expert Syst. Appl. **225** (2023)
21. Doshi-Velez, F., Kim, B.: Towards a rigorous science of interpretable machine learning," arXiv: machine learning (2017)
22. Saki, S., Soori, M.: Artificial intelligence, machine learning and deep learning in advanced transportation systems, a review. Multimodal Transp. (2025)
23. U. Parliament: Uganda's Data Protection and Privacy Act (2019). [Online]. Available: https://bills.parliament.ug/attachments/Data%20Protection%20and%20Privacy%20Act%202019.pdf.

Applications of AI in Health and Agriculture

Developing Fully Autonomous Wireless Monitoring Systems for Smallholder Farmers Communities

Congduc Pham(✉) and Guillaume Gaillard

E2S UPPA, LIUPPA, Universite de Pau et des Pays de l'Adour, Pau, France
{congduc.pham,guillaume.gaillard}@univ-pau.fr

Abstract. Digital innovations still have low penetration in the smallholder farmer (SHF) communities which remain reluctant to adopt such technology-based systems. In this article, we present a robust, cost-effective, power-efficient, wireless and "fully autonomous" sensor system for "out-of-the-box" deployment using long-range LoRa technology. By "fully autonomous" we mean that, by default, the system operates without Internet access and still offers advanced data processing and prediction features. We describe our wireless sensor platform, how we achieved full autonomy for out-of-the-box deployment, how transmission coverage can be improved with transparent and optimized relaying functionalities, and how edge intelligence can be added to the framework. Piloting programs with agriculture service advisors and more than 60 SHFs validated the "fully autonomous" and "out-of-the-box" deployment approach in Algeria and Morocco.

Keywords: Cost-effective IoT · LoRa · Wireless sensor · Edge-AI

1 Introduction

Digital innovation in agriculture is not new, neither is the deployment of ground sensor systems for a smarter control of various agricultural processes, such as irrigation control. However, most of the available commercial solutions from companies in the smart agriculture sector are targeting big farms with high-end sensor systems that are highly specialized, very integrated, difficult to customize and can easily cost several thousand euros. In addition, these solutions heavily rely on cloud servers and proprietary software platforms, requiring customers to be bound to the infrastructure provider.

For all these reasons, digital innovations still have low penetration in the smallholder farmer (SHF) communities. Farmers and other actors are still very reluctant to adopt such technology-based systems. In that context, the PRIMA

A. Oluwatope et al. (Eds.): AFRICOMM 2025, LNICST 713, pp. 163–177, 2027.
https://doi.org/10.1007/978-3-032-38682-3_10

INTEL-IRRIS project (https://intel-irris.eu/) started in June 1st, 2021 with the ambition to make digital and smart farming technologies more attractive and accessible to SHFs. To address the needs of this community, the proposed solutions must be affordable, able to be integrated into existing farming practices and, most importantly, able to be deployed "out-of-the-box" by farmers themselves. INTEL-IRRIS promotes the concept of "intelligent irrigation in-the-box". Through a participatory piloting approach, INTEL-IRRIS strongly involved more than 60 SHFs and stakeholders into the innovation process itself. The innovative contribution of INTEL-IRRIS is to propose a robust, generic and edge-enabled wireless sensor framework that can be simply and quickly deployed by farmers themselves.

The rest of the paper is organized as follows. Section 2 provides a quick overview of the INTEL-IRRIS's project. Section 3 presents the proposed wireless sensing systems that can be deployed out-of-the-box by farmers. Section 4 then details how INTEL-IRRIS implements the "intelligent irrigation in-the-box" concept by embedding advanced configuration features and AI-based data processing in the edge-enabled IoT gateway. We highlight a proof-of-concept demonstrating the development and integration of custom applications using edge-AI features. Conclusions are given in Sect. 5.

2 Overview of INTEL-IRRIS Project

The proposition of cost-effective sensing systems is not new and INTEL-IRRIS has been greatly inspired by makers, DIY initiatives and previous works [1–3]. There are also recent contributions in the same line than INTEL-IRRIS [4–8]. However, INTEL-IRRIS's unique feature is to propose a robust, power efficient and edge-enabled wireless sensor framework that can be simply and quickly deployed by farmers.

Therefore, INTEL-IRRIS's objective is to develop a "fully autonomous" wireless sensor framework that enables "out-of-the-box" deployments by farmers themselves, even when transmission coverage is challenging. Robustness, accuracy and power efficiency that are strong requirements of INTEL-IRRIS make the proposed system an operational wireless monitoring system at TRL7-8.

In order to operationally provide the "out-of-the-box" and "fully autonomous" features, INTEL-IRRIS implements architecture where all the control and recommendation system parts are embedded in a low-cost IoT gateway that is deployed locally in a farm, with no connection to Internet servers.

Since INTEL-IRRIS focuses on optimizing water usage, we worked with experts in soil and agriculture to integrate soil-water-plant-atmosphere complex interactions into the gateway itself for more accurate feedback to the farmers. The objective to reach would be to also integrate agricultural knowledge (crop/plant models, region-dependent climate models, evapotranspiration models, etc.) enabling corrective as well as predictive processing on collected data. For piloting purposes, INTEL-IRRIS developed a starter kit where 1 pre-configured sensor device and 1 edge-enabled gateway are ready to be deployed by smallholders. The sensor device can have a Gravity SEN0308 capacitive sensor from

DFRobots or a Watermark tensiometer WM200 from Irrometer, see Fig. 2. Additional sensor devices can be added incrementally.

3 A Cost-Effective, Autonomous Wireless Sensor System

3.1 The Cost-Effective Hardware Sensing Platform

The cost-effective and open-source hardware platform is based on a DIY design that has been initially developed and validated in 2 EU H2020 projects (WAZIUP and WAZIHUB) with piloting sites deployed in several sub-Saharan countries. When INTEL-IRRIS started, the PCB v2 in Fig. 1 was deployed. INTEL-IRRIS's partner IRD (Institut de Recherche pour le Développement) improved the initial design to easily connect various types of sensor as well as to provide support for solar panel charging leading to the latest versions: v4.1 with raw LoRa and v5 with full LoRaWAN support. The PCBs manufacturing files are available and the fully assembled PCB can be ordered online from manufacturers for a cost of about 8€/unit for 80 units and above.

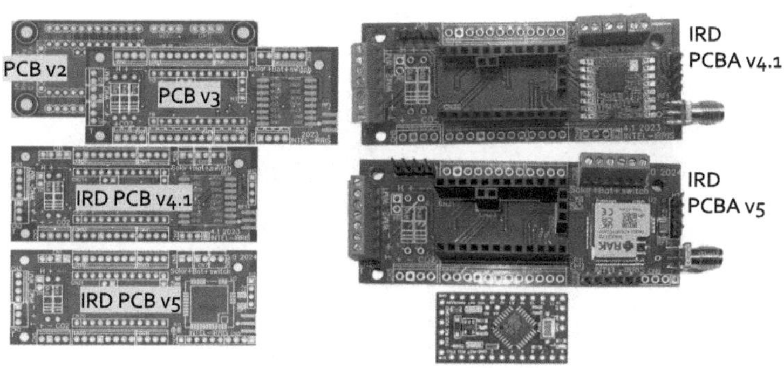

Fig. 1. The generic hardware platform evolution from v2 to v5. On the right side, the two assembled PCBs (PCBAs) allow easier deployment with terminal block connectors and header for the Arduino ProMini microcontroller.

The separate microcontroller that needs to be added (about 2€ to be added) and plugged on the PCB is the Arduino ProMini in its 3.3V and 8MHz version. Software building blocks include physical sensor management, long-range data transmission with LoRa radio technology and advanced power management that allows the device to be fully autonomous for more than 2 years when running on 2 AA batteries and transmitting data once every 60 mins [9]. Various power management mechanisms are included to prevent the board from draining the battery: mitigation of reboot loops due to low voltage, automatic increase of the data measurement period when battery levels go too low, etc. Figures 2 and 3 show the off-the-shelf but robust integration where a solar panel option can be enabled if needed. The integration steps have been validated during numerous hackathons and capacity-building events, and we have devices that have been deployed and running for more than 3 years in harsh outdoor conditions.

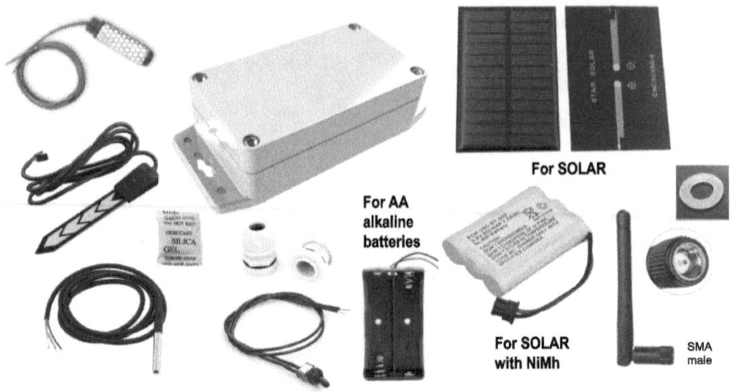

Fig. 2. Off-the-shelf integration: the device's components, including sensors, can be chosen and obtained separately and independently, thus improving flexibility.

Fig. 3. Robust integration for outdoor deployment. The device is water-proof and designed for harsh climate conditions (sun exposure, temperature changes) in the field.

3.2 Raw LoRa or Full LoRaWAN?

As shown in Fig. 1, there are 2 versions of the PCB that can be ordered from PCB manufacturers: v4.1 with raw LoRa radio module provided by an RFM95/96 and v5 with full LoRaWAN support provided by the RAK3172 radio module. The v4.1 can transmit LoRaWAN formatted uplink packets and can receive application-level downlink packets but does not have the full LoRaWAN protocol stack with link layer control such as Adaptive Data Rate nor Over-The-Air-Activation (OTAA) with Join procedure. Most of the starter kits distributed to smallholders for the piloting program are based on v4.1 where the sensor devices in the starter kit are already configured in ABP mode (Activation By Personalization) to work out-of-the-box with the IoT gateway. This will be presented in more detail in the next section on the IoT gateway. We use v5 with full LoRaWAN support in larger deployment scenarios where devices need to be registered on the local IoT gateway to enable a local OTAA procedure.

3.3 The Edge-Enabled IoT Gateway

The edge-capable IoT gateway used in the INTEL-IRRIS project builds on the WaziGate software platform, which has been progressively developed by the WAZIUP e.V. Foundation through multiple international research and innovation initiatives. This platform originates from earlier work on an open, low-cost LoRa gateway architecture created at the University of Pau around 2015, initially targeting Raspberry Pi–based deployments [11]. Since then, WaziGate has evolved into an independent and mature solution, currently assessed at Technology Readiness Level (TRL) 8–9. Its architecture is well suited to edge-centric deployments, as it supports the execution of application services directly on the gateway, including an integrated LoRaWAN network server, local application services with data storage, built-in visualization tools, and container-based application management. In typical deployments for remote rural environments, the system is configured to operate fully autonomously without reliance on external connectivity. When Internet access is available and operationally relevant, optional cloud synchronization and remote administration functionalities can also be activated.

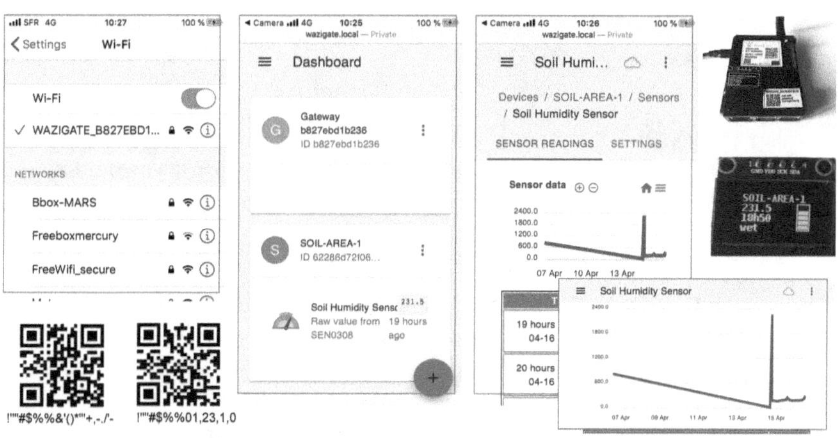

Fig. 4. The WaziGate's dashboard with generic sensor data visualization. The Gateway (top-right) hosts a WiFi cell and a dashboard the farmer can access scanning the QR (bottom-left) on a smartphone, displaying detailed data from devices and sensors.

The WaziGate Dashboard. For smallholder farmers, the primary point of interaction with WaziGate is the web-based dashboard, which provides a user-friendly interface for viewing sensor measurements through straightforward graphical displays. As shown in Fig. 4, the dashboard is accessible via a responsive web interface, enabling farmers to consult and interact with the system using a smartphone after connecting directly to the gateway's local Wi-Fi network, for instance by scanning a QR code. In addition to the web interface, the gateway includes a small built-in OLED display that continuously presents basic irrigation alerts, offering an immediate and always-visible feedback channel. The INTEL-IRRIS starter kit is delivered with a fully initialized configuration: when the WaziGate is powered on, soil moisture sensing devices are already registered, and measurement data automatically appear on the dashboard as soon as the sensors are activated, without requiring user-side setup, as illustrated in Fig. 5. This plug-and-play behavior greatly simplifies field deployment and helps lower the barriers to technology uptake by smallholder farming communities.

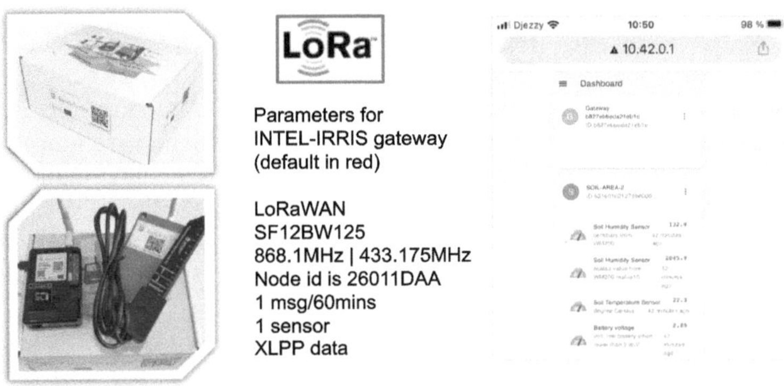

Fig. 5. The INTEL-IRRIS starter kit for out-of-the-box deployment: the pre-configuration enables a simple "power up and sense" for one Wazigate and one device.

The Gateway Radio Hardware. For a very cost-effective gateway targeting SHF communities, we use and deploy a single-channel gateway where a regular LoRa radio module provides the connectivity with deployed end-devices, most likely based on PCB v4.1. The simple RFM95/96 PCB breakout designed in the early "Low-cost LoRa IoT gateway" framework [11] can be integrated easily. An external RTC module can be plugged to provide accurate time information, required to store the collected data. A more integrated LoRa radio hat has also been designed by WAZIUP e.V. with an embedded RTC module. In case a full LoRaWAN connectivity (in particular its multi-channel feature) is required because some of the end-devices are based on the PCB v5 or come from the commercial market then a radio concentrator hat such as the RAK2245/5146 can be used with the WaziGate software without needing additional configuration.

3.4 Improving Transmission Coverage: Antennas

One of the most frequent issues when deploying a wireless sensing system is the transmission range to the gateway. Even with LoRa, transmissions from devices deployed in plots can have difficulties to reach the locally deployed gateway. This is mainly because gateways that are deployed in local farms are deployed indoor and between 1–1.8 m height (on a table or a shelf for instance) to simplify the installation process to an acceptable level by farmers. In addition to the simple antennas used by end-devices and advertised as "3dBi" (usually whip antennas) and "5dBi" (usually sleeve dipole antennas) that have very limited range (about 600 m when the gateway is indoor), we tested 2 antennas with a higher gain in an indoor configuration as illustrated in Fig. 6: (1) a commercial fiber glass 5dBi N-connector plugged in a base and (2) a DIY ground plane antenna.

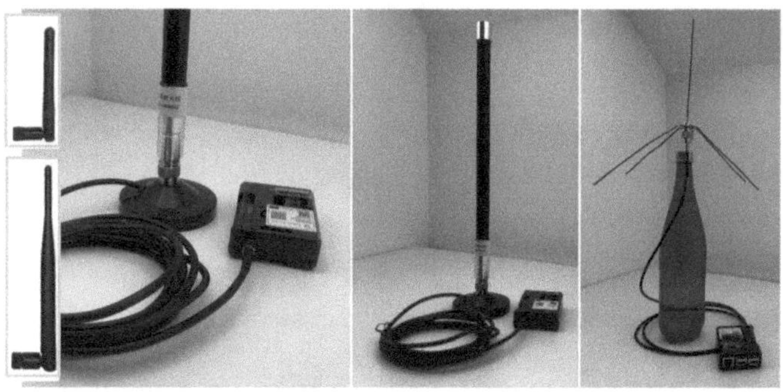

Fig. 6. Indoor higher-gain antennas at the gateway improving coverage.

Results from the tests showed that the performance of the DIY ground plane antenna is very close to those of the commercial fiber glass antenna with a cost of about 1/10th. Both can increase the reception range from about 600 m to about 2km in a typical deployment environment. The detailed test results are available from [12]. Despite the much lower cost of the DIY ground plane antenna we favored the commercial fiber glass N-connector on a base solution as the DIY solution would have introduced too much complexity and overwhelming fragility for farmers.

3.5 Improving Transmission Coverage with Relaying

During the piloting program, we observed that some farms still have plots that are too far for devices to reach the locally deployed gateway. As there is also very little alternative for the gateway location because it has to be powered, we tested the relaying feature that we developed some years ago in the H2020 WAZIUP project [13]. The PCB v4.1 can be used to build a relay node running on a 2xAA battery just like a regular end-device. In INTEL-IRRIS, it was a strong requirement to have the relay nodes only differing from end-devices by the uploaded software. The relaying principle is illustrated in Fig. 7.

The method we proposed in [13] is based on an observation phase where the relay node is added to the network after the deployment of both the end-devices and the gateway. It will then discover and learn the pattern of uplink

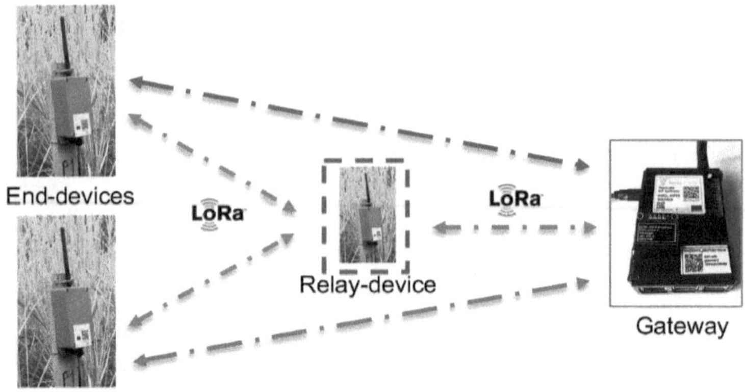

Fig. 7. Introducing intermediate and transparent relaying: shorter links (in green) are more reliable than longer ones (red). (Color figure online)

transmissions from end-devices. By default for INTEL-IRRIS, all sensing devices are configured with a fixed transmission period of 60mins although this value can be changed before deployment. Each one may be powered up at a different moment. This approach of using an observation phase is illustrated in Fig. 8 where 8 devices are covered by a unique relay node.

In addition to the observation period that determines the various wake up moments for the relay node, there is a guard time window prior to each wake up where the relay node wakes up periodically for a very short time, e.g. every 100ms, to run a Channel Activity Detection (CAD) procedure with the LoRa radio. If activity is detected, typically because of a packet preamble, then the relay node switches to receive mode in order to catch the uplink transmission. The guard time window is necessary because the clocks of the devices and relay nodes are not synchronized and can drift away quite significantly due to the low cost electronic hardware. The CAD-based mechanism limits the energy consumption during this guard time window while the observation phase allows the relay node to go into deep sleep between each wake up. Our work on LoRa relaying was realized before this issue was taken into account by the LoRaWAN specification. Recently, a LoRaWAN relay specification has been released using only the periodic CAD procedure to scan for radio activity [14]. This approach consumes more energy and is better adapted to denser traffic as found in urban IoT deployment scenarios. We believe our solution is more suitable when deploying a smaller scale sensing infrastructure for individual farms.

3.6 Reducing Further the Relaying Traffic

When introducing relay nodes in countries where there are regulations on the radio activity time per device, known as duty-cycle restrictions, there must be a mechanism to reduce the uplink traffic of the relay node which would otherwise

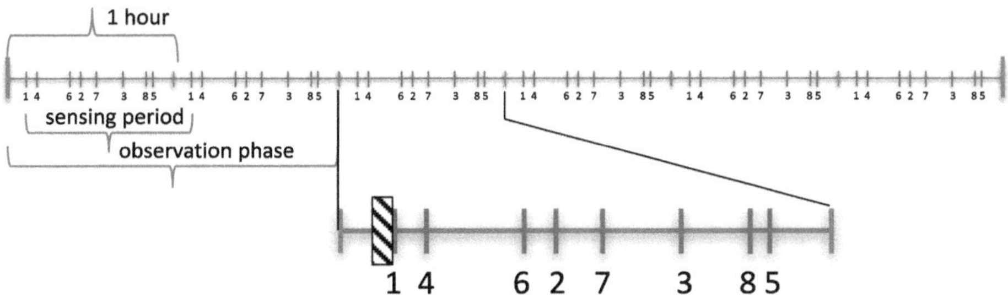

Fig. 8. Relaying with observation phase and short activity detection. The relay listens to its neighbors (observation phase) during more than a sensing period (1h), then uses Channel Activity Detection (CAD) to detect and forward frames.

be N times the traffic of a single node, N being the number of devices covered by the relay node.

There are 2 simple solutions to reduce uplink traffic: (i) increasing the time between 2 measures and transmissions at the device in an adaptive way and, (ii) the devices themselves avoiding transmitting similar values. One drawback on these solutions is the lack of global vision or knowledge that could be used to reach a given objective. For instance what "similar values" mean? Obviously an interval should be defined to consider 2 values as similar to avoid transmitting an update. If this decision is left to the device, then data coming from other devices can not be taken into account to optimize further the similarity detection towards a given objective. Therefore, we took the opportunity of the INTEL-IRRIS piloting program to integrate in the experimental deployments the uplink traffic reduction mechanism by similarity detection with data suppression proposed in [15]. The general approach of this method is described in Fig. 9 where data sent from 3 devices are considered.

At a first look, it enhances the previous relaying task of Fig. 8 with an additional data similarity detection procedure which objective is to determine the messages from devices deployed downstream that can be removed from the list of uplink transmissions to the gateway. However, by receiving data from all downstream devices, the relay node can implement a more sophisticated similarity detection and value suppression mechanism. In the approach proposed in [15], not only similarity detection can be realized for data coming from a given device, but data coming from different devices can also be considered similar under some conditions. Therefore, beyond value similarity, relay nodes can implement a device similarity leading to the concept of redundant device. Several criteria can be used to define whether data from devices can lead to device redundancy. In [15] we experimented and made a proof-of-concept using Euclidean distance but there are other metrics such as cosine distance, Jaccard similarity, Bray-Curtis distance, Canberra distance, etc. More detail on the proposed algorithm, implementation and energy consumption can be found in [15].

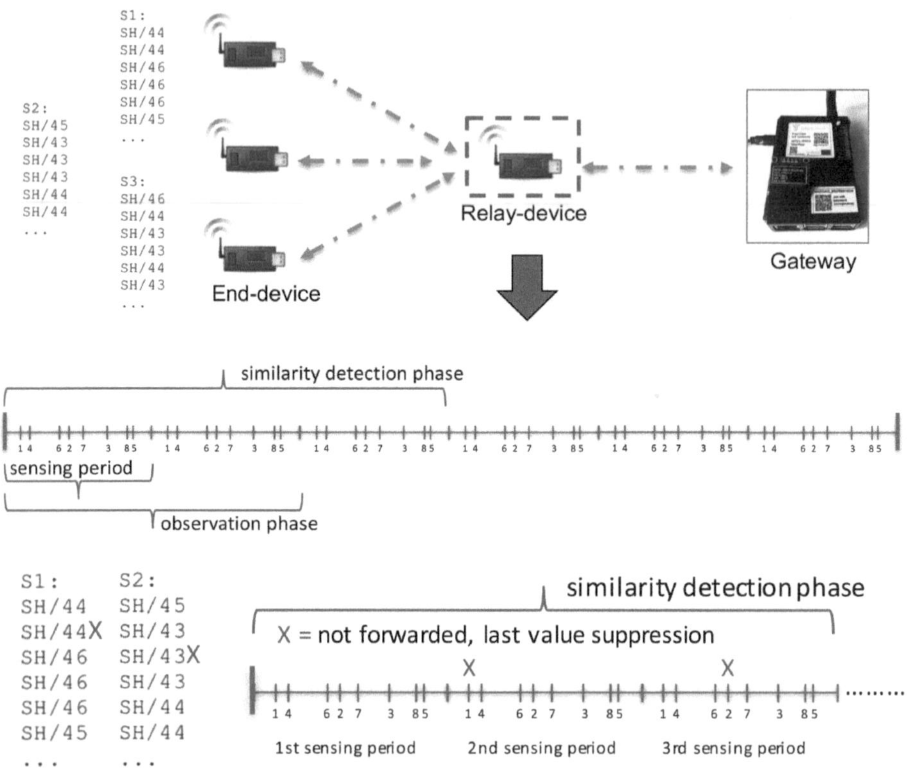

Fig. 9. Reducing uplink traffic with similarity detection. Relays avoid forwarding similar values in their covered zone, following a given criteria [15].

3.7 Results and Lessons Learned

Introducing digital technologies is always a trade-off, and this is particularly true when targeting the smallholder farmer communities that are running small scale farms. With the INTEL-IRRIS project which proposes Wireless monitoring systems to optimize the irrigation process there were a number of design choices that were dictated by this trade-off.

In addition to the obvious cost parameter, the proposed system must be simple and robust to be deployed by farmers themselves. Then, the system must be flexible enough to be incrementally scaled, again by farmers themselves. The system must run and provide information to the farmer without relying on Internet connectivity, and certainly not on cloud storage or external servers. To increase technology adoption and innovation capacities from local actors, the system should be open and interoperable, as well as being able to easily integrate systems provided by third-parties, provided that data format are available. For the particular case of irrigation addressed by INTEL-IRRIS, the system must be versatile enough to be integrated into existing irrigation infrastructures, different crop cultures and/or farming practices.

We believe the system we presented satisfies these requirements. The cost-effective design resulting in an open, robust, generic and versatile hardware platform to build efficient sensing systems can be adopted and improved by local actors. The robust, yet simple, integration has been validated and proved robust enough for outdoor harsh conditions. With long-range LoRa technology and pre-configuration of devices, the starter kit can be deployed out-of-the-box by farmers themselves. Connectivity issues can be solved by introducing a simple and transparent relay node that runs autonomously. Incremental addition of devices, including those from commercial market, is possible based on the evolution of the farmer's needs. Of course, in that case, technology support may be needed and can be provided from either governmental agriculture services, cooperatives or entrepreneurs. The "fully autonomous" approach with all data management and processing on the locally deployed IoT gateway is positively perceived by farmers who are reluctant to use Internet clouds, either because of trust or simply because a permanent Internet access is complex to be deployed by smallholders in remote rural areas as most of the farmers only connect to Internet from their smartphones.

4 Embedding Intelligence

INTEL-IRRIS's objective is also to implement the "intelligent irrigation in-the-box" concept to validate the fully edge-mode approach for the SHF communities. The project develops 2 components as proof-of-concept: (1) a web-based platform running as a separate application on the IoT gateway (previously referred to as WaziApp) and (2) the integration of AI processing on the IoT gateway.

4.1 INTEL-IRRIS Irrigation WaziApp

In addition to the standard sensor dashboard, the INTEL-IRRIS platform includes a project-specific application called the INTEL-IRRIS Irrigation WaziApp (IIWA). This specialized WaziApp extends the basic gateway services with functionalities tailored to irrigation management, such as enhanced plotting tools, domain-specific data preprocessing, and interfaces for setting application-related parameters. Integrating these capabilities directly on the gateway simplifies software maintenance and avoids the need for a standalone mobile application. Since IIWA is executed locally on the WaziGate, it can directly access all measurements stored on the device and can be used without Internet connectivity once users connect to the gateway's Wi-Fi network. Technically, IIWA is implemented as a containerized Python microservice, combining a Python backend with an HTML/CSS/JavaScript frontend, and it retrieves sensor readings through the standardized WaziGate REST interface.

To support irrigation decision-making, IIWA provides detailed calibration options and agronomic configuration settings, including sensor category, soil characteristics, salinity level, bulk density, and crop type. These settings may be applied system-wide or adjusted individually for each sensing node. In the starter-kit configuration, many values are preset to facilitate initial deployment, although users are still expected to select certain descriptors such as soil texture classes (e.g., clay, sand, silt, peat, chalk, or loam) from predefined lists. To further reduce adoption barriers, the application supports multiple languages; an example of the Arabic interface is shown in Fig. 11 (Fig. 10).

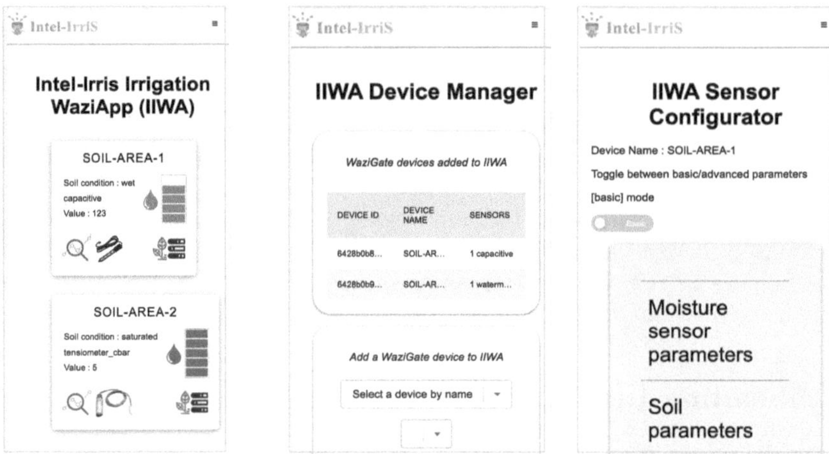

Fig. 10. The INTEL-IRRIS Irrigation WaziApp, IIWA. IIWA adds features to the interface specific to the context: e.g. crop and sensor types impact data processing.

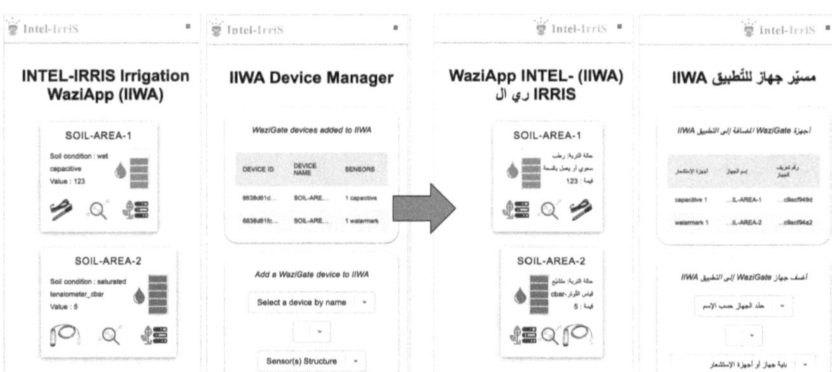

Fig. 11. Multi-language support in IIWA.

4.2 Edge-AI Processing Framework

Beyond application services, WaziGate now integrates an Edge-AI module that enables machine learning workflows to be executed directly on the gateway, with support for both connected and disconnected operation. This module provides a development environment where users can perform data analysis, model training, and inference locally, thereby facilitating experimentation and deployment of AI-based methods at the network edge. A dedicated system-oriented WaziApp with the full Jupyterlab functionality has been packaged as a Docker container where various ML packages with several regression models are available for developers. This framework is described in more detail in [16].

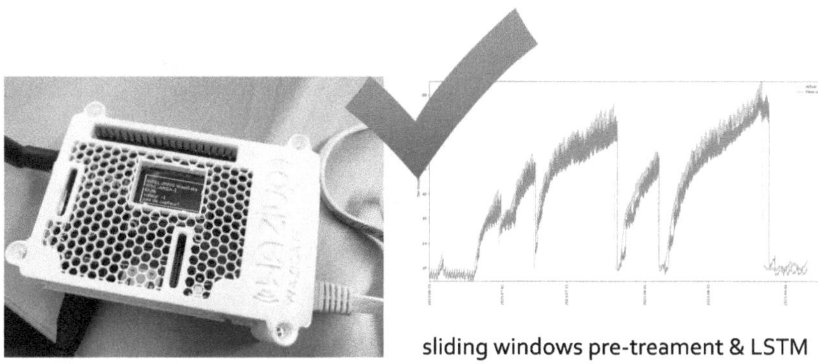

Fig. 12. Prediction of soil moisture with embedded AI. These preliminary results encourage further studies.

INTEL-IRRIS uses the WaziGate Edge-AI framework to implement a proof-of-concept of embedded soil moisture prediction based on AI/ML model: an LSTM network (Long Short-Term Memory) is applied on the time-series, e.g. from the collected soil moisture measures from devices (Fig. 12). Such predictions can then be fed back into the IIWA in order to include an AI-based prediction model in the application, and help the farmers in adjusting their irrigation plan. It is also possible to run several prediction models (in parallel on separate Wazi-Apps) and let IIWA and/or the user select which model to use depending on local conditions and needs.

4.3 Going Further with Advanced AI Methods

For the particular case of smallholder farmers and small-scale farms, 2 innovative AI/ML techniques show many promises: Federated Learning (FL) [17] and Transfer Learning [18]. The main interest of FL resides in the fact that farmers do not need to share their data with a central server in order to contribute in improving AI models for local agriculture needs. For TL, the main interest is to improve the efficiency of AI models when the size of the dataset is small. INTEL-IRRIS conducted preliminary work on FL and TL in Algerian and French farms using data collected by the various starter kits that have been deployed.

5 Conclusions

We presented INTEL-IRRIS's robust, cost-effective, power-efficient, wireless and fully autonomous sensor system for out-of-the-box deployment that was developed for the smallholder farmer communities. The proposed solution can be quickly deployed with a minimum of technological infrastructure, even in very remote and rural areas as it does not rely on Internet connectivity for remote clouds/servers. Piloting programs with agriculture service advisors and more than 60 SHFs validated the "fully autonomous" and "out-of-the-box" deployment approach in Algeria and Morocco.

The open and versatile hardware platform can be used with numerous other types of physical sensors to extend the range of applications. For instance, leveraging on INTEL-IRRIS's results, the developed framework has already been extended in the ANR PEPR AgriFutur project to develop a wider range of sensors to better qualify and quantify the impact of agroecological practices. With PCBA that can be ordered fully assembled from the PCB manufacturer, hardware availability for scaling-up should not be an issue. However, the production of starter kits would need a local technology actor that would take care of the integration.

At the moment, embedded AI is still a proof-of-concept and the starter kit can be used to build datasets that are more representative of the local conditions and farmer agricultural practices. Future work on Federated Learning and Transfer Learning, that are particularly adapted technologies for the smallholder farmer communities, will be conducted to seamlessly integrate these features into the autonomous sensor system framework.

Acknowledgment. This work is funded by PRIMA S2 2020 INTEL-IRRIS project id 1560 and ANR PEPR AgriFutur. The PRIMA Program is supported by the European Union.

References

1. Pham, C., Rahim, A., Cousin, P.: Low-cost, long-range open IoT for smarter rural African villages. In: Proceedings of IEEE ISC2, Trento, Italy, (2016)
2. Dupont, C., Bures, T., Sheikhalishahi, M., Pham, C., Rahim, A.: Low-cost IoT, big data, and cloud platform for developing countries. In: Proceedings of GECON'2017, Biarritz, France, September 19–21 (2017)
3. Briciu-Burghina, C., Zhou, J., Ali, M.I., Regan, F.: Demonstrating the potential of a low-cost soil moisture sensor network. Sensors (2022)
4. Vandôme, P., Moinard, S., Brunel, G., et al.: A low cost sensor to improve surface irrigation management. Precis. Agric. **25**, 3072–3085 (2024)
5. Dafonte, J., González, M.Á., Comesaña, E., Teijeiro, M.T., Cancela, J.J.: Soil water status monitoring system with proximal low-cost sensors and LoRa technology for smart water irrigation in woody crops. Sensors **24**, 8104 (2024)
6. Nandi, R., Shrestha, D.: Assessment of low-cost and higher-end soil moisture sensors across various moisture ranges and soil textures. Sensors **24**, 5886 (2024)

7. Steinbach, S., et al.: Low-cost sensors and multitemporal remote sensing for operational turbidity monitoring in an east African wetland environment. IEEE J. Sel. Top. Appl. Earth Obser. Remote Sens. **17**, 8490–8508 (2024)
8. Ebstu, E., Hatiye, S., Goshime, D., et al.: Development and testing of a low-cost soil moisture sensor for real-time irrigation scheduling. Irrig. Drainage 1–15
9. Pham, C. https://github.com/CongducPham/PRIMA-Intel-IrriS
10. WAZIUP e.V. Wazigate. https://github.com/Waziup/WaziGate and https://www.waziup.org/iot-edge-platform/#wazigate
11. Pham, C. https://github.com/CongducPham/LowCostLoRaGw
12. Pham, C. https://github.com/CongducPham/PRIMA-Intel-IrriS/blob/main/Tutorials/Intel-Irris-antenna-test.pdf
13. Diop, M., Pham, C.: Increased flexibility in long-range IoT deployments with transparent and light-weight 2-hop LoRa approach. In: Proceedings of WD'2019, Manchester, UK, April 23–25 (2019)
14. Alliance, L.: LoRaWAN Relay Specification. TS011-1.0.0
15. Pham, C., Makhoul, A., Diop, M.: Similarity detection for smart and transparent long-range IoT relaying. In: Proceedings of ISCC'19, Barcelona, Spain, June 30-July 3rd (2019)
16. Pham, C. et al.: Deploying low-cost and full edge-IoT/AI system for optimizing irrigation in smallholder farmers communities. In: EAISA'2022 Workshop on Edge AI for Smart Agriculture, co-located with IE'2022, Biarritz, France, June 20-23 (2022)
17. Kondaveeti, H.K., Sai, G.B., Athar, S.A., Vatsavayi, V.K., Mitra, A., Ananthachari, P.: Federated learning for smart agriculture: challenges and opportunities. In: Proceedings of ICDCECE'2024,, Ballari, India (2024)
18. Zahraa, A.S., Mariette, A.: The power of transfer learning in agricultural applications. AgriNet. Front. Plant Sci. **13** (2022)

Preliminary Result in the Detection of Four Varieties of Mangoes with YOLOv11: Amélie, Kent, Mangot vert, Brooks

Moustapha Bikienga[1], Sanguirè Pascal Somda[1(✉)], Safiatou Soré[1], Tounwendyam Frédéric Ouédraogo[1], and Corneille Drabo[2]

[1] Department of Computer Science, Norbert ZONGO University, Koudougou, Burkina Faso
bmoustaph@yahoo.fr, sanguiree@gmail.com

[2] Plant Breeding Team, Traditional Cereals Program (Corn, Wheat, and Emerging Plants), INERA/Farako-Bâ, 01 BP 910 BOBO-Dioulasso 01, BOBO-Dioulasso, Burkina Faso

Abstract. The automatic detection of mango varieties using YOLOv11 was explored in order to evaluate the performance of this *deep learning* model in an agricultural context in Burkina Faso. The study focused on four representative varieties: *Brooks(Retard)*, *Mangot vert*, *Amélie*, and *Kent*. **Average Precision (AP)** was chosen as the main metric, since it combines both precision and recall, providing a comprehensive evaluation of the model's detection and classification ability.

The results reveal a high AP for *Brooks(Retard)* (73.6%) and *Mangot vert* (71.13%), indicating effective differentiation of these varieties, which display distinctive visual characteristics. In contrast, distinguishing between *Amélie* (70.9%) and *Kent* (64.4%) remains more challenging due to their strong morphological and chromatic similarity, which leads to greater confusion during classification.

Overall evaluation indicates a **mAP of 70%**, reflecting satisfactory performance under real orchard conditions, despite inter-variety variability, changes in lighting, and the diversity of shooting angles. These results highlight the robustness of the model and confirm its potential for practical application in orchard monitoring.

Keywords: YOLO algorithm · artificial intelligence · object recognition · automated agriculture · YOLOv11 · mango variety

A. Oluwatope et al. (Eds.): AFRICOMM 2025, LNICST 713, pp. 178–190, 2027.
https://doi.org/10.1007/978-3-032-38682-3_11

Introduction

Mango production plays a key role in Burkina Faso's agricultural economy, representing one of the country's main export products and contributing significantly to national fruit production and economic stability. Beyond its market value, mango cultivation supports rural employment and serves as a vital source of income for many producers.

Despite its importance, harvesting still largely relies on traditional methods, which are often inefficient and labor-intensive. The integration of Artificial Intelligence (AI) and drones (*Unmanned Aerial Vehicles*, UAVs) presents an opportunity to modernize the sector by automating fruit detection and localization, thereby enabling the implementation of precision agriculture practices.

Most existing studies focus primarily on general mango detection or on distinguishing between ripe and unripe fruits [2]. However, these approaches overlook a crucial factor: **the variability among different mango varieties**. Fruits from distinct varieties may share very similar visual characteristics, making identification challenging and limiting the effectiveness of traditional models.

In this context, it is necessary to develop a system capable of accurately detecting and differentiating multiple mango varieties cultivated in Burkina Faso, in order to automate harvesting and optimize agricultural practices.

To address this need, this study focuses on the **detection of four mango varieties**: *Brooks (Retard)*, *Mangot vert*, *Amélie*, and *Kent.* We propose a modern *deep learning* approach based on YOLOv11, designed for real-time detection and capable of capturing the morphological and chromatic subtleties of each variety. The goal is to develop a reliable and efficient tool that can be integrated into UAVs to automate mango monitoring and harvesting, while promoting the diversity of local varieties and supporting sustainable agriculture.

1 Related Work

The automatic detection of fruits in orchards has attracted growing interest over the past decade, driven by advances in computer vision and deep learning. Several architectures have been explored, compared, and optimized in terms of accuracy, *mean Average Precision* (mAP), and processing speed, in order to meet the requirements of precision agriculture.

The first significant works include Sa et al. [14], who proposed *DeepFruits*, a model based on Convolutional Neural Networks (CNN) for real-time detection of multiple fruits. Their system achieved an overall accuracy above 90%, paving the way for the application of deep learning in agriculture. Similarly, Bargoti and Underwood [1] employed CNNs for the detection of apples and oranges, reaching an mAP of 91% and a speed of 25 FPS, thereby demonstrating the feasibility of large-scale harvest automation.

For mangoes, several studies have focused on detection and yield estimation. Koirala et al. [10] applied a CNN-based model that achieved 92% accuracy, while Gongal et al. [5] employed YOLOv3 to localize mangoes in real time, reaching an mAP of 94% and 30 FPS. However, these approaches did not distinguish between varieties, limiting themselves to global fruit detection.

Comparative studies between different versions of YOLO and other architectures have further confirmed the superiority of YOLO models for real-time detection. Noran and Ouf [12] showed that YOLOv4 outperformed Faster R-CNN with an accuracy of 98.5%, while Hasbi Athala et al. [6] demonstrated that YOLOv7 (98%) provided better performance than YOLOv4-tiny in banana detection. In the specific case of mangoes, the Light-YOLO model [18] achieved an mAP of 96.1%, confirming the effectiveness of optimized YOLO variants for fast and accurate fruit detection.

Recent improvements have also integrated advanced modules such as attention mechanisms and context fusion modules. For example, Lin et al. [11] combined YOLO with a *Global Context Fusion* module to improve citrus detection, achieving an mAP of 90%. In the case of mangoes, Cao et al. [3] applied YOLOv4 enhanced with a CBAM (*Convolutional Block Attention Module*), reaching an accuracy of 95.39% and a speed of 45 FPS, demonstrating the usefulness of attention mechanisms in refining localization and reducing false positives.

In summary, previous studies confirm the relevance of YOLO-based models for automatic fruit detection due to their balance between accuracy and speed. However, most studies are limited to distinguishing fruits from the background or assessing their maturity stage, without considering **inter-variety variability**. This limitation reduces the practical applicability of these approaches, particularly for crops such as mangoes where multiple varieties coexist with very similar visual characteristics.

It is in this context that our contribution is situated, focusing on the **detection of four mango varieties** cultivated in Burkina Faso: *Brooks*, *Mangot vert*, *Amélie*, and *Kent*. Unlike previous work, our goal is to **distinguish each variety**, by leveraging the potential of **YOLOv11** and evaluating its performance using **Average Precision (AP)** per variety and the overall **mAP**.

2 YOLO11 Architecture

YOLO11 (*You Only Look Once* version 11) is a real-time object detection model based on Convolutional Neural Networks (CNN), which directly detects objects in an image without a prior region proposal stage [13]. The architecture consists of three main components: the *backbone*, the *neck*, and the *head*. The *backbone* is a deep convolutional network that extracts hierarchical representations of the input image. For an input image $X \in \mathbb{R}^{H \times W \times 3}$, the backbone applies successively 23 convolutional layers: 12 convolutions of size 3×3 and 11 convolutions of size 1×1, each followed by Batch Normalization and the SiLU activation function. The first layers include a 2×2 *max pooling* with stride 2 to reduce spatial dimensions, while intermediate layers use stride-2 convolutions for progressive downsampling. The outputs of the main layers are feature maps $F_l \in \mathbb{R}^{H_l \times W_l \times C_l}$

where $H_l = H/2^{s_l}$, $W_l = W/2^{s_l}$, s_l is the downsampling factor at layer l, and C_l the number of output channels. The final output of the backbone is therefore:

$$F_{\text{backbone}} = f_{\text{backbone}}(X;\theta_b) \in \mathbb{R}^{H' \times W' \times C}, \tag{1}$$

with $H' = H/32$, $W' = W/32$, $C = 1024$, and θ_b the learned parameters. Attention modules such as CBAM [17] or SE (*Squeeze-and-Excitation*) are integrated into certain layers to enhance relevant feature extraction by reweighting feature maps both channel-wise and spatially.

The *neck* aggregates and fuses information from different backbone layers to detect objects of various sizes. YOLOv11 combines a *Feature Pyramid Network (FPN)* and a *Path Aggregation Network (PAN)*. The feature maps F_1, F_2, and F_3 from resolutions $H'/8 \times W'/8$, $H'/16 \times W'/16$, and $H'/32 \times W'/32$ are fused according to:

$$F_i^{\text{neck}} = \sum_{j \in \mathcal{S}(i)} w_{ij} \cdot \text{Resize}(F_j), \tag{2}$$

where Resize$(\cdot)$ corresponds to bilinear upsampling or stride-2 convolutional downsampling, w_{ij} are learnable weights, and $\mathcal{S}(i)$ the source maps for scale i. This multi-scale fusion allows the combination of fine and global information for detecting both small and large objects.

The *head* performs the final prediction on a grid of size $S \times S$ (typically $S = 20$ for 640×640 images), generating for each cell $B = 3$ bounding boxes with: normalized coordinates (x, y, w, h), the objectness score C, and the class probabilities p_c, $c = 1, ..., N_c$. The output of a single cell is:

$$y = [x, y, w, h, C, p_1, ..., p_{N_c}] \in \mathbb{R}^{5+N_c}, \tag{3}$$

and the overall prediction for the image is:

$$Y \in \mathbb{R}^{S \times S \times B \times (5+N_c)}. \tag{4}$$

The YOLOv11 loss function combines localization, confidence, and classification terms:

$$\mathcal{L} = \lambda_{\text{coord}}\mathcal{L}_{\text{coord}} + \lambda_{\text{obj}}\mathcal{L}_{\text{obj}} + \lambda_{\text{class}}\mathcal{L}_{\text{class}}, \tag{5}$$

with $\mathcal{L}_{\text{coord}} = \sum_{i,j} \mathbb{1}_{ij} \left((x_i - \hat{x}_i)^2 + (y_i - \hat{y}_i)^2 + (w_i - \hat{w}_i)^2 + (h_i - \hat{h}_i)^2\right)$, $\mathcal{L}_{\text{obj}}$ the Binary Cross-Entropy on objectness, and $\mathcal{L}_{\text{class}}$ the multi-class Cross-Entropy. Training is performed end-to-end to jointly optimize localization, confidence, and classification [9,13].

Finally, YOLOv11 improves upon previous versions by optimizing the backbone for multi-scale feature extraction, integrating CBAM/SE attention modules, combining FPN and PAN for small and medium-sized objects, and employing a loss function adapted to dense objects and imbalanced classes. These improvements enable high performance on complex datasets, such as the detection of mango varieties in natural orchards.

The figure (see figure 1) above illustrates the YOLO11 architecture, highlighting the three main components: the Backbone for feature extraction, the Neck for feature fusion, and the Head for object prediction across multiple tasks.

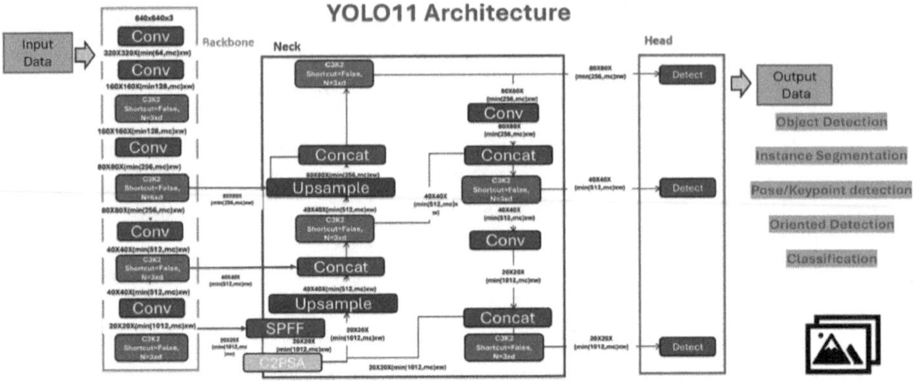

Fig. 1. YOLO11 Architecture [15].

3 Methodology

In order to carry out this study on the detection of mango varieties, we will begin with data collection and preprocessing, followed by training the **YOLO11** model. We will then proceed with the implementation and tuning of hyperparameters, conducting several experiments to optimize performance. Finally, the evaluation of the model will be carried out using indicators such as **precision**, **recall**, **F1-score**, as well as the mAP, chosen as the reference metric to validate the effectiveness of our approach.

3.1 Choice of Algorithms

Since its introduction in 2016 by Redmon et al. [13], the YOLO (You Only Look Once) algorithm has undergone rapid and continuous evolution. Each new version aimed to address the limitations of its predecessors by improving accuracy, inference speed, and model flexibility. As a result, YOLO has established itself as one of the most efficient architectures for real-time object detection.

YOLOv5, developed by Ultralytics, marked a significant transition by moving from Darknet to PyTorch, which facilitated adoption by the community thanks to a more user-friendly interface and better compatibility with modern environments [7]. Subsequently, YOLOv8 introduced more advanced tools for training and deployment, offering greater modularity and flexibility [8].

The recently released YOLOv11 stands out for its increased efficiency (approximately +22%) compared to previous versions, as well as multi-task support including detection, segmentation, and oriented bounding box (OBB) detection [9]. YOLOv12, on the other hand, incorporates spatial attention mechanisms and optimizations such as *FlashAttention*, but its comparative evaluation remains limited to date [16].

In this study, we selected YOLOv11 for its robustness, speed, and multitask compatibility, making it a good choice for mango variety detection. The main hyperparameters used for training YOLOv11 were set as follows: batch size = -1 (automatic), learning rate = 0.01, number of epochs = 100, confidence threshold = automatic, and IoU threshold = 0.7. The performance of different versions of YOLO is summarized in Figure 2.

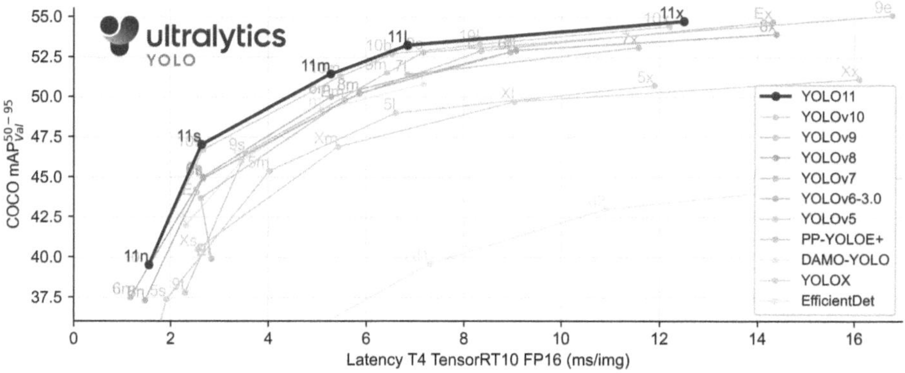

Fig. 2. Comparative performance evaluation of YOLO versions on the COCO dataset [9].

3.2 Data Preprocessing and Dataset Preparation

The mango varieties selected for this project are **Kent**, **Amélie**, **Mangot vert**, and **Retard** (see Fig. 3). They were chosen due to their strong representation in the South-West region of Burkina Faso, particularly in the Poni province around Gaoua, where the images were collected. This varietal diversity enriches the dataset and facilitates the identification and classification of mangoes during processing and model training.

Data preprocessing is a crucial step to ensure reliable identification and accurate classification of the four varieties. Figure 3, based on the study by [4], was used as a reference to distinguish mangoes according to their **morphological characteristics**, such as color, shape, texture, and size (see Table 1). This detailed analysis ensures consistent and scientifically grounded annotations, which are essential for supervised learning.

For image annotation, we used the online tool **Roboflow**[1], which provides a comprehensive platform for dataset management and preprocessing for computer vision. Roboflow allows uploading images, defining **bounding boxes** around objects of interest, labeling classes, and exporting the dataset in formats compatible with deep learning frameworks. Using this interface, each mango was precisely localized and labeled, ensuring optimal quality for training the YOLOv11 model.

[1] https://roboflow.com/.

Table 1. Qualitative characteristics of mango fruit at physiological maturity for different varieties (transposed)

Characteristics	Kent	Brooks	Amélie	Green mango
Skin color	green and purple	green	green	green
Stem cavity	deep	medium	medium	medium
Collar presence	absent	absent	absent	absent
Collar length	short	short	short	short
Ventral shoulder shape	rounded upward	rounded upward	rounded horizontal	rounded upward
Dorsal shoulder shape	rounded horizontal	rounded horizontal	abrupt break	slanted downward
Ventral shoulder groove length	short	short	medium	short
Ventral shoulder groove depth	shallow	shallow	medium	absent
Ventral shoulder protuberance	present	present	absent	absent
Sinus presence	absent	present	present	present
Sinus depth	shallow	shallow	shallow	shallow
Proximal stylar scar protuberance	present	absent	absent	absent
Stylar scar point	weak	medium	medium	medium

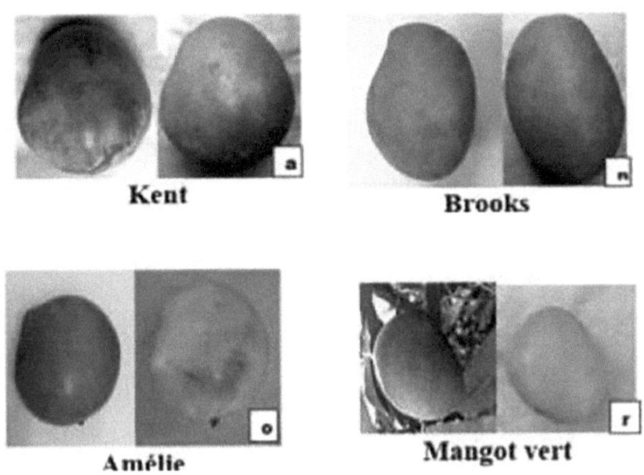

Fig. 3. Example of mango varieties used: Kent, Amelie, Green Mango and Brooks (Retard) [4] (Color figure online).

The final dataset consists of **400 images**, evenly distributed with **100 images per class**. To ensure good model generalization and prevent overfitting, the dataset was split using the **Hold-out** method into three subsets: **70%** of the images for training, **20%** for validation to tune hyperparameters, and **10%** for testing to evaluate the final model performance (see Fig. 4). This balanced distribution ensures both effective learning and rigorous evaluation, while maintaining the representative diversity of each variety across the different subsets.

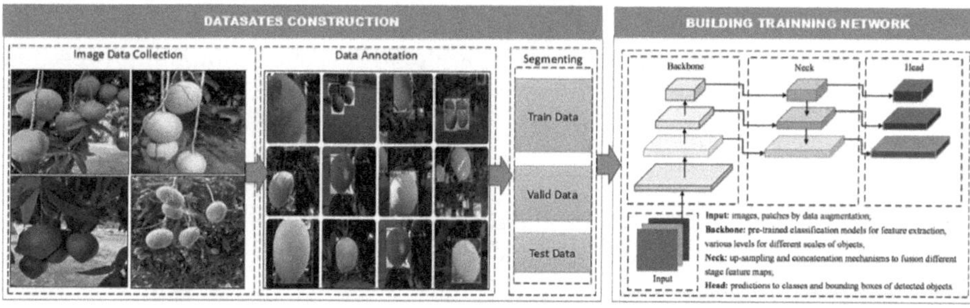

Fig. 4. Diagram of the methodology adopted for the detection of mango varieties.

3.3 Evaluating YOLO

The performance of the YOLOv11 model, used for the detection and classification of mango varieties, was evaluated using standard computer vision metrics to quantify its effectiveness. Precision measures the proportion of correct predictions among all positive predictions for a given class and is defined as

$$\text{Precision} = \frac{TP}{TP + FP}, \tag{6}$$

where TP (True Positives) represents mangoes correctly detected and classified (e.g., a Kent mango identified as such), and FP (False Positives) corresponds to incorrect detections. Recall, on the other hand, indicates the proportion of mangoes correctly detected among all mangoes actually present in the image, expressed as

$$\text{Recall} = \frac{TP}{TP + FN}, \tag{7}$$

with FN (False Negatives) denoting mangoes that were not detected or misclassified (e.g., a Retard mango not identified). The F1-score combines precision and recall to provide an overall measure of model performance, according to the formula

$$\text{F1-score} = 2 \times \frac{\text{Precision} \times \text{Recall}}{\text{Precision} + \text{Recall}}. \tag{8}$$

For the four mango varieties, the macro-average is used:

$$\text{F1}_{\text{macro}} = \frac{1}{N} \sum_{i=1}^{N} \text{F1}_i, \quad N = 4. \tag{9}$$

The Intersection over Union (IoU) evaluates the quality of the predicted bounding boxes compared to the ground truth boxes and is computed as

$$\text{IoU} = \frac{A \cap B}{A \cup B}, \tag{10}$$

where A and B represent the predicted and ground truth boxes, respectively. A detection is considered correct if the IoU exceeds a threshold, typically 0.5, which measures the localization accuracy of mangoes in the images. Finally, the Mean Average Precision (mAP) provides a global measure combining precision and recall across all classes. The Average Precision (AP) for a class corresponds to the area under the precision-recall curve, and the mAP is the mean of the APs over $N = 4$ varieties:

$$\mathrm{mAP} = \frac{1}{N}\sum_{i=1}^{N} \mathrm{AP}_i. \tag{11}$$

Two mAP variants are used: `mAP@0.5`, with IoU ≥ 0.5 for standard evaluation, and `mAP@0.5:0.95`, which corresponds to the average over IoU thresholds from 0.5 to 0.95 for a more rigorous evaluation. These combined metrics allow assessing YOLOv11's ability to accurately detect and classify the different mango varieties in the images.

4 Results and Discussion

In this section, we present the significant results obtained and discuss how these results can be used to optimize our mango harvesting project.

4.1 Results

Performance Metrics. The following Table 2 summarizes the performance indicators for *Mangot vert*, *Brooks(Retard)*, *Amelie*, and *Kent*. In this table (see Table 2), precision, recall, AP, and F1-score are expressed as percentages.

Table 2. Performance for each class

Classe	AP50	Reccal	Precision	F1-score
Amelie	70.9%	72.50%	67.44%	69.86%
Kente	64.4%	64.44%	69.05%	66.67%
MangotVert	71.13%	78.17%	87.7%	82.61%
Retard	73.6%	87.6%	78,5%	82.81%

4.2 Discussion

The results obtained for the four mango varieties reveal distinct differences in the performance of the YOLOv11 model (see Figs. 5 and 6).

For the **Amélie** variety, the model achieves an AP50 of 70.9%, with a recall of 72.50% and a precision of 67.44%. The F1-score of 69.86% indicates balanced performance, although the slightly lower precision suggests that some non-Amélie mangoes are incorrectly classified as Amélie. This misclassification is also observable in the confusion matrix (Fig. 6), where Amélie shares a significant number of false positives with Kent. This overlap likely arises from their strong visual resemblance, particularly in color and shape.

In contrast, the **Kent** variety shows weaker results, with an AP50 of 64.4%, recall of 64.44%, and precision of 69.05%. The resulting F1-score of 66.67% confirms the model's difficulty in identifying Kent consistently. The confusion matrix reveals multiple instances of Kent being misclassified as Amélie, supporting the hypothesis that morphological similarity and potentially fewer representative samples in the training set contribute to this performance gap.

The **Mangot vert** variety demonstrates the best overall performance, with an AP50 of 71.13%, precision of 87.7%, and recall of 78.17%. The F1-score of 82.61% is the highest among the four classes, indicating that the model is highly effective at detecting and classifying this variety. The PR curve (Fig. 5) confirms a strong balance between precision and recall across detection thresholds, suggesting that the distinct morphological traits of Mangot vert are well captured in the dataset.

Similarly, the **Brooks (Retard)** variety performs remarkably well, with an AP50 of 73.6%, recall of 87.6%, and precision of 78.5%. Its F1-score of 82.81% slightly surpasses that of Mangot vert, demonstrating that the model successfully detects most instances while maintaining a good trade-off between recall and precision. The corresponding region in the confusion matrix shows fewer misclassifications, confirming the model's robustness for this class.

Overall, the mAP reaches approximately 70%, reflecting satisfactory global performance (Fig. 5). Precision remains high across all classes, showing that when the model predicts a positive instance, it is generally correct. However, the variation in recall values highlights persistent detection challenges for certain

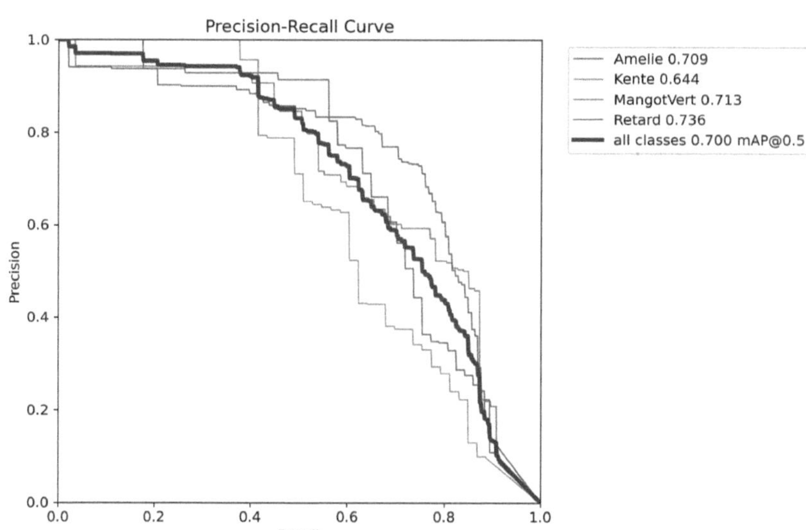

Fig. 5. Precision–Recall curves for the four mango varieties.

varieties—particularly **Kent** and, to a lesser extent, **Amélie**. Conversely, the consistently high F1-scores of **Mangot vert** and **Brooks** indicate that these classes are better learned by the model. These differences can be attributed to morphological variability, dataset imbalance, and visual similarities between some varieties, notably Amélie and Kent.

Figure 5 clearly shows that **Mangot vert** and **Brooks** achieve higher precision and recall balance compared to **Amélie** and **Kent**, whose curves lie slightly below, indicating less stable detection performance.

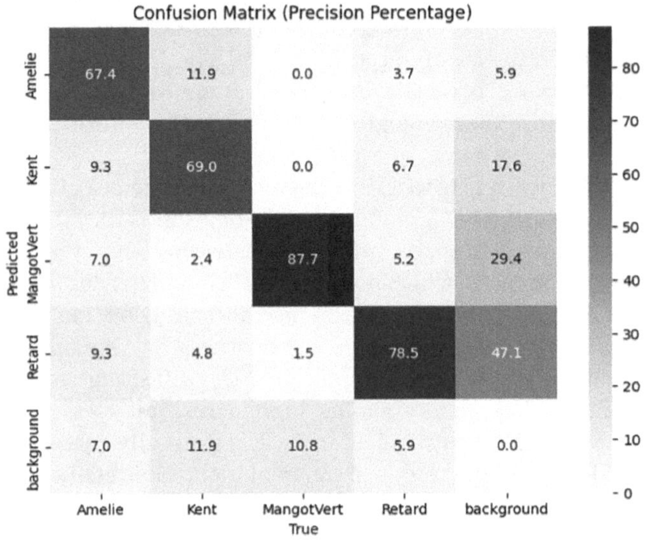

Fig. 6. Confusion matrix illustrating classification performance per variety.

The confusion matrix (Fig. 6) highlights that **Kent** and **Amélie** are the most frequently confused classes, confirming their morphological similarity. In contrast, **Mangot vert** and **Brooks** show high diagonal dominance, meaning that most of their instances are correctly classified.

Conclusion and Future Perspectives

Conclusion

This study addressed the challenge of accurately detecting and differentiating multiple mango varieties cultivated in Burkina Faso by evaluating the performance of the YOLOv11 model for automatic fruit detection. The results demonstrate that the model achieves a mean Average Precision (mAP) of approximately 70%, indicating a relatively satisfactory performance in classifying the different varieties. High precision values suggest that the model makes few errors in positive predictions. However, the detection of certain varieties, such as **Kent** and **Amélie**, remains challenging due to their strong visual similarity and morphological variability. In contrast, **Mangot vert** and **Brooks (Retard)** are more consistently identified, reflecting more reliable learning for these classes. These findings confirm both the potential of YOLOv11 as a tool for automating mango monitoring and harvesting and the limitations that arise when distinguishing visually similar varieties. Overall, this study provides a foundation for integrating AI-based detection systems into UAVs to support precision agriculture and enhance the management and sustainability of local mango varieties in Burkina Faso.

Future Perspectives

To improve model performance, several optimization avenues are envisaged. One approach is to enhance the training set by applying basic data augmentation techniques, such as rotation, cropping, color *jittering*, or horizontal flipping. These methods would increase the diversity of examples and enhance the model's robustness, particularly for morphologically similar varieties such as **Amélie** and **Kent**, which are often sources of confusion. Better differentiation between these similar classes would represent a significant improvement in the overall system accuracy.

Furthermore, although YOLOv11 has shown promising results, another alternative would be to test the performance of the more recent version, **YOLOv12**, which integrates improvements in efficiency and speed. In the longer term, it would also be relevant to consider the use of hybrid or multimodal architectures (vision + sensors) to further increase the robustness and reliability of the system under real agricultural conditions and for post-harvest sorting.

References

1. Bargoti, S., Underwood, J.: Deep fruit detection in orchards. In: IEEE International Conference on Robotics and Automation (ICRA), pp. 3626–3633 (2017)
2. Bikienga, M., Tougma, M.R., Somda, S.P., Zerbo, B.: Comparative study of YOLOv8, YOLOv9 and YOLOv10 by their ability to detect mangoes. In: International Conference on Multi-disciplinary Trends in Artificial Intelligence, pp. 77–88. Springer (2024)
3. Cao, H., al.: Real-time detection of mango based on improved YOLOv4 with CBAM attention. In: 2022 International Conference on Robotics and Automation (2022)
4. Drabo, C., Sawadogo, P., Sawadogo, N., Sanou, J., Sawadogo, M.: Leaf and fruit description of 18 varieties of mango tree (Mangifera indica L.) in Burkina Faso. Unknown J. (2024)
5. Gongal, A., Amatya, S., Karkee, M., Zhang, Q., Lewis, K.: Automated fruit detection and localization using multiple view geometry for robotic harvesting. Biosys. Eng. **146**, 129–139 (2018)

6. Hasbi Athala, M., et al.: Comparative analysis of banana detection models: YOLOv7 vs YOLOv4-tiny. In: 2022 International Conference on Computer Vision and Pattern Recognition (2022)
7. Jocher, G.: Ultralytics YOLOv5 (2020). https://doi.org/10.5281/zenodo.3908559. https://github.com/ultralytics/yolov5
8. Jocher, G., Chaurasia, A., Qiu, J.: Ultralytics YOLOv8 (2023). https://docs.ultralytics.com/models/yolov8
9. Jocher, G., Qiu, J.: Ultralytics YOLO11 (2024). https://github.com/ultralytics/ultralytics
10. Koirala, A., Walsh, K., Wang, Z., McCarthy, C.: Deep learning-method overview and review of use for fruit detection and yield estimation. Comput. Electron. Agric. **162**, 219–234 (2019)
11. Lin, Y., et al.: AG-YOLO: a rapid citrus fruit detection algorithm with global context fusion. In: 2021 IEEE International Conference on Image Processing (2021)
12. Noran, A., Ouf, F.: Leguminous seeds detection based on convolutional neural networks: comparison of faster R-CNN and YOLOv4. In: 2020 International Conference on Artificial Intelligence and Data Processing (IDAP), pp. 1–6. IEEE (2020)
13. Redmon, J., Divvala, S., Girshick, R., Farhadi, A.: You only look once: unified, real-time object detection. In: CVPR (2016)
14. Sa, I., Ge, Z., Dayoub, F., Upcroft, B., Perez, T., McCool, C.: DeepFruits: a fruit detection system using deep neural networks. Sensors (2016)
15. Sapkota, R., et al.: YOLO advances to its genesis: a decadal and comprehensive review of the you only look once (YOLO) series. Artif. Intell. Rev. **58**(9), 274 (2025)
16. Tian, Y., Ye, Q., Doermann, D.: YOLOv12: attention-centric real-time object detectors. arXiv preprint arXiv:2502.12524 (2025)
17. Woo, S., Park, J., Lee, J., Kweon, I.: CBAM: convolutional block attention module. In: ECCV, pp. 3–19 (2018)
18. Zhong, Z., Yun, L., Cheng, F., Chen, Z., Zhang, C.: Light-YOLO: a lightweight and efficient yolo-based deep learning model for mango detection. Agriculture **14**(1), 140 (2024)

AI Framework for E-Health: Validating EfficientNetV2s for Automated Diabetic Retinopathy Screening in Low-Resource Settings

Habeeb Oladimeji Oladipupo(✉) and Chika Yinka-Banjo

Department of Computer Science, University of Lagos, Lagos, Nigeria
249074147@live.unilag.edu.ng

Abstract. Diabetic Retinopathy (DR) is one of the leading causes of blindness, but its effective detection is hampered in low-resource settings by a shortage of ophthalmologists and the high computational cost of advanced Deep Learning models. This challenge creates a critical need for diagnostic tools that are highly accurate and computationally efficient. This research validates the performance of EfficientNetV2s, a lightweight architecture, for automated DR detection and grading. The model was benchmarked against three other lightweight baselines which are MobileNetV3-Small, FastViT-S12, and TinyViT on APTOS 2019 dataset. They were evaluated on two distinct tasks: a binary classification for initial detection and a five-class severity grading. The results demonstrate that EfficientNetV2s consistently outperformed all baseline models across both tasks, achieving a test accuracy of 98.5% for binary screening and 81.4% for multi-class severity grading. While being the largest and computationally most intensive of the tested models with 20.84 million parameters and an inference time of 16.75 ms, its superior diagnostic accuracy validated its position as the top-performing model for clinical applications. This study concludes that EfficientNetV2s provides an optimal balance of high diagnostic accuracy, validating its suitability as a powerful foundation for developing accessible, AI-powered screening tools to help mitigate the global burden of diabetic blindness.

Keywords: Diabetic Retinopathy · Deep Learning · Lightweight Architectures · EfficientNetV2S · Computer-Aided Diagnosis · Medical Image Analysis

1 Introduction

Diabetes, also called Diabetes mellitus, is a chronic metabolic condition that has reached global epidemic proportions, presenting a significant public health challenge ([1]). The IDF - International Diabetes Federation estimates that over 415 million adults worldwide live with diabetes, a figure projected to escalate [2, 3]. A prevalent and debilitating long-term complication of this condition is Diabetic Retinopathy (DR), a microvascular issue arising from prolonged damage to the blood vessels of the retina [4]. DR is a leading cause of vision impairment and irreversible blindness among the working-age

A. Oluwatope et al. (Eds.): AFRICOMM 2025, LNICST 713, pp. 191–204, 2027.
https://doi.org/10.1007/978-3-032-38682-3_12

population, particularly in developing nations. It is estimated that over one-third of individuals with diabetes will develop some form of retinopathy, placing millions at risk [5].

A key challenge in managing DR is its asymptomatic onset; patients typically experience no noticeable symptoms in the early stages as retinal damage accumulates [6]. Symptoms such as floaters or blurred vision only appear when the disease has progressed to advanced stages [5, 7]. The global burden of Diabetic Retinopathy disproportionately affects low-resource settings where a severe shortage of ophthalmologists creates a "diagnostic gap," leaving millions unscreened and at risk of preventable blindness [9]. This requires methodical, population scale screening programs which would be time consuming to perform in person. This reality in clinical practice warrants the design of automated diagnostic systems to ensure high-throughput, low-cost and reproducible screening. The latter stages of the disease can include more advanced symptoms and signs, such as venous beading, Intraretinal Microvascular Abnormalities (IRMAs), and neovascularization (the formation of new and weak blood vessels) [3, 8]. Based on such lesions, DR is mapped into different stages, which occur and are important in establishing a treatment. It is based on this multi-class categorisation, Grade 0 - No DR, Grade 1- Mild, Grade 2 - Moderate, Grade 3- Severe, Grade 4- Proliferative, that the diagnostic task of automated systems is defined [5]. Ophthalmologists manually interprets fundus photographs which are of the conventional standard, but are subjective, time-consuming and laborious and subject to inter-observer variability [9]. A shortage of qualified specialists, especially in low-income areas, leads to an insurmountable global shortage of specialists that would make the manual screening of large amounts of people impossible [3].

The growth and expansion of deep learning (DL), especially, the Convolutional Neural Networks (CNN), has transformed the progress of the field of automated DR detection, as it has now been shown that more consistently than conventional machine learning algorithms and models, they can outperform them in the analysis of medical images [8, 9]. While powerful, many advanced CNNs are computationally complex, with large model sizes and millions of parameters, making them unsuitable for deployment in low-resource settings. Diagnostics must be deliverable on portable, low-cost hardware like smartphones, which have limited processing power and memory. This has driven the development of "lightweight" neural networks designed for high accuracy with a small memory footprint [4, 10]. A fundamental trade-off exists between the diagnostic accuracy and computational efficiency of current DR detection models.

This creates a significant research gap for a novel CNN architecture that is both diagnostically accurate for multi-class DR grading and computationally efficient for practical deployment on standard, affordable and resource-constrained hardware. Models like EfficientNetV2s are theoretically promising, their effectiveness must be rigorously evaluated on a relevant dataset and benchmarked against other lightweight models to confirm their suitability as a real-world solution for low-resource settings. This research aims to implement & evaluate the performance of the lightweight model, EfficientNetV2s model for the early detection and severity grading of DR, using other lightweight models as a baseline to validate its suitability for deployment in low-resource settings.

The research will offer a direct performance benchmark of the state-of-the-art EfficientNetV2s model on a critical medical imaging task. This contributes valuable, practical insights into the real-world application of efficient DL models in healthcare. The findings can directly inform the development of an affordable and accessible AI-powered diagnostic tool that does not require specialized, high-cost hardware. This makes large-scale screening programs feasible, helping to bridge the "diagnostic gap" in underserved communities and making a tangible impact on public health.

2 Materials and Methods Review of Literature

2.1 The Deep Learning Paradigm Shift with CNNs

With the introduction of more powerful technology like DL and CNNs it is possible to state that the introduction of this technology in the field of defect detection was very successful. It has made a paradigmatic shift around automated DR detection. The critical innovation of CNNs is their ability to perform automatic, end-to-end features learning directly from raw pixel data, thereby circumventing the entire handcrafted feature engineering pipeline [5]. Through a hierarchical structure of convolutional layers, a CNN autonomously learns to recognize relevant patterns. Initial layers learn to identify simple features like edges and textures, while deeper layers learn to combine these to recognize highly complex and abstract pathological structures, such as the specific morphology of microaneurysms or neovascularization [6, 7]. This capacity has allowed deep learning models to consistently and significantly outperform traditional systems, achieving diagnostic accuracies that rival or even surpass those of human experts and establishing them as the new state-of-the-art [4].

2.2 Review of Related Literature

A key study on the shortcomings of transfer learning by [1] compared the performance of pre-trained ResNet-18 and ResNet-50 against a custom-designed, non-pretrained CNN. The presented CNN is a non-pretrained CNN model trained on the APTOS 2019 dataset. In their findings, they have discovered a crucial problem when the deep pre-trained models were involved as they faced catastrophic performance degradation. The size of data used was considerably too large in relation to the results obtained. The precision of ResNet-18 dropped by 70%, to 26% when in fine. tuning. In comparison, Shallow CNN uniformly gave better results than that of the ResNets. The model depicted an accuracy of 91% and showed stable learning. Regarding DR classification the study concluded that the complexity of deep ResNet models is disadvantageous though as they tend to memorize data rather than learning generalizable pathological features.

[2] introduced a new hybrid model that combined a pre-trained EfficientNet for feature extraction with an XGBoost classifier. The combination of EfficientNet with the XGBoost classifier demonstrated the best results and reached 99.1% accuracy on the APTOS dataset and 99.2% on the IDRID dataset, showing the powerful synergy of hybrid models. The combination of EfficientNet with the XGBoost classifier demonstrated the best results and reached 99.1% accuracy on APTOS set. The hybrid model reached an

accuracy of 99.29% on the IDRID dataset, which shows hybrid models come into play in a synergistic way.

With model compression in mind, [12] examined a light approach to resource-constrained settings by minimizing large models. They clustered the weights of three deep structures with VGG-19, DenseNet-121 and EfficientNet-B6. In their experiments on dataset APTOS-2019, the use of weighted clustering displayed the best results with EfficientNet-B6, making the size of the model 12 times smaller but with a stable high classification accuracy at 92%. This paper highlighted the effectiveness of model compression methods in improving the practicability of powerful, advanced models.

In one of the studies by [13], lightweight architecture MobileNetV2 was applied to build a high-performance system to detect the presence of DR. They tested their model on the APTOS 2019 dataset, and the overall accuracy is 95% in a two-stage classification task (DR vs. No Dr) and 75% for the five-stage severity classification, which is more granular. The study showed the benefits of MobileNetV2 in terms of DR analysis; the methodology was indeed showing potential to deliver high accuracy at a significantly low number of parameters as compared to deeper architectures.

In a study by [14], the authors implemented a CNN-based system, in which the DR classification into five classes resulted in an accuracy of 90%. Despite the good results with healthy and moderate DR stages, the authors indicate that it was quite a challenge in terms of the reduced recall of Proliferative and Severe DR stages. This observation clearly indicates the important problem of the imbalance of classes and the inability of deep learning models to reliably identify rare but acutely important stages of the disease.

Finally, [15] presented an approach to optimize the use of ResNet50 with transfer learning, specifically for imbalanced DR datasets. Their method incorporated data augmentation, oversampling, and an automated learning rate finder to improve training efficiency. A key contribution of their work was the use of Class Activation Maps (CAMs) to enhance model interpretability, creating heatmaps that visualize the most important regions in a retinal image that influenced the model's diagnostic decision. This approach not only achieved a high accuracy of 91.8% but also provided a valuable tool for aiding ophthalmologists in understanding and trusting the model's predictions.

2.3 The Identified Gap: Lack of Rigorous Benchmarking for Point-of-Care Deployment

Despite the clear trend towards lightweight models, a critical research gap persists. The existing literature often has one or more of the following limitations:

1. Limited Scope of Comparison: Many studies compare their proposed model against only one or two heavyweight baselines (e.g., ResNet-50) or a small selection of other lightweight models, without a comprehensive, side-by-side evaluation of the leading efficient candidates [16].
2. Focus on Accuracy Alone: While accuracy is a critical metric, many studies do not provide a holistic evaluation that includes key computational efficiency metrics such as parameter count, model size (MB), and inference time on standardized hardware [5]. This makes it hard to objectively compare the practical deployability of different types of models.

3. Underutilization of State-of-the-Art Efficient Models: While foundational lightweight models like MobileNetV2 are frequently used, there is less research that rigorously benchmarks the newer, highly promising variants like EfficientNetV2 against other top-performing lightweight models in a single, controlled experimental setup.

2.4 Research Design Architecture

This work follows a quantitative experimental research method to describe and analyze the working capabilities of a series of lightweight CNN architectures. The study design is done in such a manner that there is objectivity in the evaluation process, it can be repeated and is directly related to the research aims. The research process structure is arranged as shown in Fig. 1:

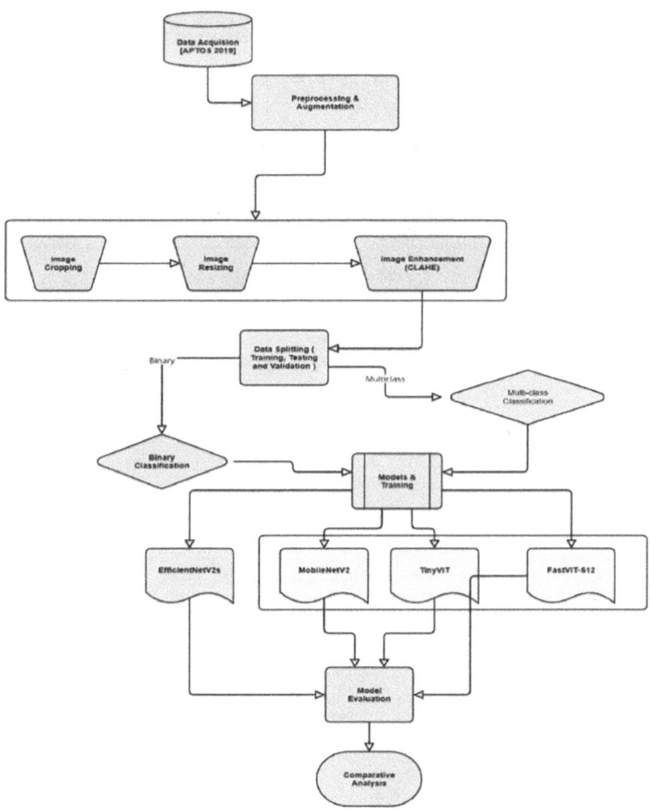

Fig. 1. Architecture of model development

2.5 Dataset Description

This research exclusively utilizes the APTOS 2019 dataset, which is a publicly available collection of high-resolution retinal fundus images sourced from Kaggle. This dataset is a widely recognized benchmark for developing and validating DR detection algorithms. It was curated by Aravind Eye Hospital in India and contains 3,662 fundus images captured under various imaging conditions, reflecting a real-world clinical scenario. Each of the photos contained in the data as shown in Fig. 2 has been rated by a qualified clinician using the International Clinical scale of diabetic retinopathy disease severity.

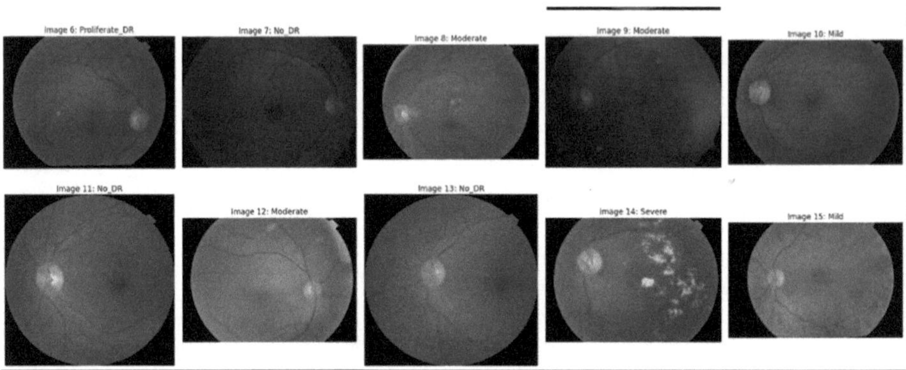

Fig. 2. Dataset from APTOS 2019 showing data classification

The pictures are sorted into five broad categories of images the stages of the disease:

Table 1. APTOS 2019 dataset from Kaggle category

Grade	Severity Level	Number of Images	Percentage
0	No DR	1805	49.29%
1	Mild - Non-Proliferative DR (NPDR)	370	10.10%
2	Moderate NPDR	999	27.28%
3	Severe NPDR	193	5.27%
4	Proliferative (PDR)	295	8.06%
Total		**3662**	**100%**

The major feature of this dataset is also its great class imbalance as presented in Table 1. The class of 'No DR' occupies almost half of the data, whereas more profound areas, especially 'Severe NPDR' and 'Proliferative DR' are underrepresented significantly. This skew creates a major challenge to training the deep learning model, which can result in bias towards the majority classes in classification. It pays to address this imbalance because it is a significant part of data preprocessing and methodology of training.

2.6 Data Preprocessing and Augmentation

To aid in the standardization of the input data, data preprocessing/augmentation pipeline has been developed, that aims at improving image quality and eliminating the risks of overfitting and class imbalance.

1. **Data Preprocessing**: The raw images were taken through a set of preprocessing procedures with the help of the cv2 library:
   - **Image Cropping**: A custom crop_image_from_gray function was used to remove the dark border around the fundus images, focusing the model on the relevant anatomical features.
   - **Image Resizing**: The cropped images were then resized to a uniform dimension of **384x384 pixels**, a standard input size for the selected models.
   - **Image Enhancement**: CLAHE, known as Contrast Limited Adaptive Histogram Equalization, was applied to the R, G, and B channels of each image to improve the visibility of key pathological features like microaneurysms and hemorrhages. This process was parallelized using a ThreadPoolExecutor for efficient processing of the entire dataset.
   - **Data Augmentation**: To address the significant class imbalance and expand the diversity of the training set, a series of data augmentation techniques were applied on-the-fly during model training using torchvision.transforms, they include Geometric Transformations, Photometric Transformations and Mixup Augmentation.

2.7 Model Selection

The selection of models was guided by the objective of this research which is to identify a CNN architecture that is both diagnostically accurate and computationally lightweight.

Primary Model: EfficientNetV2s: EfficientNetV2s was chosen as the primary model due to its state-of-the-art design, which explicitly optimizes for both training speed and parameter efficiency. It incorporates architectural improvements like Fused-MBConv blocks and a progressive training strategy, making it a strong candidate for high-performance applications on resource-constrained hardware.

Baseline Models: To establish a robust performance benchmark, three other well-established lightweight CNNs were selected for comparison. They are MobileNetV2, a TinyViT variant, and a FastViT-S12 variant. MobileNetV2 is a widely adopted lightweight architecture known for its use of depthwise separable convolutions to dramatically reduce computational cost. TinyViT is a compact variant of the Vision Transformer architecture, designed to bring the power of transformers to resource-constrained devices, chosen to benchmark performance against a non-CNN architecture. FastViT-S12 is a modern, efficient hybrid architecture that combines the strengths of convolutional layers for local feature extraction with the global context capabilities of transformers, selected for its reported balance of speed and accuracy.

Fig. 3 shows the Architecture of a CNN. It is fundamentally constructed by multiple layers of successive learning of hierarchical feature representations of images. Convolutional layers use filters to identify spatial features like edges, textures and color gradients;

pooling layers decrease the spatial dimension and preserve the necessary information and the final fully connected layers convert the extracted features into classification.

2.8 Experimental Setup

For both experiments (**Binary Classification (Early Detection)** and **Multi-class Classification (Severity Grading)**), the dataset was partitioned into training, validation, and testing sets using a stratified 70:15:15 split. This ensures the model is trained on a large portion of the data, validated on a separate set for hyperparameter tuning & early stopping, and finally evaluated on a completely unseen test set to provide an unbiased measure of its performance.

2.9 Model Architecture

This architecture, shown in Fig. 3, leverages the powerful feature extraction capabilities of a pre-trained backbone and appends a custom classification head designed to produce two distinct predictions from a single input image. The architecture consists of three main components:

1. **Pre-trained Backbone:** The core of the model is a pre-trained lightweight network. This backbone processes the 384x384 input image through its series of convolutional (Conv) and pooling (Pool) layers.
2. **Shared Fully Connected (FC) Head:** The original classifier of the pre-trained backbone is removed. In its place, the feature map is first flattened and then passed through a shared head consisting of fully connected layers. Based on the implementation, this involves a dense layer of 512 neurons with a ReLU activation function and dropout for regularization.
3. **Dual Output Head:** The output from the shared FC head is then fed into two separate and parallel linear layers, each tailored for a specific task.

During inference, a Softmax function is applied to the logits from each head to generate the final class probabilities. This dual-output design is highly efficient, as the computationally intensive feature extraction process is performed only once per image.

2.10 Model Training Procedure

All models were trained following a consistent transfer learning methodology. The process involved loading the models with weights pre-trained on ImageNet, which provides a strong foundation of general feature extraction capabilities. The final classification layer of each model was replaced with a new, dual-head architecture tailored to the specific tasks.

The training was governed by the following hyperparameters, selected based on common practices in medical image analysis and preliminary experimentation:

The training process was governed by the following hyperparameters and techniques:

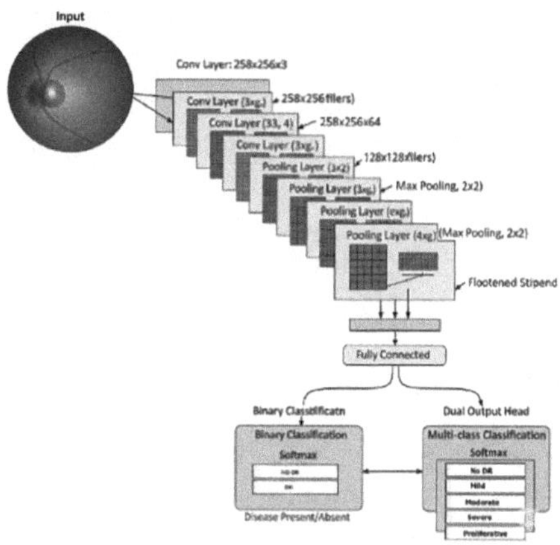

Fig. 3. The dual-output CNN architecture used for the experiments

- **Optimizer:** The AdamW optimizer was used. The core of the optimization is the gradient descent update rule, which iteratively adjusts the model's parameters (θ) to minimize the loss function (L) based on the learning rate (η):

$$\Theta := \Theta - \eta \frac{\partial L}{\partial \Theta} \tag{1}$$

- **Loss Function:** A composite loss function was employed. For the multi-class task, **Categorical Cross-Entropy** was used:

$$L = -\sum_{i=1}^{N} \cdot \sum_{c=1}^{C} [yi, c \; log \; (\check{Y}i)] \tag{2}$$

For the binary task, a weighted **Binary Cross-Entropy** was used to address class imbalance:

$$L = 1/N \sum_{i=1}^{N} [yi \; log \; (\check{Y}i) + (1 - yi) \; log \; (1 - \check{Y}i)] \tag{3}$$

- **Learning Rate and Scheduler:** An initial learning rate of 1e-4 was set, with a Cosine Annealing Warm Restarts scheduler to cyclically adjust the rate during training.
- **Batch Size:** A batch size of 32 was used to balance memory consumption and training stability.
- **Class Imbalance Handling:** A **WeightedRandomSampler** was applied to the training DataLoader to oversample the minority classes, ensuring the model sees a more balanced distribution of data.
- **Epochs and Early Stopping:** The Models were trained for a maximum of 20 epochs, and with an Early Stopping mechanism to stop the training if the validation loss did not improve for five consecutive epochs.
- **Performance Optimization: Automatic Mixed Precision (AMP)** was used to accelerate training and reduce GPU memory usage.

2.11 System Tools and Requirements

The experiment was conducted within the Google Colaboratory cloud environment using the NVIDIA GPU (Tesla T4), which provided the necessary computational resources and a managed software stack. It was implemented in Python, leveraging several key libraries and frameworks for deep learning and image processing, which are PyTorch, PyTorch Image Models (timm), OpenCV (cv2), torchvision.transforms, NumPy and Pandas.

3 Results and Discussion

This section presents the quantitative results obtained from the evaluation of the four selected lightweight models on the held-out test set.

For the primary screening task of identifying the presence or absence of DR, all models were evaluated on their binary classification performance. And the more challenging task of grading DR into its five severity levels, the models were evaluated on their multi-class classification performance. The results, including accuracy, weighted F1-Score, and the Area Under the Receiver Operating Characteristic Curve (AUC-ROC), are summarized in Table 2.

Table 2. Performance comparison of models on binary and multiclass classification task (Test Set)

Metric	EfficientNetV2-S	FastViT-S12	MobileNetV3-Small	TinyViT-11 M
Binary Classification				
Accuracy (%)	98.50%	97.30%	96.20%	96.20%
Weighted F1-Score	0.9854	0.9727	0.9617	0.9618
AUC-ROC	0.9955	0.9932	0.9941	0.9922
Multi-class Classification				
Accuracy (%)	81.40%	80.10%	80.30%	71.00%
F1-Score (Weighted)	0.821	0.795	0.807	0.709
Computational Efficiency				
Parameter Count (Millions)	20.84	8.98	2.05	10.78
Model Size (MB)	80.35	34.62	7.94	41.29
Inference Time (ms)	16.75	9.64	6.96	13.26

One of the objectives of this research is to evaluate the computational footprint of each model. Table 2 also provides a direct comparison of the models based on their total learnable parameter count, their final saved model size on disk and average CPU inference time.

The training history of the EfficientNetV2s model over 20 epochs is visualized in Fig. 4. The plots for training and validation loss and accuracy demonstrate a stable and effective learning process.

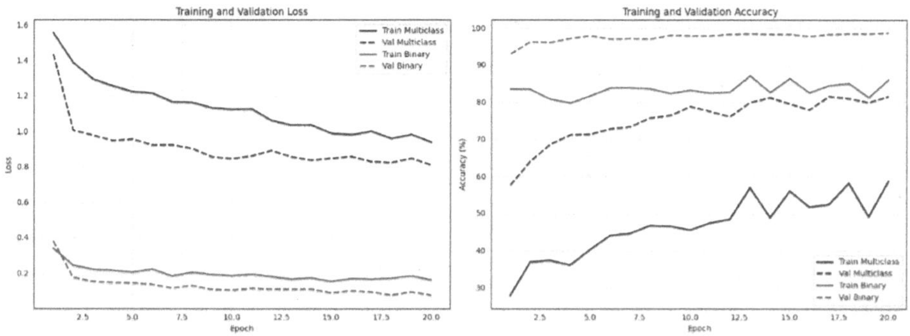

Fig. 4. The dual-output CNN architecture used for the experiments training and validation loss and accuracy for EfficientNetV2s over 20 epochs

The loss curves (left) show a consistent decrease for both training and validation sets, indicating that the model was successfully learning to minimize error. The validation loss remained consistently low, confirming that the regularization techniques (e.g., data augmentation, Mixup, weighted loss) were effective in preventing overfitting. The accuracy curves (right) show a corresponding steady increase. Notably, the validation accuracy for both tasks remained higher than the training accuracy throughout, a hallmark of well-regularized models where techniques like dropout make the training task inherently more difficult than validation. The binary task accuracy quickly converged to a high level (>95%), while the more complex multi-class task showed a smooth and continuous learning trajectory, validating the stability of the training setup.

3.1 Discussion and Analysis

The experimental results provide a clear validation of the EfficientNetV2s model's efficacy for DR classification, particularly when analyzed in the context of the baseline models and the fundamental trade-off between diagnostic performance and computational efficiency.

The superior diagnostic capability of EfficientNetV2s is evident across both tasks. In the binary screening task, it achieved an accuracy of 98.5%, demonstrating outstanding reliability. This performance is visually confirmed by its confusion matrix (Fig. 5), which shows an extremely low number of errors: only one DR case was missed (false negative) and only seven healthy cases were misclassified (false positives). This high sensitivity is critical for a screening tool.

In the multi-class grading task, the 81.4% accuracy of EfficientNetV2s again surpassed all baselines. The multi-class confusion matrix (Fig. 5) offers deeper insight

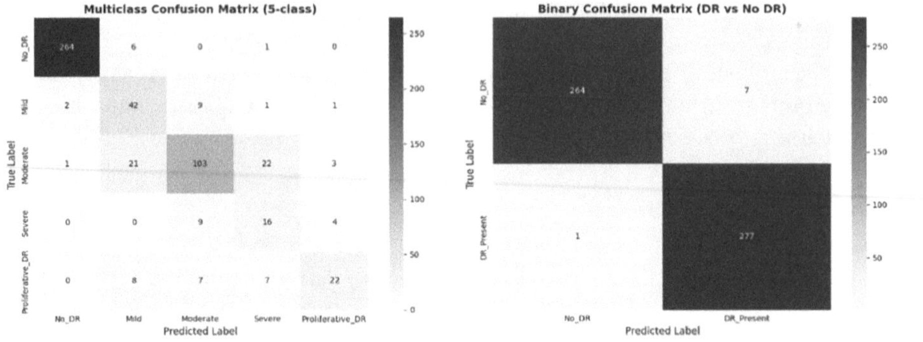

Fig. 5. Confusion matrices for EfficientNetV2s on the test set for multi-class and bi-nary classification

into its performance. The model performed exceptionally well on "No DR" cases (97% recall). While it faced challenges with the underrepresented "Severe" class, it demonstrated a strong ability to classify the crucial early and intermediate stages. For instance, its recall for "Mild" DR was 76.4%, substantially outperforming MobileNetV3-Small (65.5%), FastViT-S12 (74.5%), and TinyViT (72.7%). This enhanced sensitivity for early-stage disease is a highly desirable characteristic for a screening tool.

The computational metrics in Table 2 highlight the diversity among lightweight models. MobileNetV3-Small stands out as the most efficient, with only 2.05 million parameters, a mere 7.94 MB model size, and the fastest CPU inference time of 6.96 ms. In contrast, EfficientNetV2-S is the largest of the four, with 20.84 million parameters, an 80.35 MB footprint, and a CPU inference time of 16.75 ms. While significantly leaner than heavyweight models like VGG-16 (~138 M parameters), it carries a substantially larger and slower computational profile than the other lightweight baselines in this study.

The results confirm that EfficientNetV2-S achieves this balance most effectively. While MobileNetV3-Small offers superior computational efficiency in terms of size and speed, this comes at the cost of a tangible drop in diagnostic accuracy most critically, a lower performance in the multi-class task which is essential for grading. An inference time of 16.75 ms is still extremely fast for any practical point-of-care application, making the trade-off of slightly higher latency for significantly better accuracy a worthwhile one.

Therefore, this study validates EfficientNetV2s as a highly suitable architecture for DR screening. It successfully resolves the accuracy-efficiency trade-off by delivering the highest diagnostic performance among the tested lightweight models, confirming its value as a powerful and practical solution for deployment in resource-constrained clinical settings where diagnostic confidence is the highest priority.

4 Conclusion

The aim of this research was to implement and evaluate the performance of the EfficientNetV2s model for the early detection and severity grading of Diabetic Retinopathy, using other lightweight models as a baseline to validate its suitability for deployment in low-resource settings. Based on comprehensive experimental results and analysis, this research concludes that EfficientNetV2s is a highly effective and robust architecture for automated DR detection that provides a superior balance of diagnostic accuracy and computational efficiency compared to its lightweight peers.

Despite the successful fulfillment of the research objectives, it is crucial to recognize the study's constraints to properly contextualize the findings and guide subsequent research. They include, Single-Dataset Evaluation, although this dataset is a well-regarded benchmark, the capacity of the model to generalize images from varied patient populations, different clinical environments, or those captured with alternative fundus cameras has not been empirically verified. Also, the assessment of computational efficiency was based on parameter count and model size on disk. A more comprehensive evaluation would involve measuring real-world inference latency (time per image) and power consumption on actual low-cost hardware, such as a smartphone CPU or an edge computing device. As a computational study, this research does not include validation in a real-world clinical trial. The ultimate utility of the model depends on its performance and integration into the workflow of ophthalmologists and primary care providers.

The following recommendations are proposed for future research: External Validation on Diverse Datasets, to further confirm the model's robustness and generalization capabilities, the trained EfficientNetV2s model should be evaluated on other publicly available DR datasets without retraining. Hardware Deployment and Latency Benchmarking: A critical next step is to deploy the saved EfficientNetV2s model on a range of actual low-cost hardware platforms (e.g., smartphones, Raspberry Pi, Jetson Nano) and to measure its real-world performance in terms of inference speed (images per second) and power consumption. Model Optimization and Compression to explore the application of post-training optimization techniques, such as model quantization (e.g., converting weights to 8-bit integers) and pruning, to the validated EfficientNetV2s model.

References

1. Praneeth, D., Kumar, N.S.: Diabetic retinopathy detection and categorizing using a lightweight deep learning approach. ARPN J. Eng. Appl. Sci. **19** (2024)
2. Chandrakala, K., Tulasi, Y., Shanmukhi, D., RaveenaRai, M., SriHarshitha, D.: Efficient transfer learning model for automated diabetic retinopathy grading in resource-constrained environment. In: 2nd International Conference on Automation, Computing and Renewable Systems, ICACRS 2023 - Proceedings, pp. 1397–1404. Institute of Electrical and Electronics Engineers Inc. (2023). https://doi.org/10.1109/ICACRS58579.2023.10404251
3. Mantaqa, M.N., Anjom, J., Hossain, M.I.A.: Diabetic retinopathy detection using a lightweight edge intelligence-based technique. In: 2024 IEEE International Conference on Biomedical Engineering, Computer and Information Technology for Health, BECITHCON 2024, pp. 113–118. Institute of Electrical and Electronics Engineers Inc. (2024). https://doi.org/10.1109/BECITHCON64160.2024.10962647
4. Iluno, C.C., Sah, M.: Handling Class Imbalance Problem for Diabetic Retinopathy Fundus Image Classification. In: ICHORA 2025–2025 7th International Congress on Human-Computer Interaction, Optimization and Robotic Applications, Proceedings. Institute of Electrical and Electronics Engineers Inc. (2025). https://doi.org/10.1109/ICHORA65333.2025.11017270
5. Alif, M.A.R.: Enhancing Diabetic Retinopathy Diagnosis: A Lightweight CNN Architecture for Efficient Exudate Detection in Retinal Fundus Images (2024)

6. Hussain, M.: Exudate detection: integrating retinal-based affine mapping and design flow mechanism to develop lightweight architectures. IEEE Access **11**, 125185–125203 (2023). https://doi.org/10.1109/ACCESS.2023.3328386
7. Birajdar, U., Gadhave, S., Chikodikar, S., Dadhich, S.: Detection and classification of diabetic retinopathy using convolutional neural networks and fundus images. IJARIIE **4**, 2018 (2018)
8. Aujih, A.B., Shapiai, M.I., Meriaudeau, F., Tang, T.B.: EDR-net: lightweight deep neural network architecture for detecting referable diabetic retinopathy. IEEE Trans. Biomed. Circuits Syst. **16**, 467–478 (2022). https://doi.org/10.1109/TBCAS.2022.3182907
9. Das, D., Biswas, S.K., Bandyopadhyay, S.: Detection of diabetic retinopathy using convolutional neural networks for feature extraction and classification (DRFEC). Multimed. Tools Appl. **82**, 29943–30001 (2023). https://doi.org/10.1007/s11042-022-14165-4
10. Yi, D., Baltov, P., Hua, Y., Philip, S., Sharma, P.K.: Compound scaling encoder-decoder (CoSED) network for diabetic retinopathy related bio-marker detection. IEEE J. Biomed. Health Inform. **28**, 1959–1970 (2024). https://doi.org/10.1109/JBHI.2023.3313785
11. Patiño-Pérez, D., Armijos-Valarezo, L., Chóez-Acosta, L., Burgos-Robalino, F.: Convolutional neural networks for diabetic retinopathy detection. Ingenius 91–101 (2025). https://doi.org/10.17163/ings.n33.2025.08
12. Abood, H.R., Hamad, A.H.: Optimizing diabetic retinopathy classification with transfer learning: a lightweight approach using model clustering. Iraqi J. Comput. Inf. **50**, 90–100 (2024). https://doi.org/10.25195/ijci.v50i2.533
13. Vineela, T., Krishnave, K., Meghana, K., Lekhana, B., Swathi, M.: Diabetic retinopathy detection using mobilenetv2 model. Int. Sci. J. Eng. Manag. **02** (2023). https://doi.org/10.55041/isjem00191
14. Mittal, P., Sharma, B., Yadav, D.P., Dhaou, I.: Ben: enhancing blindness detection using deep learning with MobileNet and SE blocks. In: 2025 International Conference on Control, Automation and Diagnosis (ICCAD), pp. 1–5. IEEE (2025). https://doi.org/10.1109/ICCAD64771.2025.11099419
15. Panda, P., Sahoo, D., AP, M., Sahoo, D.: Efficient diabetic retinopathy detection using ResNet50-based transfer learning with optimized performance. In: 2025 S International Conference on Cognitive Robotics and Intelligent Systems (ICC - ROBINS), pp. 687–691. IEEE (2025). https://doi.org/10.1109/ICC-ROBINS64345.2025.11086154
16. Giraddi, S., Chickerur, S., Patil, M.S., Kanakaraddi, S., Giraddi, V.: Lightweight Convolution Neural Network for Diabetic Retinopathy Grading. In: MysuruCon 2022–2022 IEEE 2nd Mysore Sub Section International Conference. Institute of Electrical and Electronics Engineers Inc. (2022). https://doi.org/10.1109/MysuruCon55714.2022.9972448.

IoTs, Blockchain and Energy

Towards Real-Time IoT-Driven Air Condition Monitoring for Factory Environments: A Uganda Industrial Case Study

Nasser Kimbugwe(✉), Alanda Ambrose, B. Mugarura Kevin, Kirabo Jelly Rollings, Musiimenta Cynthia, and Mary Nsabagwa

Makerere University, Kampala, Uganda
nasser.kimbugwe@mak.ac.ug

Abstract. Uganda's fast industrialization has sparked serious worries about the quality of the air in factories where workers are exposed to dangerous chemicals and particles. The design, creation, and validation of FactoryAirWatch—a real-time Internet of Things (IoT)-powered air conditioning monitoring system especially suited for Ugandan industry environments—are presented in this paper. The system monitors important air quality indicators as carbon monoxide, volatile organic compounds, methane, particle matter (PM2.5, PM10), temperature, and humidity by integrating locally constructed IoT sensor nodes with a cloud analytics platform. For real-time viewing, reporting, and alerting, the current version integrates cloud storage via ThingSpeak, edge-based threshold detection, GSM-based data transfer, and a web-based dashboard developed with React and Next.js. The design also anticipates future extensions such as LoRaWAN fallback connectivity and AI-based predictive analytics. During pilot deployment, the system showed strong performance, with high system availability and end-to-end latency of less than 60 s. The system design, installation procedure, evaluation results, and wider theoretical and practical ramifications for occupational safety and regulatory compliance in East African manufacturing sectors are all covered in this study.

Keywords: Internet of Things · Air quality monitoring · Factory Environment · Edge Computing · Industrial Safety · Low-Cost Sensors · Factory Environments · Edge Computing · Occupational Safety

1 Introduction

Rapid industrial expansion across East Africa has intensified concerns about air quality within manufacturing environments. In Uganda, growing sectors—ranging from agro-processing to metal fabrication—have led to increased emissions of harmful pollutants including, volatile organic compounds (VOCs), carbon monoxide (CO) and other particulate matter (like $PM_{2.5}$ and PM_{10}), introducing significant health risks for plant workers and nearby communities [1]. According to the World Health Organization [2], long-term

A. Oluwatope et al. (Eds.): AFRICOMM 2025, LNICST 713, pp. 207–219, 2027.
https://doi.org/10.1007/978-3-032-38682-3_13

exposure to fine particulates is associated with respiratory and cardiovascular diseases, highlighting the urgent need for robust monitoring systems. Traditional periodic measurements—commonly conducted monthly or quarterly—are insufficient for identifying transient peaks in pollution that can have acute health impacts [3, 4]

Recent advances in the Internet of Things (IoT) have transformed environmental monitoring, offering cost-effective, continuous sensing solutions that can be deployed at scale [5, 6]. Low-cost sensor networks, leveraging microcontroller platforms (e.g., Arduino, ESP32) and gas sensor modules (e.g., Figaro, MQ-series), have gained considerable attention [7, 8].These systems can effectively detect PM concentrations, CO, ozone (O_3), and VOCs with reasonable accuracy after careful calibration [9, 10].

Despite their promise, deploying IoT sensor networks in industrial settings remains challenging. Harsh factory conditions—with high temperatures, humidity, dust, and electromagnetic interference—can degrade sensor performance and accelerate calibration drift [11, 12]. Connectivity challenges due to intermittent cellular network or Wi-Fi signals can further limit data reliability and real-time alerting capabilities [13, 14]. Several studies have explored industrial air monitoring using LoRaWAN or NB-IoT communications to mitigate such issues [15, 16], but these technologies remain largely underutilized in low-resource manufacturing environments.

Edge computing has emerged as a viable solution to reduce latency, conserve bandwidth, and enable near-instantaneous response to hazardous conditions [17, 18]. Integrating TinyML algorithms into IoT edge devices allows for real-time anomaly detection and event-triggered alerts without needing constant cloud connectivity [19]. Moreover, hybrid architectures—where preliminary data processing occurs on the edge before transmission to cloud platforms—strike a balance between responsiveness and comprehensive data storage [20]

Though numerous research prototypes focus on environmental or smart-city monitoring, few have been tested in factory environments within East Africa. Local challenges—such as erratic power supply, limited technical support, and scarcity of industrial-grade equipment—necessitate tailored solutions [21]. Recent pilot projects in Ghana and Kenya have demonstrated feasibility, utilizing solar-powered sensor stations and hybrid GSM-LoRa networks with edge alerts to support health and safety officers [13]. These implementations emphasize modularity, low maintenance, and user-friendly dashboards for non-technical plant personnel.

Building upon these advances, our study introduces FactoryAirWatch: a modular, GSM-based air-quality monitoring system specifically designed for Ugandan factories. The system integrates low-cost gas and particulate sensors with edge-based alerting and cloud-based analytics while addressing key constraints such as network reliability, power fluctuation, and minimal calibration capacity. By combining lessons from recent industrial IoT deployments—such as leveraging GSM fallback when LoRaWAN is unavailable, adopting *edge-based threshold detection inspired by TinyML frameworks*, and employing user-centric dashboards [15], FactoryAirWatch delivers continuous, accurate, and actionable air-quality intelligence suitable for Ugandan factory environments. Although the present version implements rule-based edge processing rather than embedded TinyML inference, its modular firmware and hardware design provide a clear pathway for future TinyML integration.

To evaluate the system, we conducted a three-month pilot in a mock factory setting, measuring latency, sensor stability, and user responsiveness. Our contribution lies in a practical, hybrid IoT architecture tuned for resource-constrained industrial settings, with insights applicable to other low- and middle-income countries. We also identify critical factors for deployment success—such as scheduled recalibration, power management strategies, and scalability considerations—and highlight implications for occupational health policy.

1.1 Research Objective

The main objective of the study was to design, implement, and validate a real-time IoT-based air quality monitoring system for factory environments in Uganda. The system aimed to:

- Continuously monitor multiple air pollutants and environmental parameters.
- Provide immediate alerts for threshold breaches through both local (buzzer and LED) and remote (web dashboard) notifications.
- Facilitate regulatory compliance through automated reporting and historical data archiving.
- Ensure high reliability, scalability, and maintainability within resource-constrained factory settings.

2 Related Works

The adoption of IoT-enabled air quality monitoring has surged over the past few years, driven by the need for low-cost, scalable, and real-time environmental sensing [5, 6] Early systems typically focused on urban applications, but recent efforts have shifted toward industrial settings where pollutant concentrations are higher and latency requirements are more stringent.

2.1 Low-Cost Sensor Networks and Calibration

Low-cost sensors like the MQ series and PMS5003 have been widely utilized due to their affordability and availability [7]. demonstrated an Arduino-PMS5003 setup that achieved PM2.5 accuracy within ± 10 μg/m^3 after laboratory calibration [9]. further improved calibration by applying machine learning regression techniques on raw sensor outputs, reducing sensor drift over 60 days. Similarly, [10] used hybrid calibration strategies with reference-grade instruments and drift compensation to maintain CO and VOC measurement accuracy in harsh conditions. However, [11] highlighted that high humidity ($>$80%) continues to negatively impact readings, necessitating sensor-specific compensation models.

2.2 Connectivity Modalities in Industrial IoT

Connectivity plays a pivotal role in system reliability [13]. evaluated GSM and Wi-Fi modules in factory settings and found that GSM consistently outperformed Wi-Fi in coverage and packet delivery, albeit at higher latency [15]. introduced a LoRaWAN prototype for industrial environments, reporting 95% data delivery rates within 1 km range [16]. corroborated these findings, noting that LoRaWAN provided reliable uplink performance in noisy electromagnetic environments typical of manufacturing floors. In the East African context, [22] designed a low-cost air-quality sensing kit which has been deployed in various locations within and outside Uganda.

2.3 Edge Computing and TinyML

Real-time alerting is critical in industrial settings [17]. integrated TinyML inference on ESP32 microcontrollers to identify VOC emissions within 30 s of onset, while [18] used on-node anomaly detection for rapid exposure warnings [19]. demonstrated that edge-based data aggregation reduced cloud communication volume by 70%, enabling cost-effective deployments over cellular networks [23]. provided a comprehensive framework for hybrid edge–cloud analytics, showing that selective cloud logging of flagged events ensures compliance reporting without burdening network infrastructure.

While several studies demonstrate the feasibility of TinyML-enabled inference at the edge [24], the present implementation of FactoryAirWatch employed a deterministic rule-based approach instead. Threshold values for pollutants such as CO, VOCs, and particulate matter were pre-configured within the node's firmware. When readings exceeded safe limits, the device triggered local LED and buzzer alerts without requiring ML inference. This lightweight approach offered similar real-time responsiveness while reducing computational complexity and power demands—an essential consideration for low-resource industrial deployments.

2.4 Application in Manufacturing and Low-Resource Settings

Factory environments present unique challenges such as dust, intermittent power, and minimal maintenance staff. Garima et al. [24] deployed solar-powered PM2.5 stations in Ghanaian factories, reporting consistent uptime (>97%) with adaptive sample-rate adjustments. Bennet and Loose [25] further demonstrated the use of user-configurable alert thresholds through simple dashboards, resulting in faster response time by health officers. Ipaki and Hosseini [26] underscored the importance of modular hardware designs to facilitate repairs using local components.

2.5 Policy, Health, and Occupational Safety

Several studies underscore the need for real-time air monitoring to meet occupational health standards [2]. has set PM and CO thresholds that must be constantly met in industrial zones. Ikechukwu et al. [28] demonstrated that real-time worker alerts reduced exposure times by 70%, helping factories achieve compliance with short-term exposure limits. Frischmon et al. [29] showed that episodic monitoring failed to capture transient spikes during peak production hours, which often exceed permissible limits by up to 200%.

Therefore, these works illustrate both the advances and remaining hurdles in industrial IoT-based air monitoring. Low-cost sensors can achieve acceptable accuracy with proper calibration; [7, 9, 10], while connectivity solutions like LoRaWAN and GSM ensure scalability and resilience in factory environments ([13, 16]; Onyango et al., 2023). TinyML and edge analytics significantly improve real-time performance [17, 19], and user-centered deployment strategies help address power and maintenance constraints faced by African manufacturers [24]. Our FactoryAirWatch system builds upon and contextualizes these advances within a Ugandan industrial setting by implementing a GSM-based architecture inspired by prior hybrid GSM–LoRa frameworks. While the current version uses GSM for simplicity and availability, the system's modular design allows future extension to LoRaWAN or NB-IoT once such infrastructure becomes feasible locally. This approach ensures immediate applicability in low-resource factories while maintaining scalability for future hybrid deployments.

3 Methodology

The system development followed a modular, incremental, and agile-based approach. Requirements were gathered from factory audits and regulatory guidelines provided by Uganda's National Environment Management Authority (NEMA) and international bodies such as OSHA and WHO. The project progressed through clearly defined versions (v1.0 to v1.4), each adding functionality from basic sensor integration to full pilot deployment readiness.

3.1 Hardware Subsystem

The IoT edge nodes utilized Arduino Mega 2560 microcontrollers interfaced with MQ-135, MQ-2, MQ-4, MQ-9 gas sensors, PMS5003 particulate sensors, DHT11 temperature/humidity sensors, and SIM800 GSM modules for data transmission.

3.2 Firmware and Power Management

Custom firmware handled sensor calibration, data acquisition, spike filtering, local alert triggering, and efficient power management through sampling interval control and low-power modes during inactivity or low battery.

3.3 Cloud and Backend

Sensor data was transmitted via GSM to ThingSpeak for initial cloud storage. A Node.js backend periodically ingested data from ThingSpeak into a MySQL 8.1 time-series database for long-term storage, analytics, and reporting.

3.4 Frontend Interface

The web dashboard, developed with Next.js 14, React 18, and Tailwind CSS, provided role-based access to live metrics, historical analytics, PDF reporting, and system administration tools. JWT-based authentication and secure HTTPS communications ensured data integrity and privacy (Fig. 1).

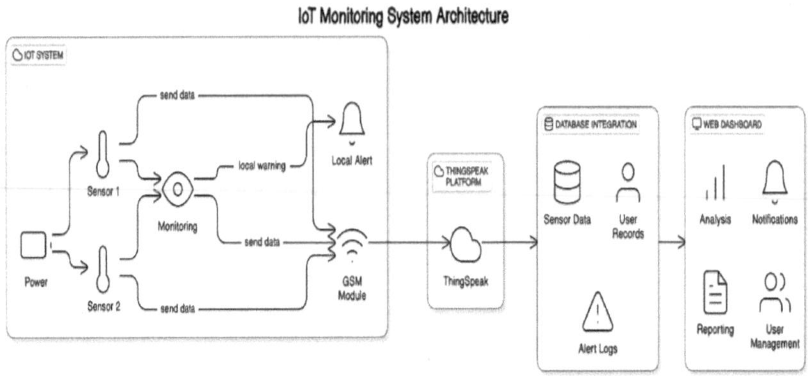

Fig. 1. High level architecture

3.5 How the System Works

- Data Collection: Sensor devices in a room or factory setting will capture key pollutants and environmental factors.
- Local Threshold Checks: If any sensor reading exceeds a configured limit, a buzzer or LED shall warn the user immediately.
- Data Transmission & Cloud Storage: The system shall send sensor data to ThingSpeak at set intervals, ensuring access to the readings from anywhere.
- Web Dashboard Analysis & Reports: Data will be fetched from ThingSpeak and then processed within the Analytics & Reporting module on the web dashboard. Users will examine metrics, generate compliance or health-focused reports, and receive notifications if thresholds are exceeded.
- Health Impact & Long-Term Trends: By enabling trend analysis and historical data visualization, users or managers will make more informed decisions about ventilation improvements, scheduling equipment checks, or adjusting occupancy levels to maintain a healthier environment.

4 Implementation, Evaluation, and Results

The system was deployed and tested in a controlled mock factory environment at Makerere University's College of Computing and Information Sciences.

4.1 Core Functionalities of the System

Core functionalities include:

- Air Quality Data Collection: IoT devices measuring temperature, humidity, VOCs, CO, PM2.5, and PM10 at regular intervals.
- Cloud-Based Analysis: ThingSpeak integration stores sensor readings and enables broader data processing or visualization if needed.
- Proactive Alerts & Notifications: Buzzer alerts and web-based notifications.

- Role-Based User Management: Control who can view, acknowledge, and configure system parameters (e.g., thresholds).
- Compliance Reporting: Generation of PDF reports to satisfy both internal audits and
- external regulatory requirements.
- MySQL Database: A relational database that stores user-related data and sensor-aggregated records for analysis

4.2 System Inputs

- Gas and particulate sensors: MQ 135, MQ 2, MQ 4, and MQ 9 deliver analogue voltages proportional to carbon monoxide, volatile organic compounds, methane, and mixed combustible gases. The PMS5003 particle sensor outputs a 32-byte digital frame containing counts for PM1.0, PM2.5, and PM10. Values beyond sensor operating ranges are flagged as invalid.
- Temperature and humidity: The DHT11 returns temperature between 0 °C and 50 °C and relative humidity between 10% and 90% RH. Readings outside these limits are discarded and logged.
- User input on the dashboard: Authenticated operators configure pollutant thresholds, acknowledge alerts, schedule reports, and administer user roles. Client-side validation blocks negative values and malformed dates, and server-side verification repeats these checks to guard against tampering.

4.3 System Output

- Real-time web dashboards showing numeric cards, spark line charts, and zone filters, refreshed every thirty seconds.
- Local annunciation through a tri-color LED (green normal, amber warning, red critical) and an 80 dB buzzer that sounds for 3 s during critical breaches.
- Cloud telemetry sent as HTTP GET requests to ThingSpeak; eight numerical fields plus a UTC timestamp are included with every record.
- Automated PDF reports containing statistics, charts, and compliance tables, branded with factory name, location, and reporting period.
- Rotating event and error logs storing sensor faults, GSM retries, user actions, and threshold edits; retained for ninety days.

4.4 Operating the Edge Node

(i) The FactoryAirWatch edge node functions primarily as a gateway and rule-based alert unit, performing threshold detection directly on the microcontroller. Upon power-up, plug the 5 V adapter or switch on the fused spur. Within 5 s, the green LED turns solid.

(ii) GSM handshake – The blue GSM LED blinks at 1 Hz while registering; a steady 3 s ON / 3 s OFF heartbeat indicates successful network attach.

(iii) Firmware log (optional) – Connect a micro-USB cable to a PC and open a serial console at 9600 baud. You will see sensor initialisation messages, APN negotiation, and live JSON payloads.

(iv) Once the message TX-OK ► ThingSpeak appears, proceed to the online dashboard.

4.5 Firmware and Connectivity

Factory Flashed Firmware: Edge nodes ship with factoryairwatch-node-v1.4.hex, SHA-256 documented on the rear label. If a re-flash is required:

(i) Download latest signed HEX from GitHub releases.
(ii) Connect micro-USB to laptop with PlatformIO.
(iii) Run pio run -t upload.
(iv) Observe console for *signature-OK*.

4.6 Performance Metrics

- End-to-end data latency: < 60 s.
- Alert notification latency: < 60 s.
- Dashboard load time: < 5 s over 3G.
- System uptime: > 99%.

4.7 Testing Procedures

- Unit and integration testing of firmware using Unity and PlatformIO.
- Backend API load testing at 1,000 requests per second with Postman.
- End-to-end functionality validation using Cypress for web interface.
- Soak tests confirmed system stability over continuous 168-h operation.

4.8 Limitations and Safety

- Network dependency: real time cloud dashboards require GSM coverage. During outages, data is cached locally and uploaded automatically once connectivity returns.
- Power autonomy: the node runs approximately eight hours on a 1,200 mAh Li ion battery; longer interruptions require mains or solar backup.
- Sensor drift: High humidity and dust can degrade accuracy; quarterly calibration is mandatory.
- Single zone coverage: one node monitors one physical zone. Multi-zone factories must deploy additional units.
- Low power mode latency: below 20 per cent battery, the transmission rate is reduced to conserve energy, delaying cloud updates.
- Safety measures include role-restricted threshold editing, full validation of every data entry, guaranteed on site alerts even if mobile data fails, dual data repositories for redundancy and HTTPS encryption with bcrypt hashed credentials.

4.9 Deployment Outcomes

- Reliable data acquisition and alerting even during intermittent GSM outages.
- Fully functional local alerts ensured immediate worker notification during network failures.
- Cloud storage and MySQL backend supported historical analytics and compliance reporting.
- The system generated branded, audit-compliant PDF reports for regulatory submissions (Figs. 2 and 3).

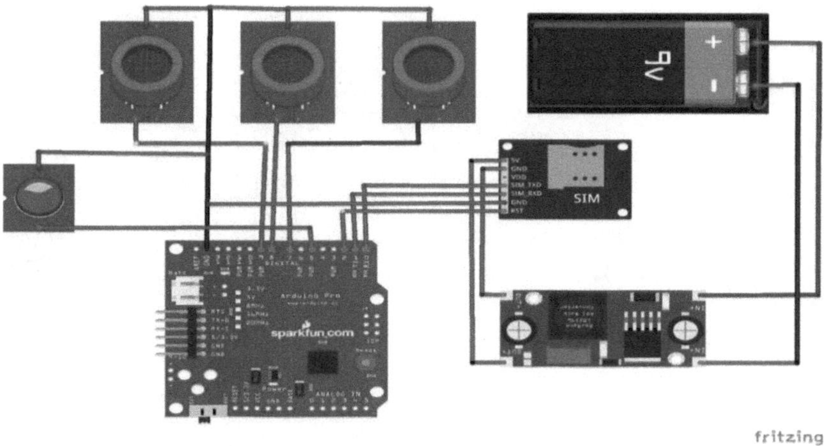

Fig. 2. Hardware schematic for the system

4.10 Real-Time Dashboard

Metric cards refresh every 30 s (colour-coded by threshold) (Fig. 4).

4.11 Historical Analytics

- Toggle Historical tab → long term trends, seasonal comparison, correlation matrix.
- Hover any data point for exact timestamp & value (Fig. 5).

4.12 Theoretical Implications

FactoryAirWatch contributes to the growing body of literature on IoT applications in developing country contexts, particularly emphasizing hybrid cloud-edge models to balance latency, cost, and infrastructure limitations. It demonstrates how modular architecture, combined with agile development and local customization, can yield highly reliable safety-critical monitoring systems even in resource-constrained settings.

4.13 Limitations

Limitations include reliance on GSM connectivity, which may not be universally stable across all industrial zones; sensitivity of low-cost sensors to environmental drift, requiring regular recalibration; and the current system's inability to handle multi-zone factory deployments from a single node. Future work will address these limitations by incorporating LoRaWAN fallback, integrating AI-based predictive analytics, developing wearable exposure monitors for workers, and enhancing cross-factory scalability through SaaS architectures.

Fig. 3. Fully assembled and working prototype IoT hardware setup with sensors and GSM module

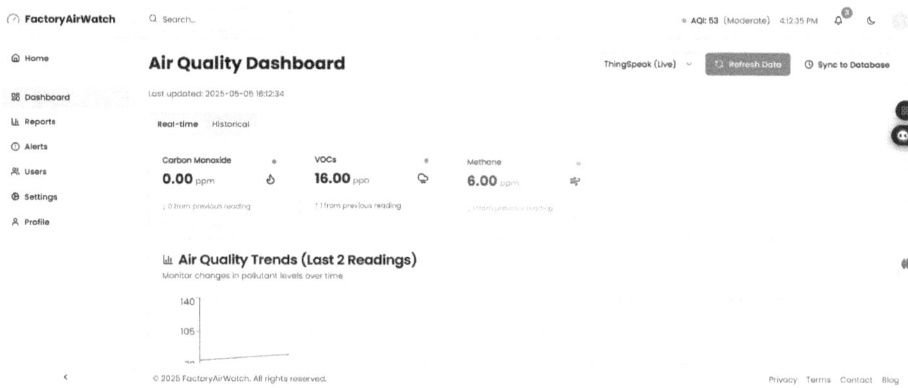

Fig. 4. Air quality dashboard

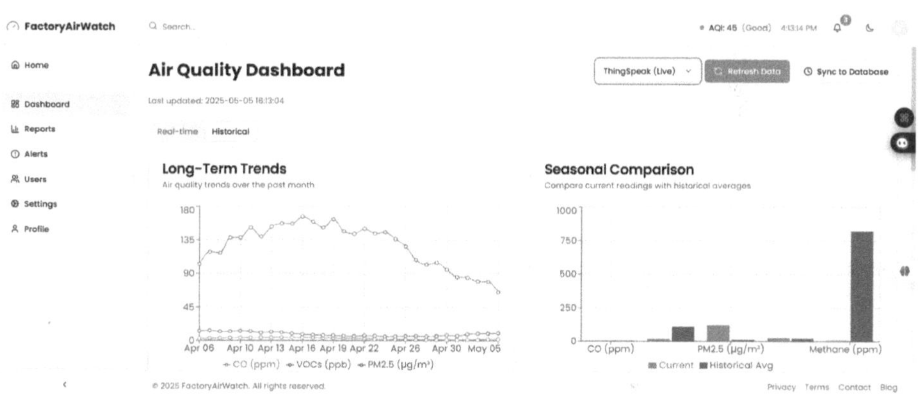

Fig. 5. Historical analytics

References

1. Obaroh, O.I., Gonzaga, A., Alum, U.E., Manjula, S.V.: Air quality in Kampala, Uganda: a review of the causes of low air quality and its impacts. Trends Environ. Sci. **1**(1), 1–7 (2025)
2. WHO: WHO global air quality guidelines: particulate matter (PM2.5 and PM10), ozone, nitrogen dioxide, sulfur dioxide and carbon monoxide. World Health Organisation, Geneva, Switzerland, (2021)
3. Ramadan, M.N.A., Ali, M.A.H., Khoo, Y.S., Alkhedher, M., Alherbawi, M.: Real-time IoT-powered AI system for monitoring and forecasting of air pollution in industrial environment. Ecotoxicol. Environ. Saf. **12** (2024)
4. Shahid, S., Brown, D.J., Wright, P., Khasawneh, A.M., Taylor, B., Kaiwartya, O.: Innovations in air quality monitoring: sensors, IoT and future research. Sensors **25**(7) (2025)
5. Anshul, S., Kiran, S.J., Divneet Singh, K., Khushal, T., Shubham, M.: The role of IoT in environmental sustainability: advancements and applications for smart cities. In: Mobile Crowdsensing and Remote Sensing in Smart Cities. springer (2024)

6. A. Kumar, M. Kumari and H. Gupta: Design and Analysis of IoT based Air Quality Monitoring System. In: International Conference on Power Electronics & IoT Applications in Renewable Energy and its Control (PARC), (2020)
7. Kelechi, A.H., et al.: Design of a low-Cost air Quality Monitoring System Using Arduino and ThingSpeak. Comput. Mater. Continua. **70**(1), 151–169 (2022)
8. Liu, T., Li, D., Chen, J., Chen, Y., Yang, T., Cao, J.: Gas-sensor drift counteraction with adaptive active learning for an electronic nose. Sensors **18**(11), 4028 (2018)
9. D. Hasenfratz, O. Saukh and L. Thiele: On-the-Fly Calibration of Low-Cost Gas Sensors. In: Wireless Sensor Networks. EWSN 2012.Lecture Notes in Computer Science, 7158, Berlin, springer, p. 228–244 (2012)
10. Araújo, T., Silva, L., Aguiar, A., Moreira, A.: Calibration assessment of low-cost carbon dioxide sensors using the extremely randomized trees algorithm. Sensors **23**(13) (2023)
11. Suriano, D., Prato, M., Penza, M.: Air quality monitoring in a Near-City industrial zone by low-cost sensor technologies: a case study †. Eng. Proc., 26 (2023)
12. Easterline, L.M., Putri, A.A.-Z.R., Atmaja, P.S., Dewi, A.L., Prasetyo, A.: Smart air monitoring with IoT-based MQ-2, MQ-7, MQ-8, and MQ-135 sensors using NodeMCU ESP32. Procedia Comput. Sci. **245**, 815–824 (2024)
13. Mohammad, A.: GSM based air quality monitoring and analysis using wireless sensor node. Int. J. Innovative Res. Sci. Eng. Technol. **5**(6) (2016)
14. Matandirotya, N.: Research trends in the field of ambient air quality monitoring and management in South Africa: a bibliometric review. Environ. Challenges **5** (2021)
15. Waheb, T.S., Jabbar, A., Ong, A.E., Shu'Ib, M.I., Wu, W., Oliveira, M.A.d.: LoRaWAN-based IoT system implementation for long-range outdoor air quality monitoring. Internet Things (2022)
16. B. Filip, A. Simo, D. Vatau, F. M. Frigura-Iliasa, S. Musuroi and P. Andea: LoRaWAN Based Real-Time Air Quality Monitoring System. In: 2020 IEEE 18th World Symposium on Applied Machine Intelligence and Informatics (SAMI), Herlany, Slovakia, (2020)
17. Shamim, M.Z.M.: TinyML model for classifying hazardous volatile organic compounds using low-power embedded edge sensors: perfecting factory 5.0 using edge AI. IEEE Sens. Lett. **6**(9) (2022)
18. Bezdek, J.C., Rajasegarar, S., Moshtaghi, M., Leckie, C., Palaniswami, M., Havens, T.C.: Anomaly detection in environmental monitoring networks [application notes]. IEEE Comput. Intell. Mag. **6**(2), 52–58 (2011)
19. Katib, I., Albassam, E., Sharaf, S.A., Ragab, M.: Safeguarding IoT consumer devices: deep learning with TinyML driven real-time anomaly detection for predictive maintenance. Ain Shams Eng. J. **16**(2) (2025)
20. Arifin, M., Ramadhan, A., Wijaya, H.: A comparative study of edge and cloud computing architectures for industrial IoT applications. Int. J. Inf. Eng. Sci., 11–15 (2024)
21. Ali, K., Johl, S.K.: Driving forces for industry 4.0 readiness, sustainable manufacturing practices and circular economy capabilities: does firm size matter? Available to purchase. J. Manuf. Technol. Manag. **34**(5), 838–871 (2023)
22. E. Bainomugisha, et al.: AirQo sensor kit: A particulate matter air quality sensing kit custom designed for low-resource settings. HardwareX 16, (2023)
23. Lilhore, U.K., et al.: Cloud-edge hybrid deep learning framework for scalable IoT resource optimization. J. Cloud Comput. (2025)
24. N. N. Alajlan and D. M. Ibrahim: TinyML: Enabling of Inference Deep Learning Models on Ultra-Low-Power IoT Edge Devices for AI Applications. Micromachines 13, (2022)
25. Raheja, G., Nimo, J., Appoh, E.K.-E., Essien, B., Sunu, M.: Low-cost sensor performance Intercomparison, correction factor development, and 2+ years of ambient PM2.5 monitoring in Accra, Ghana. Environ. Sci. Technol. **57**(29), 10708–10720 (2023)

26. Bennett, A.W., Loose, S.M.: User-centered development of an online dashboard tool for economic sustainability for small and medium enterprises. Sustainability **16**(2) (2024)
27. Ipaki, B., Hosseini, Z.: Repair-oriented design and manufacturing strategies for circular electronic products, from mass customization/standardization to scalable repair economy. Results Eng. **25** (2025)
28. CMIOSH, I.I.P., Odesola, D.A.S., Ekpenkhio, J.E.: Chemical exposure in workplace environments: assessing health risks and developing safety measures. Int. J. Res. Innovation Soc. Sci. (IJRISS), 229–238 (2024)
29. Frischmon, C., Crosslin, J., Burks, L., Weckesser, B., Hannigan, M., Duderstadt, K.: Detecting air pollution episodes and exploring their impacts using low-cost sensor data and simultaneous community symptom and odor reports. Environ. Res. Lett. **20**(4) (2025)

A Blockchain–Based Land Registration System: A Case Study of Somalia

Mohamed Nuh[1(✉)] and Mikko Ruohonen[2]

[1] Tampere University, Kalevantie, 433100 Tampere, Finland
Mohamed.nuh@tuni.fi
[2] Tampere University, Tampere, Finland
mikko.ruohonen@tuni.fi

Abstract. Somalia's land registration suffers from corruption, fraudulent sales, and prolonged disputes due to centralized and paper-based record-keeping. This paper presents a blockchain-based land registration system that enhances transparency, security, and efficiency using an Ethereum smart contract. The system creates an immutable ledger where property owners can register land titles, and buyers can verify ownership and request purchases through a decentralized web application. Smart contracts ensure that only verified owners can authorize sales, automatically executing and recording transactions without intermediaries. A prototype implementation was developed and tested in a controlled environment. Results demonstrate reduced opportunities for fraud, faster verification, and greater stakeholder trust, laying a foundation for transparent and sustainable land governance in Somalia.

Keywords: Blockchain · Land Registration · Somalia · Smart Contracts · Decentralization · Transparency · Fraud Prevention · Property Rights · Governance

1 Introduction

Land registration systems often face inefficiencies that foster corruption, disputes, and lengthy transactions. Centralized databases, weak information-sharing frameworks, and dependence on intermediaries undermine transparency and accountability, resulting in costly judicial burdens and hindering investment and development projects [1, 2].

In Somalia, these challenges are intensified by social and institutional realities. Prior research by the authors indicates that technology alone cannot resolve community-level issues without cultural integration [3]. Clan-based social structures promote cohesion and shape governance and conflict resolution. Therefore, digital solutions must reflect these socio-cultural contexts to gain public trust and sustainability. Studies highlight key design factors for digital land systems in Somalia, such as contextualization to local norms, participatory governance, transparency, and private-sector support. Yet,

A. Oluwatope et al. (Eds.): AFRICOMM 2025, LNICST 713, pp. 220–235, 2027.
https://doi.org/10.1007/978-3-032-38682-3_14

past digitization efforts have failed to curb record tampering, duplicate sales, and data-entry errors [4], revealing the limits of technical fixes applied over weak governance processes.

The absence of a unified land registry allows fraudulent sellers to resell the same property to multiple buyers, generating prolonged ownership conflicts. Although initiatives exist at the federal and state levels to promote transparency and efficiency, the current system remains vulnerable to manipulation, as shown in Fig. 1. These limitations motivate the development of a blockchain-based land registration framework that secures records, automates verification, and enhances trust in property transactions.

This paper presents the design and prototype implementation of a decentralized land registry tailored to Somalia's context. It evaluates how blockchain can address existing inefficiencies and strengthen transparency. Section 2 reviews theoretical foundations and prior work; Sect. 3 discusses blockchain adoption in African land governance and Somalia's existing process; Sect. 4 outlines challenges of centralized systems; Sect. 5 introduces the proposed framework and implementation; and Sect. 6 presents conclusions and implications for sustainable land governance.

2 Theoretical Background and Literature Review

2.1 Blockchain Technology

Blockchain technology is a decentralized, peer-to-peer distributed ledger [5] that secures transaction recording, data exchange, and network synchronization [6]. Unlike centralized systems reliant on intermediaries [7], blockchain ensures data authenticity, integrity, and security [8] through an immutable, time-stamped chain of blocks. Each block stores a header linking the previous hash, a transaction body, and a cryptographic signature [6, 9, 10]. Validated transactions are appended sequentially to the public ledger [11, 12]. Consensus protocols manage transaction order, ledger updates, and miner selection [13], maintaining a tamper-resistant network validated by trusted nodes [14, 15]. Cryptographic mechanisms such as hashing, digital signatures, and wallets prevent manipulation and identity forgery [16, 17], eliminating third-party dependence [10]. Blockchain systems are categorized as either permissionless, allowing open participation [11], or permissioned, governed by access control [13].

2.2 Blockchain for Land Management

Blockchain technology offers a promising solution to strengthen land registration systems through secure and transparent transactions. Its immutable structure enhances record reliability and minimizes traditional risks [18], while smart contracts automate and enforce agreements to improve efficiency [19]. Implementations across several jurisdictions demonstrate improved security and stakeholder trust [20], confirming blockchain's transformative potential for documenting land transactions [1, 21, 22].

Conventional property registration systems, dependent on centralized databases, remain opaque, costly, and prone to fraud [23]. Intermediaries inflate expenses and delay processes. In contrast, decentralized blockchain ledgers eliminate intermediaries, reducing corruption and improving security [24]. Since Satoshi Nakamoto's pioneering work

[25], researchers have advanced blockchain-based land solutions, such as government-integrated transfer models [26], Ethereum smart contracts for automated verification [27, 28], and frameworks enhancing registration security [29].

Other studies emphasize blockchain's capacity to improve transparency [30], reduce costs [31], enhance business safety [32], minimize fraud [33], and reinforce stakeholder trust [34]. Its immutability [35] and compatibility with Geographic Information Systems (GIS) and remote sensing further demonstrate its multidimensional value [3, 9].

3 Blockchain in Africa and Somalia

Blockchain technology is increasingly used across Sub-Saharan Africa to tackle persistent land management issues such as corruption, fraud, inefficiency, and lack of transparency in traditional systems [36, 37]. Its decentralized and immutable design provides a transparent and secure mechanism for recording land transactions and ownership [38], helping modernize registries, reduce fraud, and address documentation deficiencies [39]. Several African countries, including Ghana, Rwanda, Kenya, Liberia, and Nigeria, have piloted blockchain-based registries.

In Ghana, Bitland's Kumasi pilot sought to digitize and secure land records [1], Rwanda's Ubutaka App integrates biometric data, public key infrastructure, and blockchain for title issuance [40], and Kenya's Land Layby employs Ethereum to maintain immutable ownership records [6]. Liberia, in partnership with Medici Land Governance, is testing blockchain for administrative transparency [41], while Nigerian policymakers and scholars increasingly advocate for its adoption [42].

Across Africa, blockchain adoption aims to resolve enduring land tenure challenges rooted in colonial and post-colonial disruptions [36, 43, 44], particularly inadequate documentation, corruption, and multiple sales of single parcels caused by weak institutional oversight.

3.1 Land Registration Process in Somalia

Somalia, covering 637,337 km^2 in the Horn of Africa, occupies a strategic position linking Arabia, Southwest Asia, and Sub-Saharan Africa. Once a unitary state, the country collapsed in 1991, remaining without a stable government for nearly three decades before re-emerging as a federal system, one of the world's longest failed states. Following this collapse, extensive private-sector growth occurred, driven by deregulation and privatization that shifted the economy from central planning to a market-based model [45]. The private sector began delivering essential services such as telecommunications, water, electricity, transport, and education.

Although deregulation fostered entrepreneurial competition, the absence of strong state oversight enabled corruption and market failures—monopolies, coercive taxation, and escalating land-ownership disputes. Without an effective land registration system at either the federal or state level, vendors can sell the same parcel to multiple buyers, triggering prolonged legal conflicts [46].

Several land-management initiatives have been introduced across federal and member-state levels to reduce disputes, enhance transparency, cut administrative costs, and curb fraud. Nevertheless, as Fig. 1 illustrates, Somalia's existing land-registration process remains highly fragmented and complex, highlighting the urgent need for a more transparent, automated, and tamper-resistant mechanism.

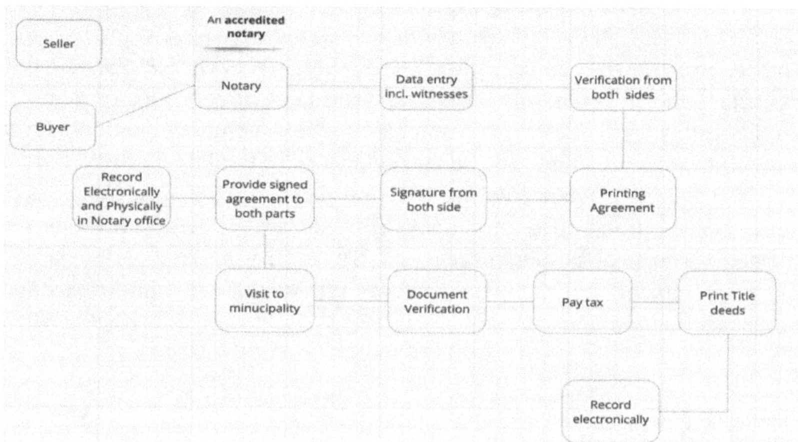

Fig. 1. Current land registration process in Somalia

4 Challenges of the Manual and Centralized System

Modern land registration systems continue to face efficiency, security, and transparency challenges [39]. These systemic weaknesses foster fraud, corruption, and prolonged ownership disputes [44]. Many registries still rely on manual, paper-based processes that cause operational delays, high costs, and data inaccuracies [47–49]. Physical records remain vulnerable to loss, damage, or forgery [50], while limited transparency impedes verification and erodes public trust [38, 51].

Centralized databases heighten security risks, being susceptible to tampering, cyber-attacks, and insider abuse [38, 52]. In several cases, individuals have fraudulently resold the same property to multiple buyers [5, 53], and weak digital identity controls leave records open to manipulation [1]. Concentrated administrative authority also introduces single points of failure and corruption [54, 55]; for instance, hundreds of fraudulent registrations were recorded in Malaysia over the past decade [56]. Lengthy procedures involving multiple intermediaries, brokers, legal offices, and notaries create additional costs and delays [37], while poor coordination across agencies causes inconsistencies that further burden users [57].

. Records are often outdated or incomplete [58], leaving large populations without formal titles [43] and generating discrepancies between records and actual ownership [59]. Moreover, outdated legal frameworks hinder innovation, delaying the recognition of digital signatures and standardized electronic documentation [60–62]. These issues highlight the urgent need for transparent, efficient, and technologically adaptive land registration reforms.

5 Proposed Blockchain-Based Land Registration System

To address the challenges outlined above, we propose a blockchain-based land-title registration system specifically designed for Somalia. The system functions as a decentralized application enabling secure property registration and transfer without a central authority. Property owners register assets on the blockchain by entering key details—location, owner's name, property size, unique title ID, and asking price. Once registered, potential buyers can search the ledger by title ID or other criteria to view verified property details.

When interested, a buyer submits a purchase request including the title ID, identification credentials, and payment. The seller reviews and, if valid, approves the request. This approval triggers a smart-contract function that automatically transfers ownership and records the transaction immutably (Fig. 2). Role-based permissions ensure only legitimate owners can authorize transfers. By automating verification and transfer through smart contracts, the framework reduces intermediaries, minimizes fraud risk, and increases transaction transparency.

Fig. 2. Architecture of the proposed blockchain-based land registration system

The system operates through a web-based decentralized application (DApp) that allows users to interact with the LandManagement smart contract on the Ethereum blockchain. Property owners and buyers access a browser interface equipped with wallets such as MetaMask to securely manage cryptographic keys and authorize transactions. When an owner registers land, the DApp invokes the smart contract's registerProperty() function, which records the title details on the blockchain ledger. Buyers can query available properties, view records fetched from the blockchain, and initiate purchases by submitting a transaction containing the property ID and payment information.

The smart contract automatically verifies that only the legitimate owner can approve and finalize a sale. Upon the owner's confirmation, ownership is transferred to the buyer, and the transaction is permanently logged on the blockchain. All updates are distributed across network nodes, ensuring transparency and resistance to tampering. In practical deployment, the system could operate on a permissioned blockchain managed by authorized institutions (e.g., Ministry of Land, municipal offices), where user roles owner, buyer, and administrator are defined within the contract's access-control layer. This architecture ensures accountability, auditability, and protection against unauthorized modification of land records.

5.1 The Development Environment for a Blockchain-Based Land Management System

We developed a functional prototype of the proposed system using Ethereum blockchain technology and modern web tools. A local Ethereum environment was established with Hardhat, which provided a private blockchain network (Chain ID 1337) and predefined test accounts for cost-free simulation. This controlled setup allowed rapid testing, debugging, and iterative refinement of smart contract logic without deploying to the public blockchain.

A simple web-based DApp interface was implemented as the user front end, served locally via Live Server at http://127.0.0.1:8080. It includes forms and actions for registering properties, searching records, and managing purchase requests. The MetaMask wallet was integrated to manage accounts and sign blockchain transactions. Connecting MetaMask to Hardhat's RPC endpoint (http://127.0.0.1:8545) enabled role-based simulations (buyer/seller) and digital signing for transaction validation.

The stack leverages JavaScript, Node.js, and Web3.js for blockchain communication. Web3.js handles contract calls (e.g., registerProperty) and event listening, while Node.js and npm manage dependencies and deployment scripts. Smart contract code (LandManagement.sol) was compiled and deployed using Hardhat tools, with supporting scripts for contract verification and account balance checks. Hardhat's console outputs and logging aided continuous inspection of state changes, ensuring functional integrity throughout testing

5.2 Smart Contract Design and Functionality

At the core of the system lies the **LandManagement** smart contract, written in Solidity and deployed on the Ethereum network. It provides the core logic for registering properties, managing purchase requests, and transferring ownership within a decentralized registry.

Data Structures and Events: The contract uses a `Property` struct containing *titleId*, *location*, *size*, *ownerName*, and *price*. Properties are stored in a mapping (`properties`) indexed by titleId, with a secondary mapping (`titleExists`) to prevent duplicate entries. A `PurchaseRequest` struct handles buyer offers, while mappings store pending transactions. Key events—`PropertyRegistered`, `PurchaseRequested`, and `PropertyOwnershipTransferred`—enable real-time updates through the front end, ensuring transparency and responsiveness.

Property Registration: The `registerProperty()` function records new properties on-chain after confirming that the *titleId* is unique. It then creates a new `Property` record, marks the title as registered, and assigns ownership to the sender's Ethereum address. Once successful, a `PropertyRegistered` event is emitted, providing on-chain visibility of the transaction. This guarantees integrity (each title linked to one verified owner) and transparency (public event logs). In the prototype interface, once confirmed, the property automatically appears among registered listings, confirming the seller's recognized ownership (see Fig. 3).

```
function registerProperty(
    string memory _location,
    string memory _size,
    string memory _sellerName,
    uint256 _titleNo,
    uint256 _price
) external {
    require(!titleExists[_titleNo], "Property title already exist
    properties[_titleNo] = Property({
        location: _location,
        size: _size,
        sellerName: _sellerName,
        titleNo: _titleNo,
        price: _price,
        owner: msg.sender,
        isSold: false
    });
    titleExists[_titleNo] = true;
    emit PropertyRegistered(_titleNo, _location, _price);
}
```

Fig. 3. Implementation of the property registration

Property Search and Query: Although not implemented as a separate smart-contract function, property search operates off-chain by reading the on-chain mappings. Any buyer can retrieve the list of properties marked for sale by calling a view function or querying the properties mapping for known IDs. The prototype DApp includes a simple search dialog where the buyer enters a title ID, and the front-end, via Web3 calls, fetches the corresponding property details—location, owner, size, and price. If the property exists and remains unsold, the result is displayed instantly. This mechanism allows independent verification of ownership and property information without reliance on agents or centralized databases, reinforcing transparency and user trust.

Purchase Request: The requestPurchase() function enables buyers to initiate property acquisition. The buyer submits a transaction specifying the target titleId and transfers cryptocurrency equal to or greater than the listed price. The function verifies three conditions: (1) the property exists, (2) it has not been sold or reserved, and (3) the payment meets the price requirement. Failure of any check reverts the transaction, ensuring user protection. When conditions are satisfied, the buyer's address and offer amount are recorded in the PurchaseRequest mapping, and a PurchaseRequested event is emitted to notify the network and interface. Storing this data on-chain locks the buyer's offer and provides an auditable payment trail. Once the transaction is confirmed, the seller's interface displays the pending request, identifying the buyer and offer amount (see Fig. 4).

Purchase Approval and Ownership Transfer: The final step in the transaction workflow is handled by the approvePurchase() function, which finalizes property transfer and can only be executed by the property's current owner. This restriction is enforced through a modifier resembling OpenZeppelin's onlyOwner, but scoped to property-level ownership. The function requires that msg.sender matches the stored owner address, ensuring that only the legitimate seller can authorize a sale even in a public contract.

When invoked, approvePurchase(titleId) retrieves the associated purchase request and property details, validating that the record exists, a request is pending, and the property remains unsold. Upon verification, ownership is updated—assigning the buyer's

```
function requestPurchase(uint256 _titleNo, string memory _buyerName) external payable {
    Property memory property = properties[_titleNo];
    require(titleExists[_titleNo], "Property does not exist");
    require(!property.isSold, "Property already sold");
    require(msg.value >= property.price, "Insufficient payment");

    purchaseRequests[_titleNo] = PurchaseRequest({
        buyer: msg.sender,
        buyerName: _buyerName,
        paidAmount: msg.value,
        approved: false
    });
    emit PurchaseRequested(_titleNo, msg.sender, msg.value);
}
```

Fig. 4. Implementation of the Request Purchase method

address as the new owner—and the contract disburses payment to the seller. In this prototype, transactions assume exact payment; however, refund logic could be added to manage overpayments. After state updates, the system marks the property as sold and emits a PropertyOwnershipTransferred event, confirming the title change on the blockchain (see Fig. 5).

```
function approvePurchase(uint256 _titleNo) external onlyOwner {
    Property storage property = properties[_titleNo];
    PurchaseRequest storage request = purchaseRequests[_titleNo];
    require(titleExists[_titleNo], "Property does not exist");
    require(!property.isSold, "Property already sold");
    require(request.buyer != address(0), "No purchase request");
    require(request.paidAmount >= property.price, "Paid amount insufficient");

    request.approved = true;
    property.isSold = true;
    property.owner = request.buyer; // Should transfer to buyer

    payable(owner()).transfer(property.price);
    if (request.paidAmount > property.price) {
        payable(request.buyer).transfer(request.paidAmount - property.price);
    }
    emit PropertyOwnershipTransferred(_titleNo, request.buyer);
}
```

Fig. 5. Implementation of purchase approval

The smart contract automatically and transparently executes the approve-and-transfer sequence without intermediaries. Once initiated, the code deterministically ensures that both payment and title transfer occur together. Cryptographic signatures verify the seller's identity, while on-chain logic enforces atomic exchange of funds and ownership, drastically reducing fraud.

The ownership check modifier ensures that only the legitimate owner can call the approval function. Even if impostors attempt off-chain manipulation, the sale cannot be completed without the private key of the rightful owner. This mechanism directly tackles Somalia's recurring issue of unauthorized land sales. In our prototype, when the verified seller authorizes a transfer through MetaMask, the blockchain instantly updates the record; if another account attempts it, the transaction is rejected.

This design replaces institutional trust with decentralized verification. Each stage, registration, purchase request, and transfer is validated by the blockchain's consensus mechanism, allowing all participants to audit property histories. Disputes can thus be resolved using immutable records, eliminating delays and corruption opportunities. Property transfers are complete within minutes instead of weeks, and tampering becomes virtually impossible without compromising network consensus.

Although the prototype runs on a local Ethereum network using cryptocurrency, a national implementation could adopt a permissioned blockchain using a stable-value token or off-chain payments. The core contribution lies not in cryptocurrency use but in blockchain-based integrity: only-owner approval and immutable logging ensure that legitimate owners control transfers and that each title's history remains incorruptible—critical safeguards for preventing duplicate sales and resolving competing claims in Somalia's land registry.

5.3 User Interface and Workflow Demonstration

To validate the smart contract's functionality and demonstrate end-to-end user interaction, a simple graphical interface was developed to connect the front end with the blockchain backend. The system includes two principal user roles: the seller (iibiye, property owner) and the buyer (iibsade, prospective purchaser). Each role was represented using separate Ethereum accounts—Account A (0xcd3B7…4Ce71) for the seller and Account B (0xdF3e1…C7097) for the buyer. Both accounts were configured in MetaMask, allowing seamless switching between roles during testing and illustrating the full transaction workflow (see Fig. 6).

Fig. 6. Selection of an appropriate account

The workflow begins when the seller registers a property through the DApp form (Fig. 7) by entering its details and unique title ID. Once the *Register* command is executed, MetaMask confirms the transaction and submits it to the blockchain. Within seconds, the property is immutably recorded on the ledger, displayed in the public listings, and the seller's wallet is verified on-chain as the registered owner.

Fig. 7. Register property dialog

Next, the buyer searches available properties using the *Search* function (Fig. 8), which displays each property's details, seller address, and asking price. To proceed, the buyer opens the *Request Purchase* dialog (Fig. 9), enters the property's Title ID, and submits the request with the corresponding Ether payment. MetaMask prompts the buyer to authorize the transaction, and once confirmed on-chain, the request is logged and the funds are held in escrow. The seller is then notified through an event update or interface alert that a purchase request is pending for their property.

Fig. 8. Search property dialog

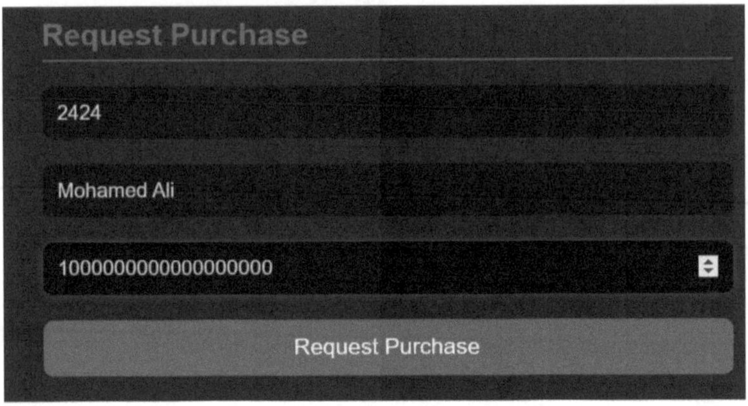

Fig. 9. Request purchase dialog

Finally, the seller approves the purchase to complete the transaction. Using the seller's MetaMask account, the pending request is opened and the Approve button selected (Fig. 10). Because the smart contract restricts this operation to the property owner, only the seller can execute it successfully. Upon approval, the approvePurchase() function updates ownership on the blockchain, transfers the escrowed payment to the seller, and emits the ownership-transfer event. The user interface then reflects the sale—removing the item from the "for sale" list or marking it as sold, and any query of that Title ID now shows the buyer's address. The buyer's MetaMask wallet simultaneously records the payment deduction and confirms ownership as registered on the blockchain.

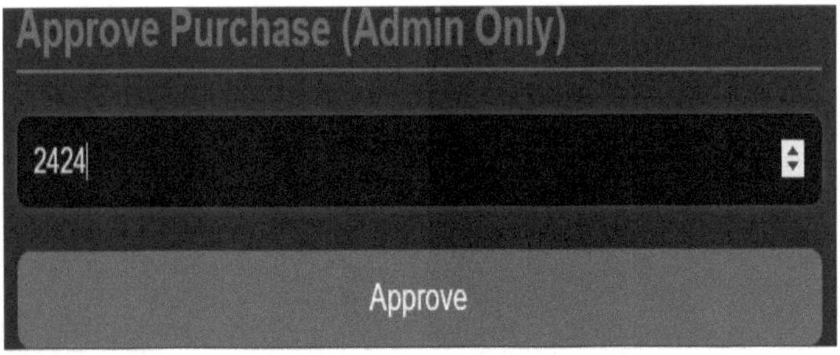

Fig. 10. Approve purchase dialog

As shown in Fig. 11, the confirmation state is where the property is now listed under the buyer's ownership.

This user interface demonstration confirmed that the smart contract and overall system logic performed reliably. Multiple registration and sale cycles were successfully executed with various test properties and accounts, validating system robustness. Constraints functioned correctly—duplicate title IDs were blocked, insufficient funds prevented purchases, and only verified owners could approve sales. Tests of invalid actions (e.g., non-owner approvals) appropriately failed, confirming that the blockchain-based

Fig. 11. Property transferred to a new owner

framework ensures title uniqueness, ownership authenticity, secure payment, and atomic transfers.

6 Conclusion

Land registration systems in Somalia currently suffer from inefficiency, insecurity, and lack of transparency, largely due to fraud, corruption, and frequent ownership disputes. Centralized record-keeping (where it exists) is prone to cyberattacks, data breaches, and unauthorized alterations. Weaknesses in identity verification have enabled incidents of double selling and record falsification, which in turn erode public trust in the land governance framework. In this paper, we proposed and prototyped a blockchain-based decentralized land registry framework to address these issues. In the proposed system, property owners register land assets on a blockchain ledger with key details (location, size, title ID, price), and prospective buyers can independently search the ledger, verify ownership, and submit purchase requests.

Only the rightful owner of a property can approve a pending sale, a transaction that is executed via a smart contract. The smart contract automates the transfer of ownership and payment, thereby eliminating the need for traditional intermediaries and significantly reducing opportunities for fraud. This blockchain-based approach enhances transparency by maintaining tamper-resistant records that are visible to all authorized participants. It also helps resolve disputes through clear, verifiable ownership histories and transaction logs, and it streamlines the overall process by cutting out unnecessary steps and delays.

This strengthens stakeholder confidence in the reliability of information. Overall, blockchain integration can reduce fraud, enhance the reliability of land records, and build public trust in Somalia's property market. By providing a secure and transparent transaction platform, the system can attract investment and stimulate development, giving landowners and buyers greater confidence in title validity.

However, implementing a blockchain-based registry in practice involves challenges beyond technical deployment. Key issues include user adoption, integration with legal frameworks, and ensuring access in remote regions. Future work will involve piloting the system with Somali authorities and communities to assess performance, usability, and acceptance.

Further considerations include scalability—handling high transaction volumes and large property datasets—privacy protection through permissioned chains, and regulatory compliance. We also plan to integrate digital identity platforms to improve user authentication and connect with GIS data for spatial referencing.

In summary, this study presents a feasible model for blockchain-enabled land registration in Somalia. The case study shows that by combining decentralization and cryptographic security, a trustworthy and efficient land registry can be achieved even in fragile institutional contexts. This work establishes a foundation for practical implementation that could advance stability and economic confidence in Somalia's land sector.

References

1. Shuaib, M., Daud, S.M., Alam, S., Khan, W.Z.: Blockchain-based framework for secure and reliable land registry system. TELKOMNIKA (Telecommun. Comput. Electron. Control) **18**(5), 2560–2571 (2020)
2. Thamrin, R.M., Harahap, E.P., Khoirunisa, A., Zelina, K.: Blockchain-based land certificate management in Indonesia. ADI J. Recent Innovation **2**(2), 232–252 (2021)
3. Nuh, M., Ruohonen, M., Pekkola, S.: Challenges of ICT4D solutions in Somalia: a case study of land management. In: Chigona, W., Kabanda, S., Seymour, L.F. (eds.) Implications of Information and Digital Technologies for Development, pp. 21–32. Springer, Cham (2024)
4. Aquib, M., Dhomeja, L., Dahri, K., Malkani, Y.M.: Blockchain-based land record management in Pakistan. In: Proceedings of the International Conference on Emerging Technologies (ICET), pp. 1–5. IEEE, Islamabad (2020)
5. Zein, R.M., Twinomurinzi, H.: Blockchain technology in land registration: a systematic literature review. JeDEM - eJournal eDemocracy Open Gov. **15**(2), 1–36 (2023)
6. Sladić, G., Milosavljević, B., Nikolić, S., Sladić, D., Radulović, A.: A blockchain solution for securing real property transactions: a case study for Serbia. ISPRS Int. J. Geo Inf. **10**(1), 35 (2021)
7. Xu, X., et al.: The blockchain as a software connector. In: 13th Working IEEE/IFIP Conference on Software Architecture (WICSA), pp. 182–191. IEEE, Venice (2016)
8. Bragagnolo, S., Rocha, H., Denker, M., Ducasse, S.: SmartInspect: solidity smart contract inspector. In: 2018 International Workshop on Blockchain Oriented Software Engineering (IWBOSE), Campobasso, pp. 9–18. IEEE (2018)
9. Akinyemi, O., Sibiya, M., Oladimeji, O.: Communication model enhancement using electronic health record standard for a tertiary hospital. SA. J. Inf. Manag. **24**, 1 (2022)
10. Indhuja, E., Venkatesulu, M.: A survey of blockchain technology applications and consensus algorithms. In: Karuppusamy, P., Perikos, I., Shi, F., Nguyen, T.N. (eds.) Sustainable Communication Networks and Application, Singapore, pp. 173–187. Springer (2021)
11. Alsaqqa, S., Almajali, S.: Blockchain technology consensus algorithms and applications: a survey. Int. J. Interact. Mobile Technol. **14**(15), 142–156 (2020)
12. Zheng, Z., Xie, S., Dai, H.-N., Chen, X., Wang, H.: Blockchain challenges and opportunities: a survey. Int. J. Web Grid Serv. **14**(4), 352–375 (2018)
13. Ismail, L., Materwala, H.: A review of blockchain architecture and consensus protocols: use cases, challenges, and solutions. Symmetry **11**(10), 1198 (2019)
14. Tosh, D.K., Shetty, S., Liang, X., Kamhoua, C.A., Kwiat, K.A., Njilla, L.: Security implications of blockchain cloud with analysis of block withholding attack. In: Proc. 17th IEEE/ACM International Symposium on Cluster, Cloud and Grid Computing (CCGRID), Madrid, pp. 458–467. IEEE (2017)

15. Zheng, Z., Xie, S., Dai, H., Chen, X., Wang, H.: An overview of blockchain technology: architecture, consensus, and future trends. In: Proceedings of the 2017 IEEE International Congress on Big Data (BigData Congress), Honolulu, pp. 557–564. IEEE (2017)
16. Xu, X., et al.: A taxonomy of blockchain-based systems for architecture design. In: Proceedings of the 2017 IEEE International Conference on Software Architecture (ICSA), Gothenburg, pp. 243–252. IEEE (2017)
17. Lepore, C., Visconti, A., Shah, K.A., Zanolini, L.: A survey on blockchain consensus with a performance comparison of PoW, PoS, and pure PoS. Mathematics **8**(10), 1782 (2020)
18. Zhang, Y., Xue, Y.: Blockchain technology and its applications in land registration: a case study of China. J. Real Estate Res. **40**(3), 309–323 (2018)
19. Christidis, K., Devetsikiotis, M.: Blockchains and smart contracts for the internet of things. IEEE Access **4**, 2292–2303 (2016)
20. Wong, R., Zhai, L., Li, Y.: Blockchain technology in land administration: a review of global practices and implications for China. Land Use Policy **128**, 105826 (2023)
21. Lemieux, V.: Evaluating the use of blockchain in land transactions: an archival science perspective. Eur. Property Law J. **6**(1), 31–47 (2017)
22. Spielman, A.: Blockchain: Digitally rebuilding the real estate industry. Master's thesis, Massachusetts Institute of Technology, Cambridge (2016)
23. Syed, T., Al Hassan, A.N., Alzahrani, A., Jan, S.: A transparent and trusted property registration system on permissioned blockchain. In: Proceedings of the 13th IEEE International Conference on Open Source Systems and Technologies (ICOSST), Lahore, pp. 1–6. IEEE (2020)
24. Kumar, K., Sahil: Decentralization through blockchain: opportunities and challenges. J. Current Res. Bus. **1**(1), 1–12 (2025) https://jcrb.net/index.php/Journal/article/view/14
25. Xu, M., Chen, X., Chen, H.: A systematic review of blockchain. Financ. Innov. **5**(1), 27 (2019)
26. Mittal, A., Sharma, B., Ranjan, P.: Real estate management system based on blockchain. In: Proc. 4th International Conference on Computing Communication and Automation (ICCCA), Greater Noida, pp. 1–6. IEEE (2020)
27. Thosar, A., Hame, M., Sarode, A., Kaur, P.: Land registry management using blockchain. In: Proc. IEEE 5th International Conference on Computing Communication and Automation (ICCCA), pp. 335–340. IEEE, Greater Noida (2020)
28. Mirza, D., Qureshi, M., Shaikh, A., Shaikh, P., Khan, I.: Secure real estate registry system using blockchain. Int. J. Adv. Res. Sci., Commun. Technol. **11**(3), 509–513 (2023)
29. Humdullah, S., Othman, S.H., Razali, M.N., Kutty Mammi, H.: Secured data storage framework for land registration using blockchain technology. In: Proceedings of the 2021 3rd International Cyber Resilience Conference (CRC 2021), pp. 1–6. IEEE (2021). Virtual
30. Ozcelik, A.: Blockchain-oriented geospatial architecture model for real-time land registration. Surv. Rev. **56**(407), 1–17 (2022)
31. Yadav, A., Kushwaha, D.: Query optimization in a blockchain-based land registry management system. Ingénierie des Systèmes d'Information **26**(1), 13–21 (2021)
32. George, R., Peterson, B., Yaros, O., Beam, D., Dibbell, J., Moore, R.: Blockchain for business. J. Investment Compliance **20**(2), 130–135 (2019)
33. Aborujilah, A., Yatim, M.N.M., Al-Othmani, A.: Blockchain-based adoption framework for an authentic land registry system in Malaysia. TELKOMNIKA (Telecommun. Comput. Electron. Control) **19**(6), 2038–2048 (2021)
34. Alkan, M., Polat, Z.: Design and implementation of a LADM-based external archive data model for land registry and cadastre transactions in Turkey: a case study of municipality. Land Use Policy **77**, 467–482 (2018)
35. Hofmann, F., Wurster, S., Ron, E., Böhmecke-Schwafert, M.: The immutability concept of blockchains and benefits of early standardization. In: Proceedings of the 2017 ITU Kaleidoscope: Challenges for a Data-Driven Society (ITU K), Nanjing, pp. 1–8. IEEE (2017)

36. Mintah, K., Boateng, F.G., Baako, K.T., Gaisie, E., Otchere, G.K.: Blockchain on stool land acquisition: lessons from Ghana for strengthening land tenure security other than titling. Land Use Policy **109**, 105635 (2021)
37. Ameyaw, P.D., de Vries, W.T.: Toward smart land management: land acquisition and the associated challenges in Ghana – a look into a blockchain digital land registry for prospects. Land **10**(3), 239 (2021)
38. Paavo, J.P., Rodríguez-Puentes, R., Chigbu, U.E.: Practicality of blockchain technology for land registration: a Namibian case study. Land **14**(8), 1626 (2025)
39. Saari, A., Vimpari, J., Junnila, S.: Blockchain in real estate: recent developments and empirical applications. Land Use Policy **121**, 106334 (2022)
40. Hughes, A.K.: Harnessing technology to advance citizen-centric land administration in Rwanda. Afr. J. Land Policy Geospatial Sci. **5**(2), 344–354 (2022)
41. Home, R.: History and prospects for African land governance: institutions, technology and 'land rights for all'. Land **10**(3), 292 (2021)
42. Osuolale, A.F., David-Daniel, O., Oluwasogo, S.: Property (land) registration management using blockchain in Nigeria. Commun. Appl. Electron. **7**(40), 1–10 (2024)
43. Boone, C.: Legal empowerment of the poor through property rights reform: tensions and trade-offs of land registration and titling in sub-Saharan Africa. J. Dev. Stud. **55**(3), 384–400 (2019)
44. Edwin, D.A., Glover, E.K.: When tradition meets modernity in land registration: evidence from Dagbon, Ghana. Land **9**(11), 416 (2020)
45. UNDP: Human Development Report: Somalia 2001. United Nations Development Programme, Nairobi (2001)
46. Tahir, A.I.: Post-conflict statecraft, land governance and exclusion in Hargeisa: urban land dynamics in Somaliland. Environ. Urban **35**(1), 46–63 (2023)
47. Bennett, R.M., Unger, E.-M., Lemmen, C., Dijkstra, P.: Land administration maintenance: a review of the persistent problem and emerging fit-for-purpose solutions. Land **10**(5), 509 (2021)
48. De Vries, W.T., Georgiadou, Y., Lewis, J.: The cost of land registration: a case study of cost efficiency in Namibia. Aust. Surveyor. **48**(1), 7–20 (2003)
49. Syaputra, R.: Legal aspects of digitalization in land registration. JILPR: J. Indonesia Law Policy Rev. **3**(3), 123–130 (2022)
50. Panda, S.K., Mohammad, G.B., Mohanty, S.N., Sahoo, S.: Smart contract–based land registry system to reduce fraud and time delay. Secur. Priv. **4**(1), e172 (2021)
51. Ameyaw, P.D., de Vries, W.T.: Transparency of land administration and the role of blockchain technology: a four-dimensional framework analysis from the Ghanaian land perspective. Land **9**(12), 491 (2020)
52. Blin, P., Aditya, T., Santosa, P., Claramunt, C.: Exploring cyber threat intelligence in land administration systems for enhanced cyber resilience. J. Geogr. Inf. Syst. **17**(2), 45–65 (2025)
53. Nakayi, R.: Certificate of title: contemporary challenges to the protection of land interests in Uganda. J. Afr. Law **67**(1), 23–43 (2023)
54. Shuaib, M., et al.: Identity model for blockchain-based land registry system: A comparison. In: Wireless Communications and Mobile Computing, 5670714, 17 pp. Hindawi, (2022)
55. Goel, A., Rahulamathavan, Y.: A comparative survey of centralised and decentralised identity management systems: analysing scalability, security, and feasibility. Future Internet. **17**(1), 1 (2025)
56. Abu Bakar, N., Omar, H., Ab Hamid, N.: Securing land registry by blockchain: at the crossroads against land fraud registration. Int. J. Acad. Res. Econ. Manag. Sci. **11**(2), 382–396 (2022)

57. Nega, W., Tenaw, M., Hunie, Y., Agegnehu, S.K., Mansberger, R.: Evaluating institutional dichotomy between urban and rural land administration in Amhara region, Ethiopia. Sustainability **13**(16), 9431 (2021)
58. Chehrehbargh, F.J., Rajabifard, A., Atazadeh, B., Steudler, D.: Current challenges and strategic directions for land administration system modernisation in Indonesia. J. Spat. Sci. **69**(4), 1097–1129 (2024)
59. Fetai, B., Tekavec, J., Fras, M.K., Lisec, A.: Inconsistencies in cadastral boundary data—digitisation and maintenance. Land **11**(12), 2318 (2022)
60. Stöcker, C., Bennett, R., Koeva, M., Nex, F., Zevenbergen, J.: Scaling up UAVs for land administration: towards the plateau of productivity. Land Use Policy **114**, 105930 (2022)
61. Kim, H.: Globalization and regulatory change: the interplay of laws and technologies in e-commerce in Southeast Asia. Comput. Law Secur. Rev. **35**(5), 105315 (2019)
62. Roić, M., Pivac, D.: Standardization of metadata of analog cadastral documents resulting from systematic cadastre establishment. Land **13**(9) (1343)

Towards a Systematic Framework for UAV Energy Model Selection

Bayaola Kolaïgué Israel[1], Fendji Kedieng Ebongué Jean Louis[1,2](✉), Yenke Blaise Omer[1], and Atemkeng Teufack Marcellin[3]

[1] University of Ngaoundere, P.O. Box 454, Ngaoundere, Cameroon
{israel.bayaola,yenke.blaise}@univ-ndere.cm

[2] Stellenbosch Institute for Advanced Study (STIAS), Stellenbosch, South Africa
jl.fendji@egcim-univ-ndere.cm

[3] Rhodes University, P.O. Box 6140, Grahamstown, South Africa
m.atemkeng@ru.ac.za

Abstract. The rapid proliferation of unmanned aerial vehicles (UAVs) in applications ranging from surveillance and agriculture to logistics underscores the critical need for precise energy consumption models to enhance mission planning, operational efficiency, and battery management. Yet, model selection is hindered by diverse factors, including data availability, accuracy demands, experimental resources, and UAV-specific constraints. This paper proposes a systematic decision-tree framework to streamline the selection of energy estimation models for UAV simulations. It classifies them into physics-based white-box models, ideal for scenarios with detailed dynamic data and access to facilities like wind tunnels—and data-driven black-box models, which excel in empirical, resource-limited contexts. By integrating UAV types (fixed-wing, rotary-wing, hybrid), operational requirements, and trade-offs between transparency, computational demands, and flexibility, the framework guides users toward optimal choices, such as adapting existing white-box models for high-precision tasks or developing black-box alternatives using operational datasets. Validated against 23 previous studies, the approach aligns well with established methodologies while addressing gaps in environmental dynamics and emerging technologies. Ultimately, this framework optimizes resource allocation, mitigates risks in real-world deployments, and fosters advancements in UAV energy modeling across domains.

Keywords: Unmanned Aerial Vehicle · Energy consumption · Model Selection · Decision framework · White-box models · Black-box models

1 Introduction

Unmanned Aerial Vehicles (UAVs), or drones, have become essential tools in various sectors such as surveillance, data collection, delivery, agriculture, aerial

A. Oluwatope et al. (Eds.): AFRICOMM 2025, LNICST 713, pp. 236–249, 2027.
https://doi.org/10.1007/978-3-032-38682-3_15

imaging, and disaster response [1–4], showcasing their potential to transform industries with efficiency and precision. However, estimating UAV energy consumption is a critical challenge [5–7]. This process is complicated by factors such as budgetary limitations, available resources, and the specific requirements of the intended application. In this paper, we seek to present our findings and insights gained from addressing the challenges associated with selecting an appropriate energy consumption estimation model.

Understanding UAV energy consumption is paramount to optimize their performance and operational range, ensuring successful mission planning and execution [5,8]. Given the growing dependence on UAVs, an accurate estimation framework is vital for both theoretical advances and practical applications. The objective of this paper is to review current energy consumption estimation models and propose a systematic decision-making framework to select the most suitable model. By integrating critical factors such as data availability, accuracy needs, and resource constraints, the framework provides a comprehensive guide for practitioners and researchers alike.

The structure of this paper is as follows. Section 2 reviews related work and foundational concepts in UAV energy modeling. Section 3 presents the proposed decision-making framework, detailing its components and application. Section 4 discusses the practical implications and limitations of the framework. Finally, Sect. 5 concludes with recommendations for future research directions.

2 Background and Related Work

2.1 Overview of UAV Types and Operations

Unmanned Aerial Vehicles (UAVs), or drones, are generally classified by design and operational capability into fixed-wing, rotary-wing, and hybrid types, each with distinct performance and energy profiles.

Common UAV Types

- **Fixed-Wing UAVs** resemble conventional aircraft, using wings for lift and offering long endurance and large-area coverage (Fig. 1a). Typical uses include agriculture, mapping, and reconnaissance. Their aerodynamic efficiency yields a lower in-flight energy use compared to rotary-wing types. Propulsion may be fuel-based or electric, and battery-powered systems are becoming more common [9].
- **Rotary-Wing UAVs**, such as helicopters and multirotors, generate lift through rotating blades, allowing vertical take-off and landing (VTOL) (Fig. 1b). They are suited for photography, surveillance, rescue, and delivery. Continuous lift generation increases energy demand, influenced by rotor count and payload mass [10,11].

- **Hybrid UAVs** integrate fixed and rotary wings capabilities, enabling VTOL with efficient forward flight (Fig. 1c). They serve in logistics and defense applications that require both endurance and operational flexibility. Energy efficiency is mode-dependent: comparable to fixed wings in cruise, but higher during vertical operations [10,11].

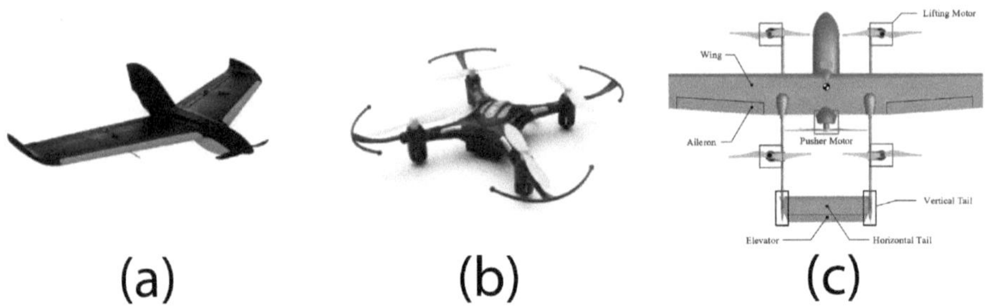

Fig. 1. Common UAV types: (a) Fixed-wing [6], (b) Rotary-wing [12], (c) Hybrid [13].

Modeling Energy Consumption Characteristics of Fixed-Wing, Rotary-Wing, and Hybrid UAVs: Energy consumption modeling varies across UAV types due to differences in flight mechanics, operational capabilities, and efficiency strategies. UAV energy usage is shaped by four main factors:

- **Lift generation**: Fixed-wing designs rely on aerodynamic lift during forward motion, offering high cruise efficiency [14]; rotary-wing designs use rotor blades for VTOL and hovering; hybrids employ both, switching as required.
- **Energy focus**: Fixed-wing models emphasize trajectory optimization for long-range efficiency [14,15], rotary-wing models address hover and maneuvering demands [16], and hybrid models target efficiency during flight-mode transitions.
- **Maneuverability**: Fixed-wing UAVs have limited turning due to aerodynamic dependence [17]; rotary-wing UAVs excel in agility and stationary hover [18,19]; hybrids achieve balanced agility and stability.
- **Control strategy**: Fixed-wing models optimize flight angles for lift, rotary-wing models manage rotor speed for lift and maneuvering, and hybrids require dual-mode control for smooth transitions between flight modes.

2.2 Importance of Energy Modeling in UAV Simulations

Energy modeling is essential for optimizing Unmanned Aerial Vehicle (UAV) performance, improving operational efficiency, and ensuring mission success. Given typical flight times of only 20–40 min due to high power demands and battery constraints, accurate models enable precise estimation of range and endurance by accounting for payload, altitude, and wind conditions [10,11]. Such predictions enhance mission planning and support energy-efficient path planning by quantifying the power costs of maneuvers like hovering, climbing, and cruising.

Energy modeling also drives performance optimization by revealing how variables such as speed, altitude, and maneuvering affect consumption, allowing engineers to address inefficiencies through design or operational changes [20,21]. It underpins effective battery management, predicting power needs for given flight profiles and environments, reducing mid-flight failure risk, and enabling integration of alternative energy sources (e.g., solar cells) to extend endurance [20,22].

Furthermore, it supports application-specific optimization: agricultural monitoring, search-and-rescue, and package delivery each impose distinct energy requirements [23]. Accurate models also enhance safety and reliability by anticipating shortages, enabling fail-safes or controlled returns before depletion [21].

2.3 Factors Affecting UAV Energy Consumption

Several factors influence the energy consumption and efficiency of UAVs. Weather conditions are significant, as highlighted by Thibbotuwawa et al. [16,24]. Flying speed also plays a crucial role, as noted in various studies [16,24–26]. Additionally, the weight and payload of the UAV directly impact its energy use, as explored in research by Abeywickrama et al. [23], Thibbotuwawa et al. [16,24], and Tseng et al. [27]. Flying altitude is another critical parameter, with studies such as Gao et al. [21] providing insights into its effects. The rotor number is also a determining factor, as discussed by Gong et al. [8]. Finally, communication systems contribute to energy consumption, as shown in the works of Abeywickrama et al. [23], Xie et al. [25], Sallouha et al. [28], and Zeng et al. [29].

2.4 Classification of UAV Energy Consumption Models

UAV energy consumption models are broadly classified as *white-box* or *black-box* [30].

White and Black-Box Models White-box models utilize physics-based equations derived from UAV structural, aerodynamic, and operational parameters, delivering high transparency, interpretability, precise scenario simulations, "what-if" analyses, and design optimization support; drawbacks include requiring domain expertise, high computational demands, and potential omission of dynamic environmental effects. Conversely, black-box models apply data-driven techniques, such as machine learning, to map inputs to outputs without internal dynamics modeling, offering flexibility, ease of implementation, and post-training computational efficiency for real-time applications, albeit dependent on data quality/quantity, lacking interpretability, and necessitating extensive datasets for robust performance.

Model Choice: Selection depends on application requirements, data availability, and trade-offs between accuracy and adaptability. White-box models are preferred for precise engineering tasks, while black-box models are advantageous in contexts requiring rapid deployment and adaptability.

Table 1 compares these approaches, and Table 2 summarizes recent works classified by model type and UAV platform.

Table 1. Comparison of White-Box and Black-Box Models

Feature	White-Box Models	Black-Box Models
Transparency	High	Low
Basis	Physics-based	Data-driven
Accuracy	Generally high	Variable, data-dependent
Complexity	High	Low
Computational Demand	High	Low (post-training)
Flexibility	Low	High

3 Proposed Framework for Model Selection

3.1 Framework Structure

Fig. 2 presents a refined decision tree for selecting an appropriate model to estimate energy consumption in UAVs. This systematic approach integrates UAV type, data availability, experimental resources, and accuracy needs. For widely used UAV models (e.g., DJI, Parrot), model selection depends on dynamic data access and accuracy demands: if high accuracy is crucial, experimental validation using facilities like wind tunnels is recommended to collect dynamic data; in the absence of such facilities, it is advised to utilize dynamic data based on the literature or develop a black-box model with UAV-collected datasets; for lower accuracy needs, adapting existing models from relevant studies is suggested. For custom UAVs, the choice of the model involves reviewing the related empirical models: high-accuracy requirements suggest adopting an existing white-box model incorporating UAV dynamics or deriving a new white-box model using system equations and physical principles; for moderate accuracy, black-box models based on data from the literature or operational data sets are recommended; if existing analytical models lack sufficient accuracy, developing new white-box models with detailed formulations (e.g., motor dynamics, aerodynamics, energy systems) is necessary.

Table 2. Works Utilizing White-Box and Black-Box Models

Ref	Authors	Year	Drone Type	Model Type
[31]	Akram et al.	2025	Multirotor	Black-Box
[1]	Qi et al.	2025	Multirotor	White-Box
[32]	Zhuo et al.	2024	Multirotor	White-Box
[33]	Liu et al.	2024	Multirotor	White-Box
[25]	Xie et al.	2023	Multirotor	White-Box
[8]	Gong et al.	2023	Multirotor	White-Box
[34]	Alyassi et al.	2023	Multirotor	Black-Box
[35]	Gora et al.	2022	Multirotor	Black-Box
[2]	Fendji et al.	2020	Multirotor	White-Box
[3]	Fendji et al.	2020	Multirotor	Black-Box
[36]	Umair et al.	2020	Multirotor	White-Box
[28]	Sallouha et al.	2018	Multirotor	White-Box
[23]	Abeywickrama et al.	2018	Multirotor	Black-Box
[37]	Abeywickrama et al.	2018	Multirotor	Black-Box
[29]	Zeng et al.	2018	Multirotor	White-Box
[38]	Prasetia et al.	2019	Multirotor	Black-Box
[16]	Thibbotuwawa et al.	2019	Fixed-wing, Multirotor	White-Box
[27]	Tseng et al.	2017	Multirotor	Black-Box
[39]	Paredes et al.	2017	Fixed-wing, Multirotor	White-Box
[40]	Mozaffari et al.	2017	Multirotor	White-Box
[41]	Rizoug et al.	2017	Multirotor	White-Box
[42]	Zorbas et al.	2013	Multirotor	White-Box
[43]	Carmelo et al.	2015	Multirotor	Black-Box

3.2 Framework Alignment with Prior Studies

To evaluate the contribution of the actual state of the proposed decision framework, Table 3 summarizes its alignment with the studies listed in Table 2. The alignment assessment is based on the model type employed (white-box or black-box) and the decision paths recommended by the framework.

- **Akram et al. (2025)** analyze flight time for micro quadrotors using a voltage-based polynomial regression model (a black-box formulation fitted to empirical battery voltage data across ground, takeoff, hover, and move modes). Their approach aligns with the framework's recommendation to"Develop black-box model using own UAV-collected dataset" for custom, high-accuracy scenarios with experimental access but limited physical modeling feasibility.

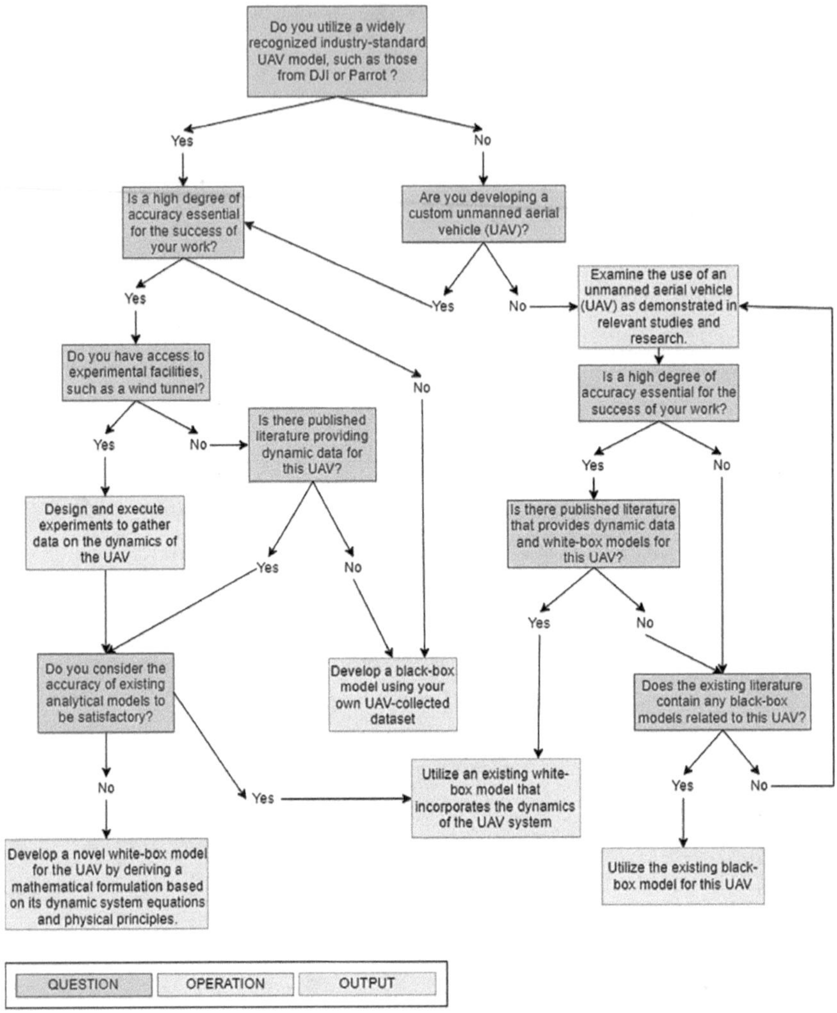

Fig. 2. Decision Tree for Choosing Energy Consumption Models in UAV Simulations.

- **Qi et al. (2025)** develop multi-UAV path planning for data collection using a detailed energy model (a white-box formulation for multi-rotor UAVs accounting for steady flight, acceleration/deceleration, turning, and climbing phases). Their approach aligns with the framework's recommendation to "Develop a novel white-box model" for high-accuracy, custom scenarios lacking extensive experimental facilities.
- **Zhuo et al. (2024)** minimize energy consumption in RIS-assisted UAV-MEC systems using a physics-based energy model (a white-box formulation for computing, transmission, and flight power). Their approach aligns with

Table 3. Energy Model Types used in some literature's and Alignment with the Decision Framework

Ref	Author	Year	Model Type	Alignment ?
[31]	Akram et al.	2025	Black-Box	**Yes**
[1]	Qi et al.	2025	White-Box	**Yes**
[32]	Zhuo et al.	2024	White-Box	**Yes**
[33]	Liu et al.	2024	White-Box	**Yes**
[25]	Xie et al.	2023	White-Box	**Yes**
[8]	Gong et al.	2023	White-Box	**Yes**
[34]	Alyassi et al.	2023	Black-Box	**Yes**
[35]	Gora et al.	2022	Black-Box	**Yes**
[2]	Fendji et al.	2020	White-Box	**Yes**
[3]	Fendji et al.	2020	Black-Box	**Yes**
[36]	Umair et al.	2020	White-Box	**Yes**
[28]	Sallouha et al.	2018	White-Box	**Yes**
[23]	Abeywickrama et al.	2018b	Black-Box	**Yes**
[37]	Abeywickrama et al.	2018c	Black-Box	**Yes**
[29]	Zeng et al.	2018	White-Box	**Yes**
[38]	Prasetia et al.	2019	Black-Box	**Yes**
[16]	Thibbotuwawa et al.	2019c	White-Box	**Yes**
[27]	Tseng et al.	2017	Black-Box	**Yes**
[39]	Paredes et al.	2017	White-Box	**Yes**
[40]	Mozaffari et al.	2017	White-Box	**Yes**
[41]	Rizoug et al.	2017	White-Box	**Yes**
[42]	Zorbas et al.	2013	White-Box	**Yes**
[43]	Carmelo et al.	2015	Black-Box	**Yes**

the framework's recommendation to "Develop a novel white-box model" for high-accuracy, custom scenarios lacking extensive experimental facilities..

- **Liu et al. (2024)** investigate cooperative arrival and energy optimization in multirotor UAV formations using a derived physics-based flight energy model (a white-box formulation for propulsion and hovering power, extending [29]). Their approach aligns with the framework's recommendation to "Develop a novel white-box model" for high-accuracy, custom scenarios lacking extensive experimental facilities, but with existing or custom dynamic data.
- **Xie et al. (2023)** optimize energy and delay in drone-enabled WSNs using a speed-related flight energy model, citing [29] (a White-Box model for rotary-wing UAVs). Their approach aligns with the framework's recommendation to "Use an existing white-box model" for high-accuracy needs.

- **Gong et al. (2023)** develop theoretical energy consumption models for multi-rotor UAVs, validated experimentally but fundamentally derived from physical principles, a classic white-box approach consistent with the framework's advice to "Develop a new white-box model."
- **Alyassi et al. (2023)** employ machine learning regression (black-box) for energy estimation on commercial drones, citing the impracticality of white-box modeling due to lack of facilities like wind tunnels. This matches the framework's suggestion to "Develop a black-box model using your own UAV data" when white-box modeling is infeasible.
- **Gora et al. (2022)** use ML-based black-box modeling on a custom hexacopter, emphasizing universality without requiring construction knowledge. Their data-driven method aligns with the framework's guidance for custom UAVs lacking access to advanced facilities.
- **Fendji et al. (2020)** incorporate environmental constraints via a theoretical model [16], exemplifying a white-box approach suited for precise optimization [2]. In subsequent work [3], they employ a commercial UAV (3DR Solo) and an empirically validated energy model with ~0.4% estimation error. This aligns with the framework's recommendation to use established industrial UAV models and white-box or experimentally supported energy models that capture UAV dynamics (velocity, acceleration, payload, wind), prioritizing accuracy through physically interpretable, data-driven modeling.
- **Umair et al. (2020)** optimize UAV transmission power and altitude using detailed physical parameters referenced from [29]. The framework supports such precise white-box modeling for high-accuracy requirements.
- **Sallouha et al. (2018)** incorporate a simplified yet physically derived energy model for UAV-assisted node localization, consistent with the framework's endorsement of existing white-box models for complex optimization.
- **Abeywickrama et al. (2018b, 2018c)** present black-box empirical models based on battery performance data from commercial drones, justifying avoidance of complex physical modeling due to lack of sophisticated setups. This matches the framework's advice for black-box modeling in standard UAV contexts without advanced facilities.
- **Zeng et al. (2018)** derive an analytical propulsion energy model grounded in aeronautical physics, exemplifying the white-box approach encouraged by the framework.
- **Prasetia et al. (2019)** propose a black-box model for a custom hexacopter using regression on experimental data, consistent with the framework's recommendation for custom UAVs when white-box modeling is impractical.
- **Thibbotuwawa et al. (2019c)** review physically based UAV energy models relevant for routing, supporting the use of existing white-box models when detailed physical phenomena must be captured.
- **Tseng et al. (2017)** apply a regression black-box model on commercial drone battery data, favoring practical data-driven methods without complex facilities, aligning with the framework's black-box guidance.

- **Paredes et al. (2017)** derive altitude-dependent power equations from propeller physics, validated with flight data, representing a white-box model in line with the framework.
- **Mozaffari et al. (2017)** employ existing white-box models [29] for UAV deployment and power control optimization, consistent with the framework's recommendation.
- **Rizoug et al. (2017)** develop a comprehensive white-box model including UAV motion, motor, and battery dynamics, aligned with the framework's advice to derive mathematical models based on physical system equations.
- **Zorbas et al. (2013)** address energy-efficient UAV planning for tracking in complex 3D terrains using a white-box model, fitting the framework's criteria for high-accuracy physical modeling.
- **Carmelo et al. (2015)** derive polynomial interpolation-based models from measurement data on an IRIS quadcopter, preferring a black-box experimental approach due to difficulties in white-box modeling, in line with framework recommendations when advanced facilities are unavailable.

4 Discussion

4.1 Insights and Practical Implications

The proposed decision tree framework for the selection of the UAV energy consumption model provides operational value by guiding systematic model choice, optimizing R&D allocation, and avoiding unnecessary complexity while ensuring adequate accuracy. This directly supports efficient flight planning, mission scheduling, battery management, and risk mitigation through application-specific accuracy requirements. For example:

- **Target Tracking and Surveillance**: Precise energy estimation enables sustained target engagement without premature resource depletion [44].
- **Mobile Edge Computing**: For UAVs serving as aerial base stations, particularly in AI-supported IoT contexts, estimation errors can cause service delays or connectivity loss [45].
- **Wireless Rechargeable Sensor Networks**: Accurate forecasts are critical for periodic coverage, efficient flight paths, and charging schedules to prevent sensor node failure, often relying on heuristic optimization [46].

The framework also strengthens cost-benefit analyses, clarifies scenarios warranting simple versus complex models, and supports balanced resource allocation for improved UAV performance prediction.

4.2 Limitations and Future Research Directions

Current Framework Limitations. The framework assumes steady-state conditions, excluding dynamic environmental factors (e.g., wind, temperature) affecting energy use. Its binary classification of experimental facility availability oversimplifies validation, ignoring partial capacities. Rapid UAV technological advances (e.g., propulsion, energy sources) demand frequent updates. Furthermore, reliance on a limited set of reviewed studies constrains on a complete generalizability and methodological coverage.

Future Research Directions. Enhancements should include hybrid white-box/black-box modeling, standardized validation protocols, benchmark datasets, and machine learning for real-time adaptation. Models should incorporate environmental variables, emerging propulsion systems, and energy harvesting while remaining lightweight for autonomous use. Broadening the literature and data sources will improve accuracy, validity, and applicability.

Recommendations for Implementation. Effective adoption requires coordinated industry–academia–research collaboration [47], prioritizing standardized protocols, UAV performance databases, and accuracy thresholds. Training materials, case studies, and workshops should facilitate uptake, while a feedback-driven improvement loop with automated model-selection tools will sustain technological relevance.

5 Conclusion

This paper tackles the challenge of selecting appropriate UAV energy consumption models by introducing a systematic decision-tree framework that guides choices based on data availability, experimental resources, accuracy needs, and UAV standardization. Validated against 23 previous studies, it recommends physics-based white-box models for high-precision applications with detailed dynamics and setups, while data-driven black-box models suit empirical data-rich but physics-limited scenarios. The framework streamlines selection, optimizing resource allocation, mission planning, and operational efficiency across UAV applications. Limitations include overlooking dynamic environments, evolving technologies, and emerging energy systems, plus reliance on a limited review set, potentially limiting generalizability. Future research will expand this via:

- Broader consultation of research papers and data for enhanced accuracy and validity across UAV scenarios.
- Hybrid white-/black-box approaches integrating both strengths.
- Standardized validation protocols for consistency.
- Machine learning for adaptive, real-time adjustments.
- Incorporation of environmental factors, novel propulsion, and energy harvesting.
- Validation against one or two case studies using real UAV flights or open datasets with standard metrics.

References

1. Qi, Y., Jiang, H., Huang, G., Yang, L., Wang, F., Yunjian, X.: Multi-UAV path planning considering multiple energy consumptions via an improved bee foraging learning particle swarm optimization algorithm. Sci. Rep. **15**(1), 14755 (2025)
2. Fendji, J.L.E.K., Bayaola, I.K., Thron, C., Fendji, M.D., Förster, A.: Cost-effective placement of recharging stations in drone path planning for surveillance missions on large farms. Symmetry **12**(10) 2020
3. Ebongue, J.L.F.K., Kolaïgué, I.B., Thron, C., Förster, A., Stations, C.: Placement in Drone Path planning for large space surveillance. In CARI,: Colloque Africain Sur La Recherche En Informatique et En Mathématiques Apliquées, p. 2020. Thies, Senegal (2020)
4. Vargas Tamayo, L., Thron, C., Louis Kedieng Ebongue Fendji, J., Thomas, S.-K., Förster, A.: Cost-minimizing system design for surveillance of large, inaccessible agricultural areas using drones of limited range. Sustainability **12**(21), 8878 (2020)
5. Cabuk, U.C., Tosun, M., Dagdeviren, O., Ozturk, Y.: Modeling energy consumption of small drones for swarm missions. IEEE Trans. Intell. Transp. Syst., 1–14 (2024)
6. Velusamy, P., Rajendran, S., Mahendran, R.K., Naseer, S., Shafiq, M., Choi, J.G.: Unmanned aerial vehicles (UAV) in precision agriculture: applications and challenges. Energies **15**(1), 217 (2022)
7. Del Cerro, J., Cruz Ulloa, C., Barrientos, A., de León Rivas, J.: Unmanned aerial vehicles in agriculture: a survey. Agronomy **11**(2), 203 (2021)
8. Gong, H., Huang, B., Jia, B., Dai, H.: Modeling power consumptions for multirotor UAVs. IEEE Trans. Aerosp. Electron. Syst. **59**(6), 7409–7422 (2023)
9. Zhang, B., Song, Z., Zhao, F., Liu, C.: Overview of propulsion systems for unmanned aerial vehicles. Energies **15**(2), 455 (2022)
10. Sharma, P., Singh, S., Tayal, V.: An overview of classification, requirements, path planning algorithms and improvement areas of unmanned aerial vehicle. Int. J. Comput. Appl. **180**(47), 19–24 (2018)
11. Thibbotuwawa, A., Bocewicz, G., Nielsen, P., Banaszak, Z.: Unmanned aerial vehicle routing problems: a literature review. Appl. Sci. **10**(13), 4504 (2020)
12. Radoglou-Grammatikis, P., Sarigiannidis, P., Lagkas, T., Moscholios, I.: A compilation of UAV applications for precision agriculture. Comput. Netw. **172**, 107148 (2020)
13. Gu, H., Lyu, X., Li, Z., Shen, S., Zhang, F.: Development and experimental verification of a hybrid vertical take-off and landing (VTOL) unmanned aerial vehicle(UAV). In 2017 International Conference on Unmanned Aircraft Systems (ICUAS), pp. 160–169 (2017)
14. Wang, S., Qin, X., Xu, W., Zhang, Z., Li, H., Ma, N.: Aerodynamic-aware energy saving for fixed-wing UAV under data collection requirements (2021)
15. Zhu, Y., Yang, B., Liu, M., Li, Z.: UAV trajectory optimization for large-scale and low-power data collection: an attention-reinforced learning scheme. IEEE Trans. Wireless Commun. (2024)
16. Thibbotuwawa, A., Nielsen, P., Zbigniew, B., Bocewicz, G.: Energy consumption in unmanned aerial vehicles: a review of energy consumption models and their relation to the UAV routing. In Jerzy Ś., Leszek B., Zofia W., (eds.), Information Systems Architecture and Technology: Proceedings of 39th International Conference on Information Systems Architecture and Technology–ISAT 2018, pages 173–184. Springer International Publishing, Cham (2019)

17. Wang, Y., Shan, M., Wang, D.: Motion capability analysis for multiple fixed-wing UAV formations with speed and heading rate constraints. IEEE Trans. Control Netw. Syst. **7**(2), 977–989 (2020)
18. Zhao, T., Li, W: Design configuration and technical application of rotary-wing unmanned aerial vehicles. Mechatron. Intell. Transp. Syst. **1**(1) (2022)
19. Zhang, J., An, Y., Cao, J., Ouyang, S., Wang, L.: UAV trajectory planning for complex open storage environments based on an improved RRT algorithm. IEEE Access **11**, 23189–23204 (2023)
20. Beigi, P., Rajabi, M.S., Aghakhani, S.: An overview of drone energy consumption factors and models. In: Fathi, M., Zio, E., Pardalos, P.M., (eds.), Handbook of Smart Energy Systems, pp. 1–20. Springer International Publishing, Cham (2021)
21. Gao, N., et al.: Energy model for UAV communications: experimental validation and model generalization. China Commun. **18**(7), 253–264 (2021)
22. Hendrarini, N., Sani, M.I.: Unmanned aerial vehicle (UAV) predictive control energy management model. In: Proceedings of the 2024 7th International Conference on Software Engineering and Information Management, ICSIM '24, pp. 147–152. Association for Computing Machinery, New York, NY, USA (2024)
23. Abeywickrama, H.V., Jayawickrama, B.A., He, Y., Dutkiewicz, E.: Empirical power consumption model for UAVs. In: 2018 IEEE 88th Vehicular Technology Conference (VTC-Fall), pp. 1–5 (2018)
24. Thibbotuwawa, A., Nielsen, P., Zbigniew, B., Bocewicz, G.: Factors affecting energy consumption of unmanned aerial vehicles: an analysis of how energy consumption changes in relation to UAV routing. In: Jerzy Ś., Leszek B., Zofia W., (eds.) Information Systems Architecture and Technology: Proceedings of 39th International Conference on Information Systems Architecture and Technology–ISAT 2018, pp.228–238. Springer International Publishing, Cham (2019)
25. Xie, J., Qiyong, F., Jia, R., Lin, F., Li, M., Zheng, Z.: Optimal energy and delay tradeoff in UAV-enabled wireless sensor networks. Drones **7**(6), 368 (2023)
26. Hwang, M.H., Cha, H.R., Jung, S.Y.: Practical endurance estimation for minimizing energy consumption of multirotor unmanned aerial vehicles. Energies **11**(9), 2221 (2018)
27. Tseng, C.M., Chau, C.K., Elbassioni, K.M., Khonji, M.: Flight Tour Planning with Recharging Optimization for Battery-operated Autonomous Drones (2017)
28. Sallouha, H., Azari, M.M., Pollin, S.: Energy-Constrained UAV Trajectory Design for Ground Node Localization (2018)
29. Zeng, Y., Xu, J., Zhang, R.: Energy Minimization for Wireless Communication with Rotary-Wing UAV (2018)
30. Tseng, C.-M., Chau, C.-K.: Personalized prediction of vehicle energy consumption based on participatory sensing. IEEE Trans. Intell. Transp. Syst. **18**(11), 3103–3113 (2017)
31. Akram, N., Khoshrangbaf, M., Challenger, M., Dagdeviren, O.: Energy consumption modeling and flight time analysis of micro drones. IEEE Access **13**, 109854–109866 (2025)
32. Zhuo, Z., Dong, S., Zheng, H., Zhang, Y.: Method of minimizing energy consumption for ris assisted uav mobile edge computing system. IEEE Access **12**, 39678–39688 (2024)
33. Liu, H., Chen, R., Yan, X., Zhang, J., Nian, Y.: Research on cooperative arrival and energy consumption optimization strategies of UAV formations. Drones **8**(12), 722 (2024)

34. Alyassi, R., Khonji, M., Karapetyan, A., Chau, S.C.K., Elbassioni, K., Tseng, C.M.: Autonomous recharging and flight mission planning for battery-operated autonomous drones. IEEE Trans. Autom. Sci. Eng. **20**(2), 1034–1046 (2023)
35. Góra, K., Smyczyński, P., Kujawiński, M., Granosik, G.: Machine learning in creating energy consumption model for UAV. Energies **15**(18), 6810 (2022)
36. Umair, M., Joung, J., Cho, Y.S.: Transmission power and altitude design for energy-efficient mission completion of small-size unmanned aerial vehicle. Electron. Lett. **56**(22), 1219–1222 (2020)
37. Abeywickrama, H.V., Jayawickrama, B.A., He, Y., Dutkiewicz, E.: Dutkiewicz: comprehensive energy consumption model for unmanned aerial vehicles, based on empirical studies of battery performance. IEEE Access **6**, 58383–58394 (2018)
38. Prasetia, A.S., Wai, R.-J., Wen, Y.-L., Wang, Y.-K.: Mission-based energy consumption prediction of multirotor UAV. IEEE Access **7**, 33055–33063 (2019)
39. Paredes, J.A., Saito, C., Abarca, M., Cuellar, F.: Study of effects of high-altitude environments on multicopter and fixed-wing UAVs' energy consumption and flight time. In: 2017 13th IEEE Conference on Automation Science and Engineering (CASE), pp. 1645–1650 (2017)
40. Mozaffari, M., Saad, W., Bennis, M., Debbah, M.: Mobile unmanned aerial vehicles (UAVs) for energy-efficient internet of things communications. IEEE Trans. Wireless Commun. **16**(11), 7574–7589 (2017)
41. Rizoug, N., Bouhali, O., Hamerlain, M.: Optimization of Energy Consumption for Quadrotor UAV (2017)
42. Zorbas, D., Razafindralambo, T., Luigi, D.P.P., Guerriero, F.: Energy efficient mobile target tracking using flying drones. Procedia Comput. Sci. **19**, 80–87 (2013)
43. Di Franco, C., Buttazzo, G.: Energy-aware coverage path planning of UAVs. In: 2015 IEEE International Conference on Autonomous Robot Systems and Competitions, pp. 111–117. Vila Real, IEEE (2015)
44. Shen, Y., Wei, C.: Target tracking and enclosing via UAV/UGV cooperation using energy estimation pigeon-inspired optimization and switchable topology. Aircr. Eng. Aerosp. Technol. **95** (2022)
45. Deng, C., Fang, X., Wang, X.: UAV-enabled mobile-edge computing for AI applications: joint model decision, resource allocation, and trajectory optimization. IEEE Internet Things J. **10**(7), 5662–5675 (2023)
46. Lin, C., et al.: Maximizing energy efficiency of period-area coverage with a UAV for wireless rechargeable sensor networks. IEEE/ACM Trans. Netw. **31**(4), 1657–1673 (2023)
47. Suprun, E., Sahin, O., Stewart, R.A., Panuwatwanich, K.: Model of the russian federation construction innovation system: an integrated participatory systems approach. Systems **4**(3), 29 (2016)

Author Index

A. Oluwatope et al. (Eds.): AFRICOMM 2025, LNICST 713, pp. 251–252, 2027.
https://doi.org/10.1007/978-3-032-38682-3

FSC
www.fsc.org
MIX
Papier | Fördert
gute Waldnutzung
FSC® C083411

Kolibri 360 GmbH
Ferdinand-Jühlke-Straße 7
99095 Erfurt, Deutschland
produktsicherheit@kolibri360.de